HOW CAN I GET TO
HEAVEN?

2/99

HOW CAN I GET TO HEAVEN?

THE BIBLE'S TEACHING ON SALVATION — MADE EASY TO UNDERSTAND

ROBERT A. SUNGENIS

FOREWORD BY THOMAS HOWARD

Queenship
PUBLISHING COMPANY
P.O. Box 42028 Santa Barbara, CA 93140-2028
(800) 647-9882 • (805) 957-4893 • Fax: (805) 957-1631

*How Can I Get to Heaven? The Bible's Teaching on Salvation —
Made Easy to Understand* is the abridged version of *Not By Faith
Alone: The Biblical Evidence for the Catholic Doctrine of Justification* (Queenship Publishing, 1997), and was issued the:

Nihil Obstat:

>Monsignor Carroll E. Satterfield
>Censor Librorum

Imprimatur:

>Monsignor W. Francis Malooly
>Vicar General of the Archdiocese of Baltimore
>October 23, 1996

© 1998 Queenship Publishing

Library of Congress #: 97-068254

Published by:
>Queenship Publishing
>P.O. Box 42028
>Santa Barbara, CA 93140-2028
>(800) 647-9882 • (805) 957-4893
>Fax: (805) 957-1631

Printed in the United States of America

ISBN: 1-57918-007-8

DEDICATION

This book is dedicated to Maureen, whose love and devotion to God helped me through very difficult times.

ABOUT THE AUTHOR

Robert Sungenis is the president of Catholic Apologetics International, an organization dedicated to teaching and defending the Catholic faith. Born into a Catholic family in 1955, Robert left the Church and became a Reformed Protestant at the age of 19. He served as an elder, itinerant preacher, adult education director, and radio bible teacher. He converted back to Catholicism in 1992. He was educated at George Washington University (Bachelors Degree, 1979), and Westminster Theological Seminary (Masters Degree, 1982). He is presently pursuing doctoral studies at the Maryvale Institute in Birmingham, England. Publications include: *Shockwave 2000* (New Leaf Press, 1994); *Not By Faith Alone: The Biblical Evidence of the Catholic Doctrine of Justification* (Queenship Publishing, 1997); contributor to *Surprised By Truth* (Basilica Press, 1994); contributor to *Jesus, Peter and the Keys* (Queenship Publishing, 1996); general editor and contributor to: *Not By Scripture Alone: A Catholic Critique of the Protestant Doctrine of Sola Scriptura* (Queenship Publishing, 1997); various articles in Catholic Periodicals and a frequent guest on the Eternal Word Television Network.

CONTENTS

Chapter 4
Is My Justification a One-Time Event
or an Ongoing Process? 149

Chapter 5
Can I Lose My Salvation? 169

FOREWORD
BY THOMAS HOWARD

There is a sense in which one wonders why a book like this was not written 450 years ago. Robert Sungenis, with immense courtesy, circumspection, and thoroughness — biblical, theological, ecclesial, and personal — treats, with disarming forthrightness, all of the questions that loomed in the great debates carried on by Luther, Melanchthon, Dr. Eck, Cardinal Cajetan, Cardinal Bellarmine, Calvin, and the rest of them.

The "sola's" of Protestantism have been the eye, so to speak, of a hurricane that has been blowing for half a millennium now. No "sola" has proved more nettlesome than Luther's *sola fides*. By faith alone. Is this, in fact, what Scripture teaches? What is the faith spoken of in the New Testament? What is required of us mortals in order that we be saved in the end? Are works a Roman addition to the true Gospel?

Ordinarily, the debate on the highest theological level has not made much more progress than have the shouting matches amongst zealous laity over the riddle.

It is difficult to imagine just how a careful (and honest) reader of the following pages might reach a conclusion other than the one put forward by Robert Sungenis. He has left no stone unturned: a glance at the (quite lively, as it happens) Table of Contents ought to assure any potential reader that he has in his hand a volume that sweeps nothing under the rug. Scripture has been combed with a very fine-toothed comb — both Testaments, it may be pointed out. Every question that troubles a Protestant over what they suppose to be the Roman teaching about salvation by works has been canvassed. Merely the first two chapter titles find us off and running:

"Did Paul Teach I Can be Saved By Faith Alone" and "Did James Teach I'm Justified By My Works?"

The great advantage of this volume is that it is written quite consciously for the lay Christian. Mr. Sungenis's prior book, *Not By Faith Alone*, is an exhaustive and heavily-footnoted treatise on the same topic. Anyone with a certain salting of theological stamina and courage is urged most heartily to go on from this present volume to the bracing highlands of the bigger book.

INTRODUCTION

How Can I Get To Heaven? That is a question that has been asked thousands of times in the course of human history — but not always with the same answer. Many years ago a Philippian jailer asked a similar question of Paul the apostle. Acts 16:31 records Paul's response, "Believe in the Lord Jesus and you shall be saved." Believe! That seems plain enough. In reading that simple statement one might wonder why someone would have to write a book, such as this one, to explain what it means. Then we read the rest of Acts 16:31: "...you and your household." Immediately, questions rush to our head. Did the jailer have children? If so, does this verse teach that the children were saved upon the belief of the jailer? More questions surface as we read verses 32-34 where we find Paul baptizing the jailer and his whole household sometime after midnight. Why, we wonder, did Paul insist on baptizing them, and so soon, in the middle of the night? Was the baptism a necessary part of being saved? What prompted the jailer to inquire about salvation? Did he do so of his own free will or did God predestinate him to do so, or both? And what happened to the jailer and his family afterward? Did they remain steadfast to the Christian faith or fall away? For that matter, what did Paul really mean when he said, "believe in the Lord Jesus"? What is it about Jesus we are supposed to believe? Are we required to do anything else? In fact, how do we explain Paul's simple answer to the Philippian jailer in light of Jesus's more involved answer to the Rich Young Man in Matthew 19:16-26 who, after inquiring how one obtains eternal life, Jesus demanded nothing concerning faith; rather, he told the young man to obey the commandments and give to the poor?

Theology, by nature, can often be very complicated. When we add to this the limitations, biases, and false presuppositions of men and groups that are invariably brought to the study of Scripture, making sense out of theology can indeed be very perplexing, as history itself has proven. In the last few hundred years alone, thousands of churches and denominations have been created from that seemingly simple yet paradoxically difficult question, "How Can I Get To Heaven?" Today there remains a cacophony of voices, each telling us something a little different.[1]

Despite this confusion, this author believes God did not leave his Church with a confusing assortment of competing answers. From the beginning of his dealings with men, we will show that God made it very plain how they could be saved. We reason that it is certainly not a stretch of the imagination to purpose that if God desired men to be saved he would have given, and still does give, the precise truth he wanted them to know and live out. If we can't depend on that premise, then Christianity certainly doesn't have much to offer the world — except the same confusion by which it is surrounded.

Before he left the earth, Jesus told the apostles he would lead them into all truth (John 16:13). He told them that he would be with them and the Church till the end of the age (Matthew 28:20; John 14:16-17). Through Paul the apostle, he told us that these same truths should be passed down to other like-minded men (2 Timothy 1:13-2:2; 2 Thess. 2:15); that the Church would be "the pillar and ground of the truth" (1 Timothy 3:15). In light of these promises, we must start from the conviction that Jesus could not abandon his Church, leaving them in the dark groping for the truth of salvation that he

---

[1] According to the *Oxford World Christian Encyclopedia*, in 1982 there existed 20,800 organized churches and denominations within Christendom, "...with a projected 22,190 by 1985." The authors attribute this to "...local disagreements in how to indigenize and inculturate the Christian faith. The inevitable result has been a vast increase in the number of distinct, discrete, separate and divergent Christian denominations in many countries of the world...The present net increase is 270 denominations each year (5 new ones a week). In many countries this produces serious overlapping, competition, rivalries, clashes, violence, and even lawsuits and protracted litigation" (ed. David B. Barrett, Oxford University Press, 1982, pp. 15-18). If the projection rate continued since 1985, this would amount to over 28,000 churches and denominations at the present date.

said he would give them. It is Christ's Church, his bride, and he cherishes her as a loving husband cherishes his wife.

The book you are holding will simplify and thoroughly explain this issue for you. When all is said and done, I hope you can agree with me that the question, "How Can I Get To Heaven?" is not really complicated at all.

Robert Sungenis

CHAPTER 1

PART A:

DID PAUL TEACH THAT I CAN BE SAVED BY FAITH ALONE?

At first glance, Paul's teaching on salvation seems very complex. Because of this apparent difficulty, many conflicting views of his teaching have been proposed.

Today, a common teaching exists among various Protestant denominations. It is the teaching that man is justified before God by *faith alone*. Protestants claim that man must simply believe that Christ has done all that is required for justification. Once man believes in Christ, he is saved forever. Consequently, Protestants understand good works merely as the fruit of one's justified state, but not meritorious for justification. Likewise, bad works do not threaten one's justified state. They have already been forgiven.

Catholic theology teaches that although faith is very important, it only begins the process of justification, a process which also has a middle and an end. Justification is not a single event of faith alone, nor are works merely the fruit of such faith, but a process whereby the individual grows in justification before God by his faith and good works, a growth which can be retarded, and even terminated, by faithlessness and bad works, ending in damnation.

First, let's clarify what we mean by the word *justification*. Basically, justification is the theological term used to denote the reason or basis upon which man can go to heaven. Because God is perfect, transcendent and holy, but man is imperfect, mortal and sinful, there must be a "justifiable" reason why God would allow such a lowly creature to live with him forever. Because God must preserve his honor and holiness, he cannot just accept men into heaven without a good and justifiable reason for doing so, otherwise he would be compromising his own divine character. In order to justify our entrance into heaven, God must also remain just, honorable and holy. The remainder of this book will explain how God accomplished that feat.[1]

To get directly into the issues and controversies surrounding justification, let's start by raising the question: Did the apostle Paul teach justification by *faith alone*? For those who propose that he did, a very haunting question remains: *Why didn't Paul use the specific phrase "faith alone" anywhere in his New Testament writings*? A thorough study of his epistles reveals that Paul used the word *faith* over two hundred times in the New Testament, but not once did he couple it with the words *alone* or *only*. What would have stopped him from such an important addition if the solitude of faith in regard to justification was at the forefront of his mind?

A second reason that leads us to pose this critical question is that Paul used the word *alone* more frequently than did any other New Testament writer. Many of these instances appear right alongside the very contexts that contain teachings on faith and justification.[2] Thus it is obvious that even while Paul was teaching about the nature of justification he was keenly aware of the word *alone* and its qualifying properties. This would lead us to expect that if Paul wanted to teach clearly that man was justified by *faith alone*, he would have utilized that phrase, since it would have made his point indisputable. Moreover, since Paul's writings were inspired, we must also acknowledge that the Holy Spirit likewise knew of the word *alone* but had specific reasons for prohibiting Paul from using it in connection with faith.

Thirdly, although the Holy Spirit prohibited *Paul* from using the phrase *faith alone*, he allowed James to make a clear and forceful point to the contrary, declaring that "man is justified by works and **not** by faith alone" (James 2:24). This negative statement comes at the precise point in the epistle where James questions whether faith, by itself, is sufficient for justification. We can only conclude that the Holy Spirit's inspiration of the phrase *faith alone*, preceded by the equally important inspired phrase *not by*, clearly shows God was concerned that some would misinterpret Scripture's stress on faith to be *faith alone*.

Comparing Paul and James leads us to conclude that Paul avoids using the phrase *faith alone* because: (1) his use of the word *faith* is pregnant with theological meaning which absolutely precludes it from being coupled with the word *alone*; and (2) it would have created an obvious and acute contradiction in holy writ for one author to say, "man is justified by faith alone," while another is saying the exact opposite, namely, "man is *not* justified by faith alone."

With these facts from Scripture in the background, the burden of proof rests upon those who insist that the doctrine of justification be taught by using language that Scripture itself does not use. Although some believe that the wording "justified by faith alone" is appropriate to use because of the specific nature of justification, it is obvious that Scripture intentionally chooses not to use such language. Since Scripture deliberately uses the opposite phrase (*"not by faith alone"*) when the issue of the solitude of faith is questioned, it apparently has concluded that the expression "justified by faith alone" is not the correct way to teach people how man is justified before God. We are forced to think about this issue ever more seriously when we realize Scripture's insistence that its words are chosen very carefully, and it makes such choices precisely because it "foresees" the impact of its teaching.[3] Moreover, Scripture teaches that Paul "...wrote to you with the wisdom given to him..." (2 Peter 3:16). It was this God-given "wisdom" which prevented him from joining the word *alone* with *faith,* wisdom that is as good for us as it was for him.

OKAY, BUT HOW DO MY "WORKS" FIT IN?

If Paul did not intend to teach *faith alone*, then how do we explain his statement in Romans 3:28, "that a man is justified by faith apart from works of the law"? Could one not argue that the phrase *"apart from"* is very similar to the word *alone,* and thus conclude that Paul really did teach that faith is alone in justification? To answer this, we must first point out that "justified by faith alone" does not mean the same thing as "justified by faith apart from works of the law." Just based on grammar, the phrase "faith alone" means that faith is the *only* instrument for justification, while the statement "faith apart from works of the law" merely means that "works of the law" — whatever they are — are the only thing that cannot be coupled with faith for justification. In other words, "faith alone" excludes anything from being added to faith, while "faith apart from works of the law" excludes only "works of the law" from being added to faith. This leaves open the possibility that perhaps something may be added to faith that is not considered "works of the law," or that we could understand "faith" as being associated with other virtues that are not technically related to "works of the law."[4] In light of this reasoning, we never find Paul saying, "man is justified by faith apart from love," or "man is justified by faith apart from obedience," or "man is justified by faith apart from hope." In fact, in speaking of justification, in Galatians 5:6 Paul creates an intimate bond between faith and love by the statement "faith working through love." In addition, in Romans 1:5 and 16:26 Paul demonstrates an intimate link between faith and obedience by the unique phrase, "the obedience of faith." By the same token, Paul never says "faith working through works of the law." Apparently, there is something very important to be discovered concerning Paul's meaning of *works of the law* which prohibits him from joining it with faith. Hence, although we must give due justice to Paul's dictum that faith must be apart from *works of the law,* this does not necessarily mean that faith is completely alone, especially from other virtues like love and obedience. According to certain Scriptures, there is something about the concept of *works of the law* which forces Paul to separate it from his concept of faith, yet dissimilar Scriptures allow, or even require, one to add other virtues, which are not necessarily associated with *works of the law*, in order to achieve justification.

Suppose someone were to argue, however, that love cannot be coupled with faith in justification because love itself, or even obedience or hope, should be classified as a *work of the law*. From this stance, someone can make the claim that if love, obedience, and hope are not separated from faith in regard to justification then there would be a contradiction between what Scripture says in one place and what it says in another. It is precisely on this particular point that Martin Luther (1483 -1546) decided to divorce love, hope, and obedience from faith, opting to use the phrase *faith alone* and put these three virtues on the side of *works of the law* that cannot justify. Other Protestants disagreed with Luther and leaned more toward defining faith in terms of love and obedience. Therein lies the controversy — a controversy not only between Catholics and Protestants, but among Protestant denominations themselves. Much of the controversy hinges on just how one defines and understands Paul's reference to *works of the law*.

But even if one insists on using the language "justified by faith alone" to express the uniqueness of faith in justification, one must still admit that the individual who exercises faith in God, at least in one sense, is "doing something" in order to be justified, regardless of whether that "something" is classified as an act, a work, or a mere mental process. It cannot be denied that even faith requires some effort from the individual, despite how one wishes to classify that effort, or however large or small that effort may be. It is no surprise that one's understanding of faith, either as a "work" or a "non-work," "qualified" or "non-qualified," becomes a great source of contention among various Protestant churches and denominations.

✗ And the issue is not over. Consider this: If the justification of the person requires that faith be apart from works of the law, then what did Paul mean when he wrote just one chapter earlier in Romans 2:13, "For it is not the hearers of the law that are just with God, but the *doers of the law* will be justified"? In this passage Paul says precisely that the *law* (not love or obedience) justifies, while in Romans 3:28 he says specifically that justification comes apart from works of the law. From reading these two passages Paul suggests that there is a particular sense in which works or law justify and another sense in which they do not. To many, these passages seem somewhat confusing.

We are beginning to see why the answer to the question posed above (i.e., "OK, but how do my works fit in?") cannot be solved by simply separating faith from works, nor adding a phrase such as "faith alone" into the interpretation. In fact, if we fail to address this issue properly, a cursory study of Paul's teaching appears contradictory at some points and leads either to total confusion, or worse, leads to premature and erroneous conclusions as to what he actually taught on this subject.[5] However, despite what may appear to be a confusing assortment of facts and ideas regarding Paul's view of justification, Paul himself gives us a very simple principle that enables us to understand his teaching, which we will now introduce.

PAUL'S PRINCIPLE OF "OBLIGATION"

To begin to uncover the true relationship between faith and works, the first thing we need to understand is one of the most fundamental principles in the theology of Paul. That principle concerns the matter of *legal obligation* or *debt*. We see this principle established in that most famous of passages, Romans 4:4: *"To the one working, the wage is not reckoned according to grace but according to obligation."* To help us understand this principle, Paul uses the example of the employer who is obligated to pay his employee for his work. In the way Paul is using the term "obligation," it refers to a measured compensation which is legally owed by one party to another. The party in debt is obligated to pay the party owed, or the party who performs work is legally entitled to be paid for his services from the party for whom the work is done. Since we understand work as something which requires the strenuous use of one's faculties, the worker is someone who must be remunerated, in some manner, equal to his efforts. Commonly speaking, for an hour's work, he must be paid an hour's wage. Unless the employer wants to break the law, he is legally required to pay the worker what is due him. It does not matter whether the employer loves or hates, likes or dislikes, the employee. He is under obligation to pay him.

Establishing this principle of *obligation*, Paul introduces the foundational rule regarding anyone who attempts to "work" his way to God. If the appeal to God is based on obligation, then the relationship between God and man becomes one in which the party who works (man) is legally *obligating* the party for whom the work is done (God) to pay for the work performed. Hence, in regard to justification, a man who approaches God expecting legal remuneration for his efforts thus puts God in a position of being "obligated" to deem him righteous and acceptable, worthy of living with God and being blessed by him for eternity. Since in this situation God would be forced to owe a *legal* debt to the man who works, then the relationship is one based on law, i.e., a legal contract. If it is based on law, then it cannot be based on God's personal benevolence, otherwise known as *grace*. This is precisely why Paul, in Romans 3:28, says, "a man is justified by faith apart from works of the law." In the larger picture, "works of law" refers to "works done solely under legal contract" which demand payment or reward for performance, regardless of whether or not the person doing the work believes in and loves his benefactor. Conversely, if man appeals to God's graciousness, God would repay out of benevolence, but he is not legally obligated to do so.[6] This is the primary distinction between grace and works. Paul reiterates this principle in Romans 11:6 by saying: "And if by grace, then it is no longer by works; if it were, grace would no longer be grace."[7]

THE STORY OF ADAM AND EVE

To understand the contrast between grace and works a little better, we need a theological backdrop to the principle of *obligation* that Paul is establishing in Romans 4:4. What God possesses that everyone desires is to be like God and to live eternally. In the very beginning, Adam and Eve wanted to be like God and live in eternal bliss. Deceived by the devil, they became convinced that the easiest way to obtain this blessed state was to eat immediately of the tree of the knowledge of good and evil — a tree that God had forbidden. After they sinned by eating of the fruit, God, knowing that Adam and Eve might attempt again to gain eternal life by eating from the *tree of life*, placed an angel to guard it with a flaming sword (Genesis 3:22-24). God subsequently banished them from the Garden. Although God prohibited Adam and Eve from gaining eternal life the quick and easy way, in his gracious love God still made it possible for them to obtain heavenly bliss. He promised them a redeemer who would suffer for Adam's sin and once again open the pathway to God's kingdom (Genesis 3:15). Accordingly, the primary purpose for all God's work on earth is that man can one day receive the blessing of heaven and live with God eternally. Heaven is, or should be, the ultimate goal of every person.

Under the terms Paul uses in Romans 4:4, he indicates two ways in which eternal life is obtained: (1) that which one receives as a *gift* from God, or (2) that which is *owed* to the individual for work performed. If heaven is a gift, then it comes by grace. Conversely, if heaven is given because it is owed, then it is no longer by grace, since the giver is legally obligated to bestow it on the one who works. In either case, whether by grace or by works, there must be a justifiable reason why an imperfect and untested creature can be permitted to enter the dwelling of a perfect, holy, and transcendent Creator. If by works, the person must fulfill all the legal requirements to justify his entrance into heaven. If by grace, the person receives heaven as a gift — a gift that the giver is not obligated to give but does so only because of his kindness and mercy. Of the two options before man, grace or legal obligation, Paul goes on to explain that the problem with attempting to attain heaven based on obligation is two-fold. First, since God is the transcendent Creator, and the heaven in which he dwells is perfect, then those who wish to work under the terms of a legal contract in order to justify their entrance into heaven must work perfectly.[8] Under a contractual arrangement, only when the work is perfect can man put God in a position of being *obligated* to pay him. Essentially, perfect work would earn a perfect payment.

The second problem with attempting to enter heaven based on obligation is the reality of sin.[9] This fact brings us back to Adam and Eve. Once Adam and Eve failed the test in the Garden of Eden, God's precepts required that they and all their progeny come under the curse of sin and death. Paul explains this principle in Romans 5:12: "Therefore, as through one man sin entered into the world, and through sin came death, and so death passed to all men, upon which all sinned." Paul also says something similar in Romans 3:9-11: "...We have previously accused Jews and Gentiles of being all under sin. As it is written, 'There is not a righteous man, not even one. There is not one who understands, there is not one who seeks God.'" Again in Romans 3:19 and 23 Paul says: "...and the whole world is held accountable to God...for all have sinned and fall short of the glory of God." It is quite clear that Adam and Eve created a serious problem. They forced God to withdraw himself from the human race to the extent that everyone created had to come under the reign of sin and death. All of mankind would inherit the stain of sin from Adam and continue to sin by their own will. They lost the complete protection of God from the forces of nature. They would also face physical death.[10] Hence, with the curse of sin and death as part of their very nature, trying to work their way to heaven by attempting to legally obligate God to bless them would be an impossible task. No one could ever perform the work required to constrain God to pay one with eternal life. In fact, under law, God's judgments are so penetrating and uncompromising that anyone attempting to work his way to heaven while in the state of sin and death would only obligate God to pay with eternal punishment. As Paul says in Romans 6:23, "For the *wages* [i.e., legal payment] of sin is death..." Consequently, obligation can never serve as the basis upon which we gain entrance into heaven. Salvation can only come as a result of grace wherein man does not put God in a position of being legally obligated to pay him. Because of the specific nature of God's relationship to man, God must bestow salvation upon man as a gift.[11]

WHO IS THIS GOD WHO JUSTIFIES?

GOD IS TRANSCENDENT, HOLY AND HONORABLE

In correlation with Paul's principle of wages and obligation, a second key to understanding justification is to understand the God behind it. As noted above, God is a totally transcendent and perfect being. Because of his transcendent status, God owes nothing to anyone. Those who attempt to obligate God to favor them are woefully inadequate for the task. As Paul says in Romans 11:33-35:

> Oh, the depth of the riches of the wisdom and knowledge of God! How unsearchable his judgments, and his paths beyond tracing out! Who has known the mind of the Lord? Or who has been his counselor? *Who has ever given to God that God should repay him*? For from him and through him and to him are all things.

In the words, "Who has ever given to God that God should repay him" we have one of the most succinct statements of Paul's theology. God is not obligated to repay anyone for their work simply because no one has ever given anything to God that deserves legal payment. Paul is saying the same thing in Romans 11:35 that he said in Romans 4:4, that is, one cannot put God in a position of obligation to repay. Therefore, one cannot establish his relationship to God based on working for pay. This was true of Adam and Eve and it is certainly true for us today.

Other instances that emphasize God's transcendent nature are the frequent descriptions of his holiness. In Isaiah 6:3 the prophet records, "Holy, Holy, Holy is the Lord Almighty, the whole earth is full of his glory." To stress its significance, God's holiness is repeated three times. We understand from statements like these that God is perfectly pure; with not the slightest presence of evil. The extent of God's holiness is seen, for example, when he is dealing with the Israelites at the giving of the Ten Commandments in Exodus 19. God is so holy he will not even allow any of the people to *touch* the mountain that Moses ascends to receive the commandments. In verse 12 God says to Moses, "Put limits for the people around the mountain and tell them, 'Be careful that you do not go up the mountain or touch the foot of it. Whoever touches the mountain shall surely be put to death'" (cf. Hebrews 12:18-21). Similarly, in Isaiah 55:9 God contrasts his awesome transcendence to man's lowliness and sinful condition with the words, "As the heavens are higher than the earth, so are my ways higher than your ways, and my thoughts than your thoughts." As for preserving his honor in the face of sin, this is portrayed no better than in the account of Phinehas who, under the Lord's command, killed those committing idolatry. Concerning Phinehas God says, "...for he was as zealous as I am for my honor among them..." (Numbers 25:11).

GOD IS VERY PERSONAL: AS A FATHER TO A SON

Right alongside God's transcendent status is his personal nature. God is an intensely personal being. He loves, he hates, he has joy, he has sorrow, he sings, he laughs, he is jealous, he is kind, he has pity, he has anger.[12] Often we think of God as being so transcendent, so totally-other, that we forget how intensely personal he is. Scripture's description of God's personality is not imaginary. God really has these personal qualities and he consistently expresses them to us. His intense emotional and passionate qualities are not signs of impetuousness and capriciousness. They are all divine qualities and as such are perfect in God. Because we are made in his image, we get a glimpse of what God is like personally. All our personal qualities derive from him, except that his personal qualities are more dynamic, without sin, and perfectly suited to his divinity. In being such an intensely personal being, God desires that we relate to him very personally. God is not interested in a superficial, mechanical, "do this—don't do that" kind of relationship. He wants us to love him as intensely as he loves us. Not surprisingly, God is personally offended when men sin. God is not to be pictured as an unemotional courtroom judge who has no vested interest or has no personal feelings for or against the criminal brought before him. No, God is a Father who has lost his wayward sons and he is intensely jealous for their return. He has a personal stake in their salvation.

As regards justification, Paul makes the personal nature of God and man a primary part of his teaching. We see a dramatic example of this dimension as Paul, speaking for God, complains of those who "boast" of their works before God and think that God owes them something for their self-styled efforts. In the heart of his teaching, Paul repeatedly mentions "boasting" in reference to the Jew's attempt to assent to God, e.g., Romans 2:17, "you rely on the law and *boast*"; Romans 2:23, "You *boast* about the law"; Romans 3:27, "Where then is *boasting*? It is excluded"; and Romans 4:2, "If, in fact, Abraham was justified by works, he had something to *boast* about but not before God." By the same token, Paul also warns the Gentiles about boasting. In reference to God's rejection of the Jews who he compares to branches that had been cut off, Paul tells the Gentile believers in Romans 11:18-22, "do not *boast* over those branches...they were broken off because of unbelief, and you stand by faith. Do not be arrogant but be afraid...Otherwise you also will be cut off." Similarly, Paul mentions grace in opposition to "boasting" in Ephesians 2:8-9: "For it is by grace you have been saved, through faith — and this is not of yourselves, it is the gift of God — not of works so that no one can *boast*." Again, to the Corinthian Gentiles in 1 Corinthians 4:7 Paul says, "What do you have that you did not receive? And if you did receive it, why do you *boast* as though you did not."

"Boasting" about one's adherence to the law conveys a proud attitude of the mind and heart, one in which the individual fails to recognize his own faults, judges the faults of others, and, most of all, attempts to place God in a position of being obligated to give payment for the work performed. Such a self-righteous individual thinks that he has performed a sufficient quantity or quality of work to *require* God to save him. But no creature can put God in a position of being obligated to save him, least of all those who out of hubris demand his blessing. Men who do not acknowledge this are a personal affront to God. God is personally offended by their arrogance and he will not save them.

FAITH : THE BEGINNING OF MY SALVATION

In contrast to works performed in an attempt to obligate God, Paul speaks of justification by God's grace through our faith. In Romans 3:22-24, Paul says:

> This righteousness from God comes through faith in Jesus Christ to all who believe. There is no difference because all have sinned and come short of the glory of God, and are justified freely by his grace through the redemption that came by Jesus Christ.

Paul often opposes *faith* to *works of law* in reference to being justified; yet we have also seen earlier from Romans 2:13 that Paul requires obedience to the law for justification. This seems to be contradictory. In order to solve this problem we must understand what Paul intends by the word "faith," what he intends by the words "works of law," and why, in spite of his doctrine in Romans 2:13, he maintains the opposition between faith and works in Romans 3:28. Simply put, the terms "faith" and "works" are extremely important to Paul because they represent two diametrically opposed ways in which one's approach to God is *grounded* or *established*. As noted above, God is a personal being who wants man to relate to him on a personal level. He is not an impersonal, unemotional, unconcerned third party. Hence, because faith is intrinsically personal, it is the ideal word to describe one who recognizes God's identity; one who takes a sincere interest in God's purposes and plans; one who trusts that God is good and looking out for everyone's best interests; one who recognizes that because God is the Creator and perfect he does not owe anything to anyone; that everything comes from his personal love and benevolence.

Conversely, Paul uses "works" or "works of law" as *contractual* terms connoting an impersonal employer/employee kind of relationship: someone who is under contract to do a job but has no interest in a personal relationship with his employer. He works for the sole purpose of remuneration but has no genuine regard for the goals and aspirations of his payer. He boasts of his accomplishments and expects to be paid handsomely for his work. Such attempts are an insult to God. If man approaches God merely as an employer, God will simply show him that, compared to God's perfection, all his work amounts to naught and subsequently he is owed nothing, except condemnation for his sins. As Isaiah 40:17 says, "Before him all the nations are as nothing; they are regarded by him as worthless and less than nothing" or Isaiah 64:6, "All of us have become like one who is unclean, and all our righteous acts are like filthy rags."

To say it another way, with respect to his principle of obligation, Paul uses the concept of faith to represent the primary element of human volition that recognizes and submits to knowing and relating to God through his grace. Paul's faith is an act performed within the mind and heart of one who willingly assents to understand truly the nature of God and what he requires of man. Paul's faith is the product of a thinking personality who comes to recognize God's benevolent nature, man's weakness, and what must be done to rectify the problem of sin. Because God is a personal being who must be approached personally, one who attempts to obligate God to pay him (as an employee does to an employer) but does not acknowledge who God really is and what he really desires, can neither please God nor establish a legitimate relationship with him. God's personal character demands that man must first recognize God's true identity and what God desires before he can ever approach God. As God told Moses in Exodus 3:5,14: "Do not come any closer...Take off your sandals, for the place you are standing is holy ground...I am who I am." Consequently, we cannot come to God by trying to obligate him through our self-righteous works because if the efforts of man are thrust in the face of God without God first establishing the proper relationship with that person — a relationship of grace and benevolence prompted by personal faith — the uncompromising principles of legal obligation will simply show, without grace, all the instances in which we have failed to measure up to God's perfect righteousness, and thus we will be condemned. Hence, since the relationship between God and man requires man's acknowledgment and appreciation of its personal quality, the first condition of justification is faith, a faith which must recognize God's grace in order to be saved. Thus, we can paraphrase a passage like Ephesians 2:8 in this way: "For it is by grace you have been saved, grace which is acknowledged by your faith; you are not saved by your own self- righteous works which attempt to obligate God; rather, salvation is a gift of God's grace so that no one will be able to boast before God that he attained salvation through his own efforts."

THE JEWISH CEREMONIAL LAWS

In several instances in Paul's writings, his objection to those who depend on works of law for justification concerns the Jewish ritual works such as circumcision, dietary laws and sabbath observance. For example, after upbraiding Peter for eating kosher food with Jews and at the same time separating himself from Gentiles, Paul says in Galatians 2:14-15, "...How is it, then, that you force Gentiles to follow Jewish customs? We who are Jews by birth and not 'Gentile sinners' know that a man is not justified by works of the law, but by faith in Jesus Christ." Obviously, Paul's concern here is on the ceremonial dietary laws of Old Testament Israel that were no longer binding on new converts to the Christian faith. Also, in Colossians 2:16-17 Paul says, "Therefore do not let anyone judge you by what you eat or drink, or with regard to a religious festival, a New Moon celebration or a Sabbath day. These are a shadow of the things that were to come; the reality, however, is found in Christ." This passage is referring to additional Jewish ceremonial laws that become obsolete. Thus, it is safe to say that one of Paul's primary concerns is that converts to the Christian faith do not practice obsolete Old Testament ceremonial rituals in order to achieve justification. This is a constant theme in Paul's writings as well as the book of Acts. This should be no surprise, since for the first time in history the Jews were being set aside as God's chosen people and replaced by the New Testament Church. Naturally, questions would surface as to which Old Testament laws and practices were no longer required. For this very reason, Acts 15 records the deliberations at the Council of Jerusalem, the first council of the budding New Testament Church, which decided that Old Testament circumcision would no longer be required of those entering the Church. In the New Testament, a new and better act of God would be instituted which would forever replace circumcision. That divine action was the sacrament of baptism. The reason is that ceremonies were under the Law; did not confer grace; and therefore could not justify a man. New Testament sacraments are under grace; confer grace; and thus can justify.[13]

In reality, God never desired the ceremonial laws of Israel to perpetuate. Although they were originally given as a sign of Israel's separation from the nations (Exodus 8:20-23; Romans 4:11), eventually their numerous and monotonous practices were required as a sign of penitence for their continual rebellion. As God says in Ezekiel 20:25: "I also gave them over to statutes that were not good and laws they could not live by." Similarly, Paul says in Hebrews 10:3,8: "But those sacrifices are an annual reminder of sins, because it is impossible for the blood of bulls and goats to take away sins... Sacrifices and offerings, burnt offerings and sin offerings you did not desire, nor were you pleased with them (although the law required them to be made)."

PAUL'S EVALUATION OF THE LAW

Although the Jew's attempt to continue practicing the obsolete ceremonial law was one of Paul's main concerns, this was not his only concern. Paul's more basic and fundamental concern was the Jew's whole concept of law. The Jew's elevation and insistence on circumcision was merely the result of their distorted concept of law in general. In Romans 3:20 Paul says:

...because by the works of the law no one will be justified before him, for through the law is the full knowledge of sin.

Here Paul uses the phrase "works of the law." This refers to any performance of works which were stipulated by the law. For the Jews, "works of the law" consisted chiefly in performing ritual rites of ceremony in an effort to be justified before God. Circumcision was one of the more prominent rites, as noted in Paul's stress on circumcision in Romans 2:25-29 and 4:9-11.[14] However, even though Paul focuses on the Jew's performance of legal ceremonies, each time he uses "works of the law" he includes a singular reference to the "Law." For example, the latter half of Romans 3:20 says, "for through the *law* is the full knowledge of sin." Here Paul uses the singular "law" as that which makes man conscious of his sin. From this usage we can see that Paul's overarching principle is that works performed solely on the basis of law (i.e., "works of the law") cannot justify, because the "Law" from which the works are derived is designed primarily to make a man conscious of his own sin.

This principle is seen even more clearly in Galatians 3:10-12. Paul writes:

> For as many as are of the works of the law, they are under a curse; for it is written, 'Accursed is everyone who does not continue in all the things which have been written in the Book of the Law. That no man is justified by God by the law is clear, because the just man will live by faith; and the law is not of faith, but the man doing them must live by them.

Here again Paul uses the phrase "works of the law" (the same phrase he uses in Galatians 2:14-16 in reference to Jewish dietary laws), but then he shifts his focus to "Law." Why? Because Paul, as he did in Romans 3:20, is making the inadequacy of Law, in itself, the overarching reason why doing "works of the law" cannot justify. Paul's primary message is that if one tries to be justified before God by doing works based solely on the law, he then places himself back into the *system of Law* — a system that will require him to obey everything written in the Law, without fault, otherwise he will be "cursed." Conversely, Paul says a man is justified by faith. Why? Because faith denotes a relationship based on a gratuitous and personal tie between two parties, not a relationship built on legalism and contract. As Paul says in Galatians 3:12, "the law is not of faith," because law is based on an impersonal, legal contract. A man who bases his justification on law "must live by them" perfectly, otherwise he will be condemned.

WE ARE RELEASED FROM THE LAW

Later in Romans 7:6-11, using himself as an example, Paul shows us another reason why he has more than obsolete ceremonial rituals in mind when he condemns the law for justification:

> But now, by dying to what once bound us, we have been *released from the law* so that we serve in the new way of the Spirit, and not in the *old way of the written code.*

What shall we say, then? Is the law sin? Certainly not! Indeed I would not have known what sin was except through the law. For I would not have known what coveting really was if the law had not said, 'Do not covet.' ...I found that the very commandment that was intended to bring life actually brought death. For sin, seizing the opportunity afforded by the commandment, deceived me, and through the commandment put me to death.

Here Paul refers to *"the old way of the written code."* Then he goes on to explain what "written" law he has in view. It is the Decalogue itself, as noted in his specifying of the Ninth and Tenth Commandments which said "do not covet." The Ten Commandments were the moral component of the Mosaic law and it is that specific law from which Paul says he was "released." Just as a wife is released from the law binding her to the husband upon his death (Romans 7:1-3), so the Christian is released from the law which condemns him in sin. Paul says it was precisely these moral stipulations of the law which brought him death. The law was good and holy, but it could not save him, because Paul could never keep its demands perfectly. Only the grace of God could save him. Since the law was an uncompromising judge and prosecutor, Paul had to be liberated from the law in order to be saved. This agrees with what Paul said in Romans 6:14, "because you are not under law, but under grace," and what he would later say concerning the position of the law after Christ's work of redemption in 2 Corinthians 3:7: the law of Moses is "the ministry that brought death, which was engraved in letters on stone..." In Galatians 3:23 Paul says, "Before faith came, we were held prisoners by the law, locked up until faith should be revealed." Colossians 2:14 says that God "forgave us our sins, having canceled the written code, with its regulations, that was against us and that stood opposed to us." Ephesians 2:15 says Christ "...abolished in his flesh the law with its commandments and regulations." In other words, in order to live in grace we had to be released from the condemnation of the Law.

PAUL CONDEMNS A LIFE
BY THE "WRITTEN CODE"

The importance in Paul placing the moral law under the heading of "the old written code" in Romans 7:6-8 becomes even more significant as we discover it being the same phrase he used in Romans 2:29 when referring to circumcision: "No, a man is a Jew if he is one inwardly; and circumcision is circumcision of the heart, by the Spirit, not by the *written code.*" Hence, by showing us that the "written code" includes both the ceremonial and moral aspects of the law, it is clear Paul desires to supersede the *whole* Mosaic law. Paul had to revamp and completely reconstruct the true meaning and purpose of the law for the Jew. They thought the law was their ticket to heaven. In fact, they even boasted of their possession of the Ten Commandments, telling others to obey them but disobeying the commands themselves (Romans 2:17-24; Matthew 19:16-26). In reality, as Paul says in Romans 7:10-11, the law, by itself, without grace, only brings death.[15]

All in all, faith is not something which is written. It is a matter of the mind and heart. Likewise, grace, love, promise and obedience are not written. They go far beyond the written code, into areas that the written code could never penetrate. As Jesus repeatedly said in the Sermon on the Mount, "You have heard that it was said...but I say unto you," he was trying to get the people to think beyond the bare commands of law and to live a life of the Spirit which seeks to show heartfelt love to one's neighbor in every area of life. In fact, Paul teaches that if one insists in living by a written code, then God will use that same written code to judge him. For one sin against the written code, the code will eternally condemn him. As Paul says in Galatians 5:3: "Again I declare to every man who lets himself be circumcised that he is obligated to obey the whole law." And James 2:10 explains the unbearable problem in putting oneself under obligation to obey the whole law: "For whoever keeps the whole law and yet stumbles at just one point is guilty of breaking all of it."

PART B:

MY FAITH AND WORKS AS VIEWED FROM GOD'S GRACE

Although in many Scriptures Paul takes great pains to make the sharpest distinction possible between faith, on the one hand, and a written code of works performed in legal obligation, on the other hand, in other Scriptures he creates the most intimate connection between faith and obedience to God's law. This connection is so strong that it is quite biblical to state that without obedience to the law it is impossible to be justified and enter the kingdom of heaven.[16] Some may find this conclusion contradictory, since we seem to be saying that law is both condemnatory and salvific. Nevertheless, once one understands the basis for Paul's distinction between 'works done under the principle of legal obligation' as opposed to 'works performed under the auspices of God's grace,' the apparent contradiction disappears. We have stressed above the basis for the distinction Paul makes between grace and works by pointing out that man cannot obligate God to pay him for his work. Once man recognizes that any reward or blessing he receives is given strictly from the grace of God, rather than as legal payment which is owed, he will then understand the relationship between faith and works from the proper perspective.[17]

To help understand the principle of works performed under grace, or what we may now introduce as "gracious merit," we can borrow from Paul's analogy of the employer/employee relationship he used in Romans 4:4. We have already learned that if the employee contracts with the employer to be paid X amount of dollars for X amount of work, this arrangement is formalized in a written agreement and is made binding by law, i.e., it is a legal contract. Whether or not the employer likes or trusts his employee, he is nonetheless legally obligated to pay him for the work performed. If, on the other hand, the employer asks the employee to do some personal work for him outside of the legal contract — work that is "not on company time" or is "off the clock," as it were

— and promises to pay the employee an appropriate sum, such an arrangement is not under the legal contract of employment. Although we can say that the employee has "merited" payment by the mere fact that he has worked, nevertheless, for work that is "not on company time" the employer is not *contractually* obligated to pay the employee. Yet because of the employer's personal integrity, and perhaps because of a personal relationship he has cultivated with the employee, he will gladly pay what he feels the extra work is worth even though he is not legally required to do so. The employer could very easily renege on his promise to pay for work performed "off the clock," yet because he is honest and just he will not stoop to such underhanded behavior. God's relationship to man is very similar. Although man cannot put God in a position of being legally obligated to pay him for his work, outside of the legal framework God can reward man. Because of his personal integrity, and because he has cultivated a personal relationship with the individual through faith, God can repay out of his graciousness. For God, who is fair, just and compassionate, graciously rewarding man's work is the proper thing to do. This principle of God's dealing with man is stated no better than in Hebrews 6:10, "God is not unjust; he will not forget your work and the love you have shown him..."

Once we commit ourselves to view our works before God from the proper perspective, we must conclude that Paul does not teach that law, understood in the proper sense, is always antithetical to justification. We must maintain that Paul is condemning justification by law only with respect to contractual obligation, that is, when man attempts to demand payment from God for his works. Outside of the realm of contractual obligation, however, the law, as expressed and practiced in virtue, fully cooperates with grace in justification.

THE PROOF: ROMANS 2:5-10

ETERNAL LIFE: THE REWARD OF GOOD WORKS

Let us observe how Paul views the distinction between works performed under the principle of obligation as opposed to works performed under grace. He elaborates on this distinction in the way he describes God's blessing for good works and God's judgment for bad works. One of the first expressions of Paul's positive view of works in regard to salvation occurs in Romans 2:5-10:

> ...of the righteous judgment of God, who will give to each man according to his works. On the one hand, to those who persist in good work, seeking glory, honor and incorruption, [he will give] eternal life. To the others who are self-seeking and disobey the truth, who follow unrighteousness, [he will give] wrath and anger. Affliction and anguish on every soul of man who works evil, to the Jew first and also to the Greek. But [he will give] glory and honor and peace to everyone who works good, to the Jew first and also to the Greek.

Romans 2:5-10 shows that in Paul's view, God saves or condemns based on the works performed by the individual. We see this clearly in his remark, verse 7, that God will give *"eternal life"* to those who *"persist in good work."* This is quite a bold statement, tantamount to saying that one can obtain eternal life by his good works. Consequently, it must also be true that *"wrath and anger"* in the same passage refers to the opposite of eternal life, namely eternal damnation. Paul's couching of his view of good and bad works within the framework of eternal life and eternal damnation assures us that he is speaking in a salvation context. This is the same salvation context he uses in Romans 3-6 where he contrasts faith against works and concludes in Romans 6:23: "for the wages of sin is death but the gift of God is *eternal life* through Jesus Christ our Lord." Hence one may wonder after reading Romans 2:5-10 and then reading Romans 3-6:23 if there is a contradiction in Paul's thinking. Does God determine whether we receive eternal life based on our works as it seems in Romans 2, or is it by faith without works as it seems in Romans 3 and 6?

To answer this question, we have already learned Paul does not teach that a man can "earn," (in the strict, legal sense of the word), the reward of eternal life. To reiterate, Romans 4:4 makes it unquestionably clear that when one attempts to "earn" his salvation based on works he is obligating God to "pay" him with eternal life. Because of man's nature and condition, God cannot be obligated to pay any man for anything. Hence we must conclude that the works Paul requires in Romans 2:5-10 are not those he considers as putting God in a position of obligation to pay the individual with eternal life. Rather, it is presumed that those who "persist in doing good" and who "seek glory, honor, and incorruption" are doing so under the advocacy of God's grace and mercy.

That the works of Romans 2:5-10 are those which are performed under God's grace is introduced just one verse prior in Romans 2:4 where Paul says: "Or do you despise the riches of his kindness and his forbearance and longsuffering, not realizing that the kindness of God leads you to repentance?" The divine qualities of "kindness," "forbearance," and "longsuffering" are virtues of God that flow from his grace.[18] This is proven in that if God were not exhibiting grace, his response would be to show no mercy to men and thus destroy them at the first sign of disobedience. Moreover, God is not obligated to "lead them to repentance," or tolerate their sin. It is God's grace that gives men the opportunity to and leads them to repent and do good works. As Peter says in 2 Peter 3:9: "The Lord...is longsuffering toward us not wishing any to perish but for all men to come to repentance."

Since Paul speaks of "repentance" in Romans 2:4, and follows this with God giving "eternal life" to the ones who have repented and "persist in doing good," but "wrath and anger" to the ones who have not repented, all the elements of the New Testament gospel are present in this passage. Paul confirms this himself in Romans 2:16 when he says in summary, "...as my gospel declares." In light of this, we must also understand that the good works of Romans 2:5-10, being done in the context of repentance from sin, are works which presuppose faith in God, as well as an acknowledgment of personal sin. One cannot repent to God and do good works (i.e., works that are done for the purpose of "seeking immortality"), without truly believing in God. Hence, the works of Romans 2:5-10, accompanied by faith and repentance, are *not* works done under the principle of debt or obligation that Paul repudiates in Romans 4:4, but works done with the proper attitude and under the auspices of God's grace which seek their recognition and reward from within that grace. We must also note that the principle in Romans 2 of being judged for bad works and blessed for good works within a context of eternal life and eternal damnation is not at all peculiar to the New Testament, especially in Paul's epistles. In Romans 14:10-12 Paul remarks about the same future judgment:

> And why do you judge your brother? Or, indeed, why do you despise your brother? For we shall all stand before the judgment seat of God. For it is written: 'As I live, says the Lord, every knee will bend and every tongue will confess to God. So then, each one of us will give an account concerning himself to God.

If Paul lifts the doing of works for obtaining eternal life to such a height as he does in Romans 2:6-10, what, then, can we conclude about Paul's understanding of works in relation to justification? The conclusion must be that works are necessary for justification, and, in fact, are one of the principle determining factors in whether or not one obtains salvation. We say this with the proviso that Paul outrightly condemns works done from boasting with a view toward *obligating* God to pay the worker with salvation. Man can never put God in the position of being in debt to an imperfect and sinful creature. The only way God can accept our works is through his grace. Works done under the auspices of God's grace, that is, works done that do not demand payment from God but are rewarded only due to the kindness and mercy of God, are the works that Paul requires for salvation.

WHAT ELSE DID PAUL SAY ABOUT WORKS?

Do the rest of Paul's writings on the nature of works support the principle we discovered in Romans 2:4-10? Yes. We have already seen briefly that Paul holds the necessity of works in such high regard that in Romans 14:10-12 he states that all people must eventually face God's judgment throne based on their works. In the passage just prior, i.e., Romans 13, Paul specifies the basic commandments of the Decalogue as a guide for doing good works. He says in Romans 13:9-10:

> The commandments, "Do not commit adultery," "Do not murder," "Do not steal," "Do not covet," and whatever other commandment there may be, are summed up in this one rule: "Love your neighbor as yourself. Love does no harm to a neighbor." Therefore love is the fulfillment of the law.

Obviously, Paul does not downplay the commandments. He holds them up as the ideal for us to follow. What is striking about this passage, however, is that Paul speaks of love as *"the fulfillment of the law."* Paul wants the Christian to go beyond the bare *written code* of law and to come up to a higher level and understand the intent behind the law. The intent of the law is to show love to one's neighbor. Which law is this? Is it the same law that he describes in Romans 3:20 in which Paul says, "because by the works of the law no one will be justified before him, for through the law is the full knowledge of sin"? Yes it is. The law is the law. There is grace, and there is law. How, then, do we reconcile these opposing concepts? The explanation is simple. We understand that, in the sense of *strict* merit, the law cannot save us nor can we fulfill it. However, since God has put us within his grace, we are no longer under the rigid and uncompromising requirements or judgments of the *system of law.* As Paul said in Romans 6:14, "because you are not under law but under grace," and in Colossians 2:14, "having canceled the written code, with its regulations, that was against us and stood opposed to us." We are under a more lenient plan that allows us to please God by our obedience and in turn God rewards us purely from his benevolence. It is in this sense only that we "fulfill" the law.

Just how adamant is Paul about keeping the principles of law with a view toward salvation? To the Galatians he writes: "For in Christ Jesus neither circumcision nor uncircumcision has any value. The only thing that counts is faith expressing itself through love...The entire law is summed up in a single command: Love

your neighbor as yourself" (5:6, 14). Except for the preface showing circumcision to be obsolete, this statement concerning the relationship between law and love is identical to what Paul said in
Romans 13:9-10 cited above. His statement becomes even more
significant when we realize that it is said right in the midst of the
faith and works controversy occurring in the Galatian church. In
fact, almost the whole epistle to the Galatians addresses the problem between faith and works. Does Paul give the command "love
your neighbor as yourself" merely as a salutary encouragement to
the Galatians, or is there something far more serious going on here
in regard to their very salvation? As we read further in Galatians 5,
we see that Paul expressed the necessity of love because the
Galatians were attacking each other. Just prior to his mentioning of
loving one's neighbor in verse 14, Paul set up a contrast in verse 13
between "indulging in the sinful nature" and "serving one another
in love." We understand from this contrast that those who were not
loving their neighbor were indulging in sinful desires. Paul goes
on to define what he means by "sinful nature" in Galatians 5:21:

> The acts of the *sinful nature* are obvious: sexual immo-
> rality, impurity and debauchery, idolatry and witchcraft,
> hatred, discord, jealousy, fits of rage, selfish ambition,
> dissensions, factions and envy, drunkenness, orgies, and
> the like. I warn you, as I did before, that those who live
> like this will not inherit the kingdom of God.

Of the fifteen or more sins that Paul describes here, most involve hurting a neighbor or engaging the neighbor in an illicit activity. Doing such evil things shows that one is not loving his neighbor. For these kinds of sins Paul says clearly that one "will not
inherit the kingdom of God." Apparently, these kinds of sins were
a major problem with the Galatians since Paul says, "I warn you,
as I did before..." Thus, this is the second time (the first we have no
record of) that Paul had warned them about such behavior. It is
clear that for such bad works they will forfeit their heavenly inheritance. Yes, works are important to Paul, so important that he threat-
ens the Galatians with the loss of their very salvation if they persist
in such evil behavior.

Paul also threatened the Corinthians in the same manner. In 1 Corinthians 6:8-9 he writes: "Instead, you yourselves cheat and do wrong, and you do this to your brothers. Do you not know that the wicked will *not inherit the kingdom of God...*" As he did with the Galatians, Paul points out the specific sins of the Corinthians. They were cheating and doing other harmful acts to their Christian brothers, just as the Galatians were doing to their brothers. Consequently Paul gives the same warning to the Corinthians that he gave to the Galatians — that is, a loss of the inheritance of the kingdom of God. This is not just an idle threat. Paul is not the type to warn of the loss of the kingdom and not mean what he says. As Paul issues the ultimatum to the Galatians, he issues the same to the Corinthians — either show love and obedience, or suffer the eternal consequences.

Other evidence that the Corinthians were engaging in illicit behavior appears in the admonition of Paul's second letter. In 2 Corinthians 12:21, he says: "...when I come again...I will be grieved over many who have sinned earlier and have not repented of the impurity, sexual sin and debauchery in which they have indulged." That these sins directly call into question their eternal salvation is evident in the verses immediately following in 2 Corinthians 13:2,5:

> I already gave you a warning when I was with you the second time. I now repeat it while absent: On my return I will not spare those who sinned earlier or any of the others...Examine yourselves to see whether you are in the faith; do you not realize that Christ Jesus is in you — unless, of course, you are reprobates.

We must conclude, then, that works are a primary criterion in deciding whether or not the individual will be saved. We have also seen that though Paul condemns works done in an effort to obligate God to pay the individual with salvation, Paul is adamant that works, under the advocacy of grace, are absolutely necessary for our salvation. Although God does not require us to fulfill the requirements of the law from a strict and contractual arrangement of obligation, he does require that we *please* him with our faith and works, an aspect of our relationship with God that we will develop momentarily. The mere fact that we can, by God's own estimation, please him, even though our actions are far from perfect, shows that God does not evaluate earnest seekers from the standard of legal perfection but from his mercy and grace. Just as a father is pleased with the devotion and obedience of his children, so God is pleased with the efforts of his children. The father, if he were to use an uncompromising and strict measure of judgment, could pardon none of his children's disobedience, but through the eyes of grace it is possible.

PHILIPPIANS 3:9

One of the more prominent passages in Paul's writings that firmly distinguishes between personal faith and works done under legal obligation is Philippians 3:9: "...and be found in him not having a righteousness of my own that comes from the law, but that which is through faith in Christ — the righteousness that comes from God and is by faith." Most Protestants assert that Philippians 3:9 clearly indicates that Paul is opposing any and all work over against simply believing in Christ's righteousness, i.e., "the righteousness that comes from God." But this interpretation introduces a false dichotomy in Paul's thinking and fails to pinpoint the real distinction he is making. The wording "a righteousness of my own *that comes from the law*" shows that Paul is not speaking of God-honoring or God-pleasing righteousness done under grace, but rather that which is derived from the *system of law,* or as we have learned, a system which attempts to put God in a position of *legal obligation.* In other words, up until the time he encountered the grace of Christ on the Damascus road, Paul was just like many other Jews. He was seeking to be justified before God within the *system of law.* He valiantly performed his ritual laws, yet with an eye toward obligating God to reward him for his religiosity. This is made clear earlier in the same context. In Philippians 3:5-6, Paul writes of himself as one: "...circumcised on the eighth day of the people of Israel, of the tribe of Benjamin, a Hebrew of Hebrews; in regard to the law, a Pharisee; as for zeal, persecuting the church; as for legalistic righteousness, faultless."

In regard to the law, Paul likens himself to the typical Pharisee. It is common understanding, expressed in many of Jesus's contentions with them, that the Pharisees attempted to obey the *letter* of the law but did not understand the *intent* or the *purpose* of the law. They boasted to God that they were holy and righteous by keeping the law, and subsequently expected God to requite them for their self-styled efforts. Not only did they seek to obligate God, they also failed to consider all the times they disobeyed the law, nor did they sincerely seek forgiveness for those failures. Now we can see why, before his conversion, Paul says he was *"faultless"* in *"legalistic righteousness."* Again, it is clear that Paul is not speaking of a *God-pleasing* righteousness performed under grace which takes account of personal sin and produces humility, but a rigid, legalistic adherence to law which seeks to obligate God to reward him. Since he thought of himself as "faultless," he no doubt considered himself worthy of God's blessing. As noted previously, Paul would be likened to someone who "boasts" of his performance before God.[19] To him, God owed him something for "faultless" obedience. He was "better" than everyone else and thus he thought he deserved more from God. Of such pharisaical attitudes, Jesus spoke quite plainly in Luke 16:15 & 18:9:

> You are the ones who *justify yourselves* in the eyes of men, but God knows your hearts. What is highly valued among men is detestable in God's sight...To some who were confident of their own righteousness and looked down on everybody else, Jesus told this parable...

FAITH : MY OBLIGATION TO GOD

In regard to the principle of obligation, let us reiterate another dimension of the faith/works relationship. It is clear that Paul condemns justification on the basis of works because through such a relationship man puts God in an obligatory position to bless him. Conversely, justification by grace allows God to justify man from sheer benevolence. However, God does not shower man with grace for justification without requiring any effort on man's part. The first thing God requires from man in order to receive salvation is faith. Faith is the beginning of salvation. Faith will determine whether or not the grace of God is applied salvifically to the individual. But notice this. By an ironic twist of fate, the requirement of faith in order to receive God's grace personally *obligates man* to God. Whereas man would put God in a position of legal obligation if he based his appeal on works of contract, God's requirement of faith puts man in a position of obligation to God. The roles are completely reversed. In other words, God tells man that if he wants to be saved then man is personally obligated to believe in and to love God with all his heart. If man refuses to oblige God personally, then God will have no recourse but to bring legal condemnation on man for his sins. He cannot ask God to annihilate him out of existence so that he is not required to make the choice to believe. Man is stuck in God's universe and must accept the nature and duties of his existence whether he likes them or not. Having faith in God is not an option, it is a command—something that man must do in order to be saved.

Why does God choose faith as the primary vehicle to obligate man to himself? Because it was precisely for lack of faith in God that the original man fell. Adam came to the conclusion that God was not who he said he was. More specifically, Adam did not believe that God was looking out for man's best interest. He thought that God was deliberately hiding something from him. Instead, Adam believed the devil who convinced him that God was prohibiting he and his wife, Eve, from attaining divinity. Since God is a personal being, Adam's disbelief was an personal affront to God and an attack against God's veracity and character. Essentially, Adam insulted the integrity of God. Consequently, at the point where Adam succumbed to doubt, God would require that each man who came after Adam pass the test that Adam failed. In effect, each man would be placed at his own 'tree of the knowledge of good and evil' to pass the test to believe that God is who he says he is; that despite what we see on the surface, God, in his infinite wisdom, is looking out for our best interests. This, as we will see in the next section, is what God required of Abraham, the father of faith. Abraham had to believe God despite all the circumstantial evidence surrounding him that suggested God was not being honest with him or good to him. God *obligated* Abraham to believe in God, and all that God is, in order for Abraham to be saved. We will also see that God requires the same faith from us.

HOW DEEP SHOULD MY FAITH BE? LIKE THE FAITH OF ABRAHAM?

In the Roman and Galatian epistles we learned that Paul teaches that faith was the means of justification in the Old Testament. In his attempts to convince the Jews that this was God's intent from the beginning, Paul uses one of the most prominent personalities of the Old Testament to prove his case. He brings the person of Abraham to the fore. Since the Jews prided themselves in being children of Abraham, which because of circumcision set them apart from the Gentile world, Paul knows that he must probe the life of Abraham more deeply in order to expose the Jews' wrong thinking about Abraham. Although we will later discover other aspects of the significance of Abraham in understanding the nature of justification, at this point we will concentrate on Paul's view of the *depth* of faith that Abraham had before God, faith that the typical Jew of Paul's day did not have.

In Romans 4:18-21, Paul writes:

> Against all hope, Abraham in hope believed and so became the father of many nations, just as it had been said to him, "So shall your offspring be." Without weakening in his faith, he faced the fact that his body was as good as dead — since he was about a hundred years old — and that Sarah's womb was also dead. Yet he did not waver through unbelief regarding the promise of God, but was strengthened in his faith and gave glory to God, being fully persuaded that God had power to do what he had promised.

One can see clearly from this account that Abraham's concept of God was not a superficial one. All the circumstantial evidence surrounding his life and culture suggested to Abraham that things could not possibly happen as God had told him. Moreover,

Abraham had few people around to encourage or to lift him up in weak moments. In spite of this, when we read such statements as, "against all hope," "without weakening," "did not waver" and "being fully persuaded," we see that Abraham had a very deep faith. Not only did Sarah prove to be infertile in her younger years, but by the time the account in Genesis 15 to which Paul refers was occurring, Sarah was already ninety years old, far too old in anyone's estimation to be bearing children. God is asking Abraham to believe in something that is virtually impossible to believe. In his one hundred years of life, Abraham knew that the things God was proposing just didn't happen. Life was too normal, nor had Abraham been a witness to any miracles prior to this meeting with God.

So what makes Abraham take that step of faith and believe despite all the circumstantial evidence against God? Abraham's decision to believe stems from an intimate relationship he had established with God long ago. The beginning of this relationship is recorded in Genesis 11-12. Abram, as he was called then, lived with his wife Sarai and his father Terah in Ur of the Chaldeans. On their way out of Ur toward the land of Canaan, they stopped in Haran. After Terah's death in Haran, God came to Abram and told him to leave his homeland. Genesis 12:1 records: "The Lord had said to Abram, 'Leave your country, your people, and your father's household and go to the land I will show you.'" Though we cannot be sure, even this instance may not have been the origin of Abram's faith-relationship with God. As far back as Genesis 4:26 it is recorded that "men began to call on the name of the Lord" many years before Terah and Abram existed. According to the best estimates, the time span from Genesis 4:26 to Genesis 12 encompasses thousands of years. It is likely that Abram knew the Lord prior to Genesis 12; otherwise the calling of Abram to leave Haran would be considered rather abrupt. Perhaps his father Terah taught him of the Lord. Whatever the truth of this matter, Abram had a strong enough belief and relationship with God that he acted promptly on God's command to leave Haran. Genesis 12:5 records: "So Abram left, as the Lord had told him; and Lot went with him. Abram was seventy-five years old when he set out from Haran." We can conclude from this account that Abram had a strong faith-relationship with God at least twenty-five years prior to his next major encounter with God in Genesis 15-17. We would assume that the faith of Abraham continued to grow uninterrupted for the next twenty-five years until the time of Genesis 15-17 when God told Abram he would give Sarai a son to fulfill the promise he had made to him in Genesis 12.

How deep must faith be to leave one's own country, people, and customs and go to a place about which one knows nothing? It must be very deep, indeed! The companion account in Hebrews 11:8, which establishes the theological underpinnings in the call of Abraham, assures us that he had a very deep faith. Paul states: "By faith Abraham, when called to go to a place he would later receive as his inheritance, obeyed and went, even though he did not know where he was going." All the heroes of faith that Paul describes from the Old Testament exhibit the same strong faith. Prior to citing Abraham's faith, Paul remarks on the faith of Abel (11:4), Enoch (11:5), and Noah (11:7). We would surmise, then, that Abraham's faith was of the same order as these other men of God, and that all of them were included under the rubric of Hebrews 11:6: "And without faith it is impossible to please God." Hence, the passage leads us to conclude that the faith of Abraham in Genesis 12, twenty-five years before he directly encountered God again in Genesis 15, is the same faith, a faith that *pleased* God. In both Genesis 12 and 15, Abraham is asked to believe in the integrity of God, that is, that God can do what he promised to do, no matter how impossible it may seem. In Genesis 12, Abram is asked to leave his home to go to another land where God would bless him. He did this, according to Paul, "even though he did not know where he was going." He believed that God would not steer him wrong. When Abram entered the land, he saw the fierce Canaanites living there, yet he did not fear and turn back as his descendants would do years later (cf., Genesis 12:6; Deut. 2:26-36; Eccles. 16:7-8). Similarly, in Genesis 15 Abraham believed that God would give him a son even though it seemed impossible for this to occur. Both Genesis 12 and Genesis 15 prove that God keeps his word and that he can be trusted. All in all, Abram was required to believe that God's word was absolutely, positively, reliable, even though the circumstances suggested otherwise.[20]

Next, Paul gives additional information to show that the faith of Abraham in Genesis 12 was the same as the faith in Genesis 15. As mentioned above, Hebrews 11:8 speaks of the time in Genesis 12 in which God came to Abram and told him to leave his homeland to go to the promised land. Hebrews 11:9 states that when Abraham arrived in the Promised land, he lived there in tents like a stranger. Paul prefaces each of these instances with "By faith Abraham..." and then closes with the following statement in Hebrews 11:10: "For he was looking forward to the *city* whose architect and builder is God." Unlike the Genesis account which merely provides the rudimentary facts of Abraham's faith, Paul penetrates into the mind and motivation of Abraham, making us privy to an insight we would never have gleaned from the Genesis account alone. We learn an astounding truth. We discover that Abraham did not just blindly obey; rather, he had a vivid vision of the future heavenly kingdom and of the whole plan and purpose of God's dealing with him. Abraham's vision anticipated not merely owning a piece of land on earth, but also his ultimate entry in heaven in the future, "a *city* whose architect and builder is God." What kind of faith is required to envision one's entrance into the heavenly kingdom for eternity? Surely more than some crude or rudimentary understanding; rather, it is a faith that comprehends the whole purpose and meaning of existence, and that trusts God implicitly for its eventual fulfillment. According to Paul, Christians possess this same faith, since he says in Hebrews 13:14, "For here we do not have an enduring city, but we are looking for the *city* that is to come" (cf., Heb. 11:39-40). Paul then assures us that Abraham already possessed this depth of faith in Genesis 12, long before Genesis 15 (which Paul recounts in Romans 4 as the time Abraham was justified for his faith).

To reinforce that the faith of Abraham in Genesis 12 was the same kind of faith he had in Genesis 15, Paul uses additional language to describe both instances of faith. Beginning in Hebrews 11:11, Paul recounts the incident of Genesis 15 in which Abraham believed that God was going to give him a son. As he had done in verses 8-9, Paul again prefaces verse 11 with: "By faith Abraham..." to confirm that he is talking about the same faith. He goes on to say:

By faith Abraham, even though he was past age, and Sarah herself was barren, was enabled to become a father because he considered him faithful who had made the promise...All these people were still living by faith when they died. They did not receive the things promised; they only saw them and welcomed them from a distance. And they admitted they were aliens and strangers on earth.

He then continues in Hebrews 11:14-16 with the same wording he already used in Hebrews 11:10 to describe Abraham's faith in leaving his homeland and sojourning in the promised land. He writes:

People who say such things show that they are looking for a *country of their own.* If they had been thinking of the country they had left, they would have had opportunity to return. Instead, they *were longing for a better country, a heavenly one.* Therefore, God is not ashamed to be called their God, for he has *prepared a city for them.*

We see here that Paul has incorporated the same vivid vision of the future kingdom that he used a few verses prior in Hebrews 11:10. Since in both instances (i.e., Abraham's leaving of his homeland and his belief God would give him a son) he is looking forward to the heavenly kingdom, the object and meaning of faith must be the same in both instances. We also see that Paul stresses the *life* of faith in the individual. He adds in Hebrews 11:13, "all these people were *still living by faith when they died.*" In this way, he confirms what we have already seen: The faith that saves is not merely a faith that begins salvation but a faith that lasts until one's death.

Paul also shows us that the faith of Abraham in Genesis 12 was the same justifying faith of which he speaks in other contexts. For instance, in Galatians 3:7-9 Paul writes:

Understand, then, that those who believe are children of Abraham. The Scripture foresaw that God would justify the Gentiles by faith, and announced the gospel in advance to Abraham: 'All nations will be blessed through you.' So those who have faith are blessed along with Abraham, the man of faith.

Here Paul speaks of Abraham as "the man of faith," but adds that this faith is the same faith which the Gentiles now possess and which justifies them. The quote, "All nations will be blessed through you" is taken from Genesis 12:3, not Genesis 15:6. This shows that the faith Abraham possessed in Genesis 12:3 was the same justifying faith he had in Genesis 15:6, the same faith through which the Gentiles can now believe and be justified. It is "the gospel announced in advance," yet the gospel already exercised by Abraham in Genesis 12:3, the gospel of justification by faith. To make the link between the faith of Genesis 12:3 and the faith of Genesis 15:6 even stronger, Paul begins his argumentation in Galatians 3:6 by quoting from Genesis 15:6: "He believed God and it was credited to him as righteousness." Paul consistently juxtaposes the Genesis narratives in his writings precisely to show that they are all speaking about the same justifying faith that he wishes to bring to the debate against his Jewish opponent.

Although we will visit Abraham several more times in this discourse, for now we have been introduced to the idea that when Paul says Abraham was justified by faith, he has in view a faith which incorporates the whole of Abraham's life, a faith that believes God in spite of the circumstantial evidence that militates against believing, and a faith that envisions the ultimate glory of the heavenly kingdom. We must understand, then, that when God asks Abraham to believe, he is not merely asking him to assent to God's existence, but to believe in nothing less than the *full integrity* of God to provide for him not only in this life but in the life to come. God could have made it easy for Abraham to believe by changing the circumstances and allowing Abraham to see in actuality more of what God intended. Instead, God purposely frames the situation to test Abraham's inner faithfulness. God is trying to draw something out from very deep within Abraham's personality. It will take every ounce of will-power that Abraham possesses to believe a God who seems to be leading him down a wrong path. In contrast to our first father, Adam, who did not believe in the integrity of God, Abraham must become our new father of faith. Later, we will address the supreme test of Abraham in which God asks him to sacrifice the very son God promised, a time when perhaps Abraham is wondering just what kind of a God he is dealing with. Is he a blood-thirsty murderer who has fiendishly led Abraham along so that he could have the blood of his son, or is he a loving, kind, and benevolent God who is seeking to give his treasures to faithful men and their progeny? Abraham must believe, as Paul says in Romans 4:17, "...the God who gives life to the dead and *calls things that are not as though they were.*"

Paul assures us that those who believe as Abraham did will receive the same promises as he. Paul says in Romans 4:16: "Therefore, the promise comes by faith, so that it may be by grace and may be guaranteed to all Abraham's offspring — not only to those who are of the law *but also to those who are of the faith of Abraham."* Earlier, in Romans 4:12, Paul said: "And he is also the father of the circumcised who not only are circumcised *but also walk in the footsteps of the faith that our father Abraham* had before he was circumcised." The faith Paul is seeking from those who come after Abraham is a "walk in the footsteps of the faith that our father Abraham had..." The expression "walk in the footsteps" denotes an ongoing life of faith, a strong robust faith that has been tested and refined, a faith similar to that of Enoch's and Noah's who also "walked with God." When the New Testament uses the metaphor of "walking," it refers to an ongoing process in someone's life (cf., Gal. 5:25; 6:16). The imagery is one in which Abraham has gone before us and left his footprints in the sand, as it were, and we come after and place our feet in the impressions he has made until we reach our destination. At each impression, Abraham was tested and at each impression we are likewise tested. Either our faith is made stronger, or we succumb to doubt.[21]

Is Paul really asking us to believe in the same way Abraham believed? Or, as some suggest, is Paul simply asking us to accept Jesus into our heart and think that from then onward we are inevitably guaranteed to enter the kingdom of heaven? Does Paul expect us to believe in the same God who tests us with seemingly impossible promises like Abraham, or do we just believe in the "alien righteousness of Christ alone" and then let God take care of the rest? We sense that it would be superfluous for Paul to describe the faith of Abraham in such vivid and exacting detail in Romans 4:17-21, and require us to "walk in the footsteps" of Abraham's faith in Romans 4:12, if this were not what he expected us to practice as well.

Paul sheds more light on this in Romans 4:23-24: "The words 'it was credited to him' were written not for him alone, but also for us to whom God will credit righteousness — *for us who believe in him* who raised Jesus our Lord from the dead." We notice here that Paul's concept of faith is not merely believing in the historical fact of Jesus' resurrection. The resurrection is certainly a grand part of our belief system, but it is not what Paul is trying to point out here. Rather, Paul specifies the one who, even Jesus said, was more important: "for us who believe *in him*..." Paul emphasizes belief "*in him*" (God) who raised Jesus; not only on the fact that Jesus was raised. This is a crucial difference. In effect, we are believing in a God who, as Paul said earlier in Romans 4:17, "gives life to the dead and calls things that are not as though they were." Abraham believed so firmly in God that he reasoned that if God allowed Isaac to die, he would then raise him from the dead (Heb. 11:19); likewise, we believe so firmly in the integrity of God that if God made his Son to die, he would then raise him from the dead. From human standards, both the resurrection of Isaac and the resurrection of Christ seem impossible. The negative influences in life lead us to doubt that such stupendous things could happen. Yet like Abraham, we believe in the integrity of God — that he does what he says he will do. This is the kind of faith that *pleases* God and it is this faith that allows us to become righteous in God's eyes, i.e., "he credits us with righteousness." He credits us with righteousness because we have shown ourselves acceptable, under his grace, by believing in God despite the circumstantial evidence all around us that compels us not to believe in him. As Paul says in 2 Corinthians 4:13-14, "It is written: 'I believed; therefore I have spoken.' With that same spirit of faith we also believe and therefore speak, because we know that the one who raised the Lord Jesus from the dead will also raise us with Jesus..." Or as 1 Peter

1:21 says, "Through him you believe in God, who raised him from the dead and glorified him, and so your faith and hope are in God." If we have this kind of faith, a faith that *pleases* God, he will bless us with the promise he gave to Abraham. He will apply to our lives the work of his Son who was "delivered over to death for our sins and was raised to life for our justification" (Romans 4:25).

What tests of faith does God give us in our lives that may resemble God's tests of Abraham? The tests are many and varied. As the apostle says in 1 Peter 1:7-9:

> These [trials] have come so that your faith...may be proved genuine and may result in praise, glory, and honor when Jesus Christ is revealed. Though you have not seen him, you love him; and even though you do not see him now, you believe in him...for you are receiving the goal of your faith, the salvation of your souls.

The supreme test of faith, of course, is believing in the things of God which cannot be seen. This is a test of faith, however, that extends over one's whole lifetime. In the face of evil, disease, persecution, poverty, discouragement, and any other negative influence, the real test of faith is manifested as one persists in believing despite all the circumstantial evidence that tells one not to believe: more specifically, in not doubting that God is who he says he is. Many, for example, ask the question: if God is so powerful, why doesn't he just make everything nice right now so we don't have to go through all this tragedy on earth? The answer is that God has a plan, a plan that takes time to work out, a plan that respects our free will, a plan that is the best possible way to rid the world of evil and bring us to eternal life. We must wait, wait on God, believing that he can and will do what he says, and will do so in the best method and most suitable timing possible for everyone involved. That is the way Abraham believed. It is believing in a God who "calls things that are not as though they were"; a believing that requires one's whole being for one's whole lifetime.

WHO ELSE BELIEVED LIKE ABRAHAM?

As noted in the biblical accounts of Abel, Enoch, and Noah, each of these Old Testament personalities received the grace of God. Their salvation through grace is confirmed by the New Testament in Hebrews 11 and other passages. This raises an important theological question. How could the saints of the Old Testament receive salvation considering the fact that Christ did not accomplish the atonement till many years after they lived on earth? The New Testament provides the answer. Although the formal establishment of the system of grace was put in place at Christ's death and resurrection, the application of the system of grace was already active before Christ came. In Romans 3:25, for example, Paul says: "God presented him as a sacrifice of atonement, through faith in his blood. He did this to demonstrate his justice, *because in his forbearance he had left the sins committed beforehand unpunished...*" This passage speaks primarily of all those who existed prior to the coming of Christ. Since the system of grace was not formally established until Christ's death and resurrection, only the *principle* of its future accomplishment could be applied to those who died before Christ. In order to include them in the redemptive plan, God held their sins in abeyance and did not punish them according to the strict standards of the law (e.g., death or eternal damnation). God put them on the shelf, as it were, until the formal accomplishment of redemption could deal with them. The Old Testament anticipated the redemption provided by Christ and based its hope for salvation on the anticipated grace provided by that salvific act. The Old Testament prophets knew that Christ's atonement and resurrection was planned by God and that it was their only hope. As Peter writes in 1 Peter 1:10-11:

> Concerning this salvation, the prophets, who spoke of the grace that was to come to you, searched intently and with the greatest care, trying to find out the time and circumstances to which the Spirit of Christ in them was pointing when he predicted the sufferings of Christ and the glories that would follow.

THE FAITH OF HABAKKUK

One of the most important passages in Paul's writings concerning the type of faith that pleases God is Romans 1:17: "For in it [the gospel] a righteousness of God is revealed from faith to faith, as it is written, 'the just man by faith will live.'" Habakkuk 2:4, from which Paul quotes in Romans 1:17, asserts that "the just man by his faith [or faithfulness][22] will live." Since the verse is expressing the type of faith one must live by in order to be justified, Paul's sudden spotlighting of Habakkuk becomes very important in the whole discussion of justification. Habakkuk, however, is a somewhat obscure and small book of the Old Testament. On the surface it does not seem to have too much to say about justification by faith. Nowhere else does the Old Testament mention the prophet Habakkuk, his particular era of prophecy, his birthplace, or his parentage. One who has not been alerted to the relevance of Habakkuk in the discussion of faith and justification might skip right over the book without a second thought. In fact, one might wonder if indeed Habakkuk was the best book from which Paul should quote to support his teaching of the nature of faith. Yet as obscure as Habakkuk is, its significance is heightened in that he is quoted three times in the New Testament (Rom. 1:17; Gal. 3:11; Heb. 10:37-38). Only a handful of Old Testament passages share this distinction. We will understand its significance when we examine the whole context of what prompted Habakkuk to write such a simple yet powerful statement: "the just shall live by his faith."

The reason the book of Habakkuk is so important to the discussion of faith is that, in actuality, the prophet *himself* is the man of great faith spoken of in the biblical text. Habakkuk's faith was the type that continued from one moment to the next, (i.e., from "faith to faith"); did not seek to obligate God through law; and a faith that endured to the end. Similar to Abraham, it was a faith that had to believe in God in spite of the circumstantial evidence surrounding him that suggested that God really wasn't fair or didn't know what he was doing.

As the book opens, Habakkuk is complaining that God seems to ignore the evildoers of that day. Habakkuk complains that the

Jews go on their merry way cutting a swath of destruction and violence in their path and persecuting the righteous (Hab. 1:1-4). After Habakkuk registers his complaint, God answers him. He says that in a little while he is going to send the Babylonians to punish Israel. God remarks that the Babylonians are feared and dreaded as if to impress Habakkuk with the anticipated outcome (Hab. 1:5-11). Habakkuk retorts, however, that it seems unjust for God to use the Babylonians, who are themselves a wicked people, to punish wicked Israel. Why doesn't God punish the Babylonians, too? (cf., Hab. 1:12-2:1). Habakkuk waits for a reply. The Lord answers by enumerating all the sins and treachery of the Babylonians throughout the years. For their wickedness, God says that he will punish them too (Hab. 2:2-20). In the midst of his explanation to Habakkuk, in chapter 2:4 (the verse in question), the Lord says, "see he is puffed up, his desires are not upright...but the righteous will live by his faith." It is the Babylonians who are "puffed up" and "not upright," but Habakkuk must "live by faith" and wait on God in spite of their haughtiness. God will use the Babylonians to accomplish his purposes to punish Israel, but in the end he will destroy the Babylonians too. The challenge for Habakkuk is that he must wait on God's timing, however long it may seem, to punish *both* Israel and the Babylonians. He teaches Habakkuk this truth in 2:3: "For the revelation awaits an appointed time; it speaks of the end and will not prove false. Though it linger, wait for it; it will certainly come and will not delay."

This is the real test of faith for Habakkuk. He sees all the sin around him that at that very instant is worthy of severe punishment. He sees righteous people being killed, maligned, extorted, and afflicted by the wicked Israelites. The temptation is to think that God doesn't care; that he has given up on them; that he is insensitive to their plight; in short, that he is not the God he claims to be. Like Abraham, Habakkuk must not "weaken in his faith" nor "waver in unbelief regarding the promise of God" (Romans 4:19-20). Habakkuk must be "fully persuaded that God had power to do what he promised" (Romans 4:21). Habakkuk must realize that God has his reasons for holding back judgment. One reason for God's delay is a principle he established long ago in his dealing with man, one which holds God back from destroying man until his iniquity reaches its full measure (cf., Genesis 15:16; 2 Maccabees 6:14; 1 Thessalonians 2:16).

In the end, Habakkuk shows great faith in God. Habakkuk 3:1-19 records how he reminds himself of all that he knows of God from the past; of God's ancient fame and awesome deeds. He prays that God would bring these mighty deeds to his own day. To confirm that eventuality, God shows him a vision of his wonderful works. The vision, which Habakkuk describes in vivid detail, convinces him that God's wrath will surely come. The precise timing he does not know, but it will come. Until then he must live in faith, believing in God's integrity and that God does care for his righteous people.

From these personalities, we see that Paul picks examples of men (e.g., Abraham and Habakkuk), who believed God in spite of all the evidence that would cast doubt on God's integrity. Moreover, as with Abraham's faith recorded in Genesis 15:6, Habakkuk's faith in Habakkuk 2:4 does not represent the first time he believed in God. Habakkuk lived a life of faith. To use Paul's phrase in Romans 1:17, Habakkuk lived "from faith to faith," that is, from one moment or test of faith to the next, until his last breath.

CAN I REALLY PLEASE GOD?

As God views the faith and works of those who earnestly seek him from his eyes of fatherly grace, he still expects a high degree of trust and obedience that is *pleasing* to him. The principle of pleasing God is no better stated than in Hebrews 11:6—the very passage that speaks of faith: "And without faith it is impossible to *please* God, because anyone who comes to him must believe that he exists and that he rewards those who earnestly seek him." This passage denotes that God desires sincere and sustained effort from those who want to know him and please him. He wants to be pleased, since as we have noted previously God is a very personal being who desires a very personal relationship with him. By the same token, however, God is not an ogre to whom nothing is acceptable.

Just prior to enunciating the principle of *pleasing* God, Paul gives an illustration of one man who did just that. In Hebrews 11:5 he writes: "By faith Enoch was taken from this life, so that he did not experience death; he could not be found, because God had taken him away. For before he was taken, he was commended as one who *pleased* God." Ecclesiasticus 44:16; 49:14 records: "Enoch pleased the Lord and was taken up, an example of repentance to all generations...Few have ever been created on earth like Enoch"; and Genesis 5:24: "Enoch walked with God; then he was no more because *God took him away*." Clearly the "taking away" of Enoch is due directly to the fact that he "walked" with God, since the first statement is in immediate proximity to the second. According to Paul, his "walking" describes his lifestyle that "pleased God." It shows that God and Enoch had a daily and intimate relationship. Yes, Enoch was a sinner and had no claims on God. In fact, Sirach tells us that it was the *repentance* of Enoch that stood out as the example to all generations. Like everyone else, he was saved by grace. God was not obligated to bless Enoch. Yet Enoch lived such a life of faith and holiness that God, being the personal being that he is, was *so well-pleased* with Enoch that he couldn't resist taking him to himself, something that we do not find explicitly recorded of anyone one else in Scripture, except, perhaps, Elijah.

Paul mentions two facets of the faith that pleases God: 1) One must believe that God exists, and 2) that he rewards those who diligently seek him. The former is the beginning; the latter is the continuation. Of the two descriptions, it is significant that Paul specifies that the faith which pleases God is the kind that believes God *rewards* those who seek him. This speaks implicitly of a gratuitous relationship between God and his followers. God is pleased by man's seeking and subsequently rewards him. Moreover, the "seeking" is not to be confined to those who already have become Christians. It can be applied to those initially seeking God. God is not obligated to reward them but does so because he loves them and has mercy on them.

Pleasing God is a concept taught throughout Scripture: "When a man's ways are *pleasing* to the Lord he makes even his enemies live at peace with him" (Proverbs 16:7); "...offer your bodies as living sacrifices, holy and *pleasing* to God...approve what God's will is — his good, *pleasing* and perfect will" (Romans 12:1- 2); "So we make it our goal to *please* him, whether we are at home in the body or away from it. For we must all appear before the judgment seat of Christ..." (2 Cor. 5:9-10); "...and find out what *pleases* the Lord." (Ephesians 5:10); "...an acceptable sacrifice, *pleasing* to God." (Philippians 4:18); "And we pray this in order that you may live a life worthy of the Lord and may *please* him in every way: bearing fruit in every good work..." (Colossians 1:10); "Children, obey your parents in everything, for this *pleases* the Lord" (Colossians 3:20); "We are not trying to *please* men but God, who tests our hearts" (1 Thess. 2:4); "...Because we obey his commands and do what *pleases* him" (1 John 3:22); "And do not forget to do good and to share with others, for with such sacrifices God is *pleased*" (Hebrews 13:16); "...and may work in us what is *pleasing* to him" (Hebrews 13:21). The same language is also used in the negative sense to describe those who are evil: "Those controlled by the sinful nature *cannot please* God" (Romans 8:8), or, "Nevertheless, God was *not pleased* with most of them; their bodies were scattered over the desert" (1 Corinthians 10:5). "The thing that David had done *displeased* the Lord" (2 Sam. 11:27). "The one whose service is pleasing to the Lord will be accepted, and his prayer will reach to the clouds" (Ecclesiasticus 35:20; 45:19). "To the man who pleases him God gives wisdom, knowledge and happiness; but to the sinner he gives the task of gathering and storing up wealth to hand it over to the one who pleases God" (Ecclesiastes 2:26).

In all of these passages we notice that there is a high level of faith and obedience expected by God from those who seek him and decide to follow him. We must fight against the sinful nature, and in turn, live by the Spirit. As we move on in our walk with God, the more faith we exercise and the more good works we do, the more God is pleased with us. God evaluates us by how we are living by the law of the Spirit. If we live by the Spirit, repenting each time we sin; loving God and our neighbor with all diligence, God is pleased by such faith and good works, even as he was with Enoch. Such individuals are "just" before God.

GOD GIVES US "GRACIOUS MERIT"

At this point, we will investigate other support Scripture supplies concerning the concept of *gracious merit* we have introduced.

For evidence, we can start with Hebrews 11. It gives us the running commentary of the many Old Testament personalities whose faith and works were accepted by God and rewarded with eternal life. For example, Hebrews 11:4 says of Abel: "By faith, Abel offered God a better sacrifice than Cain did. By faith he was commended as a righteous man, when God spoke well of his offerings." Genesis 4:4-5 specifies how God was able to speak well of Abel: "The Lord *looked with grace* on Abel and his offering, but on Cain and his offering he *did not look with grace.*" Here we are introduced to the specific phrase "looked with grace." In effect, because of his gracious viewing of Abel's faith and work, God is personally pleased with Abel and states that he produced a "better sacrifice" than Cain. Apparently, Abel had built a strong relationship with God which allowed God to look with favor upon his sincere offering. God, in strict terms, certainly did not owe anything to Abel. Abel could never attain to the perfect righteousness demanded by the law and the standard of God's perfection. Yet within the realm of God's grace, which anticipates redeeming Abel from the curse of sin by the atonement of Christ, God can look upon the intent of Abel's heart and the subsequent manifestation of his good works, graciously making these the criteria which determines the degree to which Abel pleases God and therefore the kind of blessing God will give him.

As noted above, a significant feature of this account is the specific language chosen by the writer to describe how God views Abel. The words "looked with grace" are translated literally from the Hebrew text, thus we are certain that the issue at hand is the specific way God perceives Abel. This wording denotes a specific *frame of reference* from which God evaluates and responds to Abel. Previously we had used the terms *system of grace* as opposed to *system of law*. Now we can see clearly that the system of grace corresponds to the way in which God graciously looks upon us or the gracious standards God uses to evaluate us. Through his grace, God can "look upon" our works as both pleasing to him and worthy of his blessing, since this particular system does not demand absolute perfection nor put God in a position of obligation.

Paul mentions another man of great faith, namely, Noah (Hebrews 11:7): "By faith, Noah, when warned about the things not yet seen, in holy fear built an ark to save his family. By faith he condemned the world and became heir of the righteousness that comes by faith." Genesis 6:8-9 reads: "But Noah *found grace in the eyes of the Lord*...Noah was a righteous man, blameless among the people of his time, and he walked with God." In Ecclesiasticus 44:17 it states: "Noah was found perfect and righteous; in the time of wrath he kept the race alive..." We notice here even more pertinent language regarding gracious merit. The context indicates that God, who was about to destroy the whole world because of its unrepentant wickedness, views Noah as "a righteous man, blameless among the people of his time." Genesis 7:1 is even more direct: Paul quotes God directly as saying, "because I have found you righteous in this generation." It is God who claims to be making the judgment about Noah's righteousness, and it is clear that it was for *Noah's* righteousness that God saved him and his family. We have cited earlier Noah's "walk with God," and that God himself called him "righteous." Yet Noah is important for another reason. He is another example of one who believed God in spite of circumstantial evidence casting doubt on God's integrity. Surrounded by the utter wickedness of his day, Noah is told to build an ark to save humanity. Facing Noah is the task of building a ship approximately the size of a contemporary football stadium, in the midst of a barren wasteland with not a drop of rain in sight. According to the Genesis record, Noah may have been building the ark for 120 years (Genesis 6:3). We can imagine the jeers and ridicule the people of his day must have heaped upon him. If it rained for short spans before the Flood, we can imagine the mockery that filled Noah's ears every time it stopped: "Was that the big flood, Noah?" At these times Noah could only take his solace in God. Year after year, the circumstantial evidence must have mounted against God. Genesis does not record that God ever spoke to Noah again until the 120 years were over. For Noah's enduring faith, God testified to Noah's righteousness, a continuation of the righteousness he must have displayed long before the Flood (Genesis 6:9). Noah pleased God sufficiently that God, by his grace, saved Noah and his family. Within the strict limits of law and perfection, Noah could never have merited God's favor. He, like everyone else in the human race, was born in sin. But in anticipation of his setting aside of the strict demands of the law through the atonement of Christ, God could look at Noah differently. The *system of grace* through which God can look favorably upon Noah, as it was with Abel, is implied in the phrasing "in the eyes of the Lord," which, again, is a literal translation of the Hebrew text. Noah could please God by his faith and works to the point that God, under the auspices of his grace, could reward Noah with salvation.

The Psalms present an even clearer picture of the concept of gracious merit. David declares in Psalm 18:20-24:

> The Lord has dealt with me according to my righteousness; according to the cleanness of my hands he has rewarded me. For I have kept the ways of the Lord; I have not done evil by turning away from my God. All his laws are before me; I have not turned away from his decrees. I have been blameless before him and have kept myself from sin. The Lord has rewarded me according to my righteousness; according to the cleanness of my hands in his sight.

Here David refers several times to "my righteousness." There is nothing in the text to suggest that this is a legally imputed righteousness; rather, it is a personal righteousness that God can recognize through his grace, even as a father does to a son. David speaks of his personal righteousness as "the cleanness of my hands," "I have kept the ways of the Lord," "I have not done evil," "I have been blameless," and "kept myself from sin." For all these things the Lord "rewards" him. If we take this language at face value we can see clearly that God blesses and saves David because of David's personal righteousness.

We also see gracious merit in the very beginnings of Israel's history. Deuteronomy 6:25 states: "And if we are careful to obey all this law before the Lord our God, as he has commanded us, that will be our righteousness." A similar portrayal appears in Deuteronomy 24:13: "Return his cloak to him by sunset so that he may sleep in it. Then he will thank you, and it will be regarded as a righteousness in the sight of the Lord your God." The people of Israel, like the rest of the human race, were sinners in Adam, nevertheless through the eyes of grace, God can view their obedient and merciful deeds as "righteousness." God calls the deeds "righteous" not because he enjoys speaking in spiritual platitudes, but because he truly recognizes the deeds as righteous. They are real righteous acts, accepted by God as righteousness. Further, these two passages encapsulate the whole law. Deuteronomy 6:25 exemplifies love of God, while Deuteronomy 24:13 exemplifies love of neighbor. It is the same kind of righteousness that Jesus requires (Matt. 22:37-40), that Paul requires (Rom. 13:9-10; Gal. 5:14), and that James requires (James 1:27, 2:8).

OUR SALVATION IS A REWARD FROM GOD

That salvation itself is understood as a reward is clearly evident in the New Testament. As quoted previously, Hebrews 11:6 states: "And without faith it is impossible to please God, because anyone who comes to him must believe that he exists and that he *rewards* those who earnestly seek him." The context of Hebrews 10- 11 refers not only to the earthly blessing given to those who please God but also to heavenly blessing. This is confirmed in Hebrews 10:35, in which the "reward" is that which is withheld until the very end when Christ returns to fulfill the long-awaited promise:

> So do not throw away your confidence; it will be richly *rewarded*. You need to persevere so that when you have done the will of God, you will receive what he has *promised*. For in just a little while, He who is coming will come and not delay...

The heavenly reward is also confirmed by Moses's expectation of the reward as described in Hebrews 11:26: "He regarded disgrace for the sake of Christ as of greater value than the treasures of Egypt, because he was looking ahead to his reward." Similarly, Hebrews 11:10, 16 describes the same promise as "...the city with foundations whose architect and builder is God...a better country, a heavenly one...for he has prepared a city for them."

Regarding the criteria for God's reward, Hebrews 6:10 says: "God is *not unjust*; he will not forget your work and the love you have shown him as you helped his people and continue to help them." Thus we see that in God's grace there is a certain degree of *justice* upon which he rewards us as a gift. In other words, God is benevolent because it is right for him to be so. We call this *gracious merit*. Based on *strict* or *legal merit*, God owes nothing to anyone; but based on gracious merit God will give us all that is desired.

WE MUST LIVE BY THE SPIRIT

The opposition between "Spirit" and "the sinful nature" is one of Paul's major contrasts in his epistles. In Galatians 5:16-17 he says, "So I say, live by the Spirit, and you will not gratify the desires of the sinful nature. For the sinful nature desires what is contrary to the Spirit, and the Spirit what is contrary to the sinful nature." Succumbing to the sinful nature is the way to be lost, living by the Spirit is the way to be saved. We know that Paul has salvation in view when he uses the word "Spirit," since in Galatians 6:8 he issues the ultimatum of eternal life or eternal destruction depending upon one's choice of living either by the Spirit or by the sinful nature: "The one who sows to please his sinful nature, from that nature will reap destruction; the one who sows to please the Spirit, from the Spirit will reap eternal life." In Galatians 5:19, 21 Paul issues the same ultimatum: "The acts of the sinful nature are obvious...I warn you, as I did before, that those who live like this *will not inherit the kingdom of God.*"

A similar passage is Romans 8:6: "Those who live according to the sinful nature have their minds set on what that nature desires, but those who live in accordance with the Spirit have their minds set on what the Spirit desires." In Romans 8:13, Paul again concludes with the same warning as in Galatians 5:21: "For if you live *by the sinful nature, you will die*; but if by the Spirit you put to death the misdeeds of the body, you will live..."

Paul introduced the theme of the Spirit versus our sinful nature with this opening in Romans 8:1-4:

Therefore, there is now no condemnation for those who are in Christ Jesus, because through Christ Jesus the law of the Spirit of life set me free from the law of sin and death. For what the law was powerless to do in that it was weakened by the sinful nature, God did by sending his own Son in the likeness of sinful man, in order that the righteous requirements of the law might be fully met in us, who do not live according to the sinful nature but according to the Spirit.

We understand from all of these passages that as long as one follows the ways of the Spirit and does not live according to the sinful nature, he is "in Christ Jesus" and is not under condemnation. If he goes back to living in the sinful nature, he once again comes under condemnation. As Paul said in Galatians 5:18, "But if you are led by the Spirit, you are not under the law." This means that one who lives by the Spirit will not come under the condemnation of the law. As noted earlier, the atonement and resurrection of Christ sets one free from the uncompromising and exacting system of law and places one under the protection of God's grace. This is why Paul says above, "through Christ Jesus the law of the Spirit of life *set me free* from the law of sin and death." One system is exchanged for the other. In God's grace, we live by the Spirit, a life in which God no longer holds the absolute perfection of law over our heads. For if one is under law then he is required to do "everything written in the book of the law" without fault (Gal. 3:10). One mistake and the law will condemn him. Under the Spirit, we strive to live by God's law but if we sin we can repent. God, under the principle of grace, can forgive our sin. God can provide this grace because his own Son served as a "sin offering."

Living by the Spirit as opposed to the written code of law can best be illustrated by a simple analogy. The speed limit posted in front of a school is 25 mph. This represents the law. This is a good law because it protects children crossing the street from being run over by speeding cars, and it forces drivers to check their speedometers as they enter a school zone. As Paul says in Romans 7:12, "the law is righteous and good." But the key factor in this situation is not the law but one's attitude toward the law. Do I slow down to 25 mph and stop just to avoid being ticketed by the local policeman — showing him what a "good" citizen I am —

but all the while sneering at the children as they cross the street because they have delayed me in getting to my destination? Or do I slow down to 25 mph and stop because I care for the lives of the children and don't want to see them harmed by my speeding car? The answer to this question is crucial. The law says slow down and stop, but the spirit behind the law says that the life of children is precious. Obeying the law without understanding the spirit behind the law is living merely by a "written code" without any sense of love and understanding. Those who live only by the "written code" God will condemn by the "written code." If in the analogy, for example, I travel 26 mph into a 25 mph zone, I have broken the law and an unmerciful judge would condemn me. But if I am living in the spirit of the law, even though I may go a few miles over the speed limit, the judge will not condemn me because he knows my heart and my intentions. God works with us in the same way. Under his grace, he wants us to live not by law for law's sake but by the spirit of the law. If we do, he will not bring the uncompromising standards of law against us. God, who looks graciously into our heart, is now our judge.[23] To be sure, we must *please* him, but it is as a child who pleases his father, not as a defendant who must answer to a judge.

In summary, we have seen that in Paul's understanding of faith and works there exists a dynamic relationship. On the one hand, Paul is adamant that neither works, the law, nor anything of the sort, can save mankind. The reason is that work which attempts to obligate God to pay us with salvation cannot be used in a relationship between the Creator who is perfect and the creature who is imperfect and sinful. The system of law must be replaced with an alternative system, that is, the system of grace. Within the system of grace, God can now look at us with mercy and love rather then through the exacting and uncompromising standards of the law. In the system of grace, God can forgive us our sins, hold our sins in abeyance until rectified, treat us with longsuffering, and many other wonderful things. However, within the system of grace, we must *please* God both by our faith, a faith that believes that God can do what he said he will do even though the circumstantial evidence may suggest otherwise; and our works, works that must be modeled on the Ten Commandments and summed up in the two greatest commandments: love God and your neighbor as yourself. God, who is the judge of our hearts, knows if we are truly seeking to please him. We can be confident, as Hebrews 11:6 states, that God is "the rewarder of those who diligently seek him." On the other hand, if we do not please God in the system of grace, either by falling into serious sin; not repenting; or not showing the love of the Spirit, God will again bring the exacting standards of law against us and condemn us for our sin. For Paul, then, works are a two-edged sword, depending upon the system in which they are viewed and applied. If done through grace they are graciously meritorious for salvation; if done under the law, they are absolutely condemnatory.

PART C
WHAT DID CHRIST DO FOR US ON THE CROSS?

PAUL'S TEACHING ON THE REDEMPTIVE WORK OF CHRIST

As stated previously, the means of salvation that God has established is grace. First, grace denotes that we can do nothing of ourselves to initiate salvation. As Paul levied the "charge" that the whole world is in sin (cf. Romans 3:9; 4:15; Galatians 3:22), consequently all of mankind stands condemned before God. Since the system of law is insufficient to provide the means of returning us to God, then another system had to be put into place in order to save man. Simply put, out of his kindness and mercy God would save man because he personally desired to do so. But there was a huge obstacle for God to overcome. God is perfectly just. No matter how much he desired to save man, he could not excuse the sin of man without a justifiable or satisfactory basis for doing so. As Paul says, for God to be "*just*, and the one who justifies..." (Romans 3:26), the matter of sin had to be rectified. God could neither side-step his divine character nor the moral principles he had previously put in place. Once these were satisfied, however, God could provide salvation by grace.

When God created the world, he set up certain inviolate principles. One of those principles was that of *representation* or *substitution*. This was a principle in which one person out of a group of persons would be held responsible for the good or bad that would come to the group. Paul outlines this principle of God in Romans 5:18-19:

> Consequently, just as the result of one trespass was condemnation for all men, so also the result of one act of righteousness was justification that brings life for all men. For just as through the disobedience of the one man the many were made sinners, so also through the obedience of the one man many will be made righteous.

God applied this principle when he created Adam. Adam's decision to obey or disobey God would affect the whole human race. If he obeyed, all would receive eternal life. If he disobeyed, all would be subject to eternal death. It was very simple, yet very ominous. As noted previously, Paul states in Romans 5:12 that Adam sinned, and when he sinned he initiated the curse of sin and death that fell upon the rest of humanity. He states: "Therefore, just as sin entered the world through one man [Adam], and death through sin, and in this way death came to all men, because all sinned." Paul reiterates this truth in Ephesians 2:1-3 with the words, "As for you, you were dead in transgressions and sins in which you used to live...like the rest we were by nature children of wrath."

Because God is righteous and just, he had to condemn the sinner. In order to save mankind, God had to bring the sinner out of condemnation. This was quite a difficult task, but God had a wonderful plan to resolve it. Using the same principle of *representation* he instituted when he created Adam, God planned the best possible solution. He himself would fulfill the necessary requirements for redemption, atoning for man's sin, and satisfying the demands of his own personal holiness and honor. Simultaneously, through his divine power, he would also be able to survive the ordeal so that he could live with man eternally. In order to accomplish the redemption, God had to become a man. Man had sinned; thus, according to God's law of *representation* already established, a representative of man had to atone for the transgression and satisfy the divine principles. This was accomplished as Jesus, the God-man, made satisfaction to God by his suffering and death; and in triumphing over both sin and death by his resurrection. Although the law demanded death for sin, there is one thing it did not prohibit — rising from the dead. Resurrection is outside the realm of law. This is why Paul specifies both the death *and* resurrection in Romans 4:25: "He was delivered over to death for our sins and was *raised to life for our justification.*"

Another divine quality that allowed Christ to serve as our representative was sinlessness. Since God demanded a perfect sacrifice for sin, both in his person and in his life, no other man could measure up to this requirement. Only a divine being could fulfill it. As Paul says in 2 Corinthians 5:21: "God made him who knew no sin to be sin for us, so that in him we might become the righteousness of God." Or as he says in Galatians 3:13: "Christ redeemed us from the curse of the law by becoming a curse for us, for it is written, Cursed is everyone who is hung on a tree." Or as he says in Romans 8:1-3:

> Therefore, there is now no condemnation for those who are in Christ Jesus, because through Christ Jesus the law of the Spirit of life set me free from the law of sin and death. For what the law was powerless to do in that it was weakened by the sinful nature, God did by sending his own Son in the likeness of sinful man to be a sin offering. And so he condemned sin in sinful man...

By becoming our representative in God's judgment upon sin, Christ takes away the curse imposed on us by the strict standards of the law. The law demands perfect obedience and if it does not receive perfection then it curses with sin and death. Hence, it is law as a *system* of rectifying relationships, i.e., our relationship with God, that had to be set aside (Ephesians 2:15; Colossians 2:14). In its place, Christ brings the system of grace whereby God can offer us salvation from sin and death based on a wholly different kind of relationship. Christ's atonement and resurrection provide the means by which God can fulfill his desire to save mankind while still remaining a just and honorable God who condemns sin. Christ's atonement and resurrection provided grace to the whole world, whereas before there was only law which had to condemn. As John says in 1 John 2:2: "He is the atoning sacrifice for our sins, and not only for ours but also for the sins of the whole world."

WHAT DID CHRIST'S SUFFERING AND DEATH ACTUALLY ACCOMPLISH TO MAKE MY SALVATION POSSIBLE?

What did Christ's suffering and death actually accomplish that allowed the Father to provide the human race with salvation? Did Christ take within himself the sin and guilt of mankind and suffer the specific punishment for that sin and guilt, as Protestants contend? The answer is no. The punishment for sin is first physical death, but ultimately it is eternal damnation. Obviously, Christ did not undergo the punishment of eternal damnation; otherwise he would still be in hell suffering for sin. Further, there is no Scripture specifying that Christ suffered the eternal punishment of hell for sin. If Christ had paid the eternal consequence for everyone's sin, God would have no recourse to punish anyone because the sin would have already been adjudicated. God could not demand double payment for the same sin. We must conclude then, that Christ did not take upon himself the entire punishment required of man for sin. Although the Scripture sometimes speaks of salvation being *purchased*, this refers only to the requirements Christ had to satisfy in order to make salvation *possible* for the whole world (1 John 2:1).[24]

Rather than paying the price of eternal damnation for everyone's specific sins, Scripture teaches that Christ became a "propitiation," a "sin offering," or a "sacrifice" for sins.[25] Paul writes, for example, in Ephesians 5:2 that "Christ loved us and gave himself up for us as a fragrant offering and sacrifice to God," or, as 1 John 2:2 states, "He is the atoning sacrifice [or propitiation] for our sins, and not only for ours but also for the sins of the whole world." There is one major component in what Christ's sacrifice accomplished. Since

God must remain holy and honorable in his dealings with men, he cannot merely excuse the sin of man. God must first be appeased for the sin of man. According to God's principles, only the blood of an innocent victim would be accepted for atonement. Christ, because he was guiltless, sin-free and in favor with God, could offer himself up as a means of appeasing God in order to have God relent of his wrath against the sins of mankind. Sin is a personal offense against God.[26] God is not an unemotional courtroom judge who is personally unharmed by the sin of the offender brought before him. Because God is personally offended by sin, he demands to be personally appeased in order to offer a personal forgiveness. A great satisfaction was necessary since man had sinned against a great and holy God. This dramatic plan is stated no better than in Isaiah 53:10-12:

> Yet it was the Lord's will to *crush* him and cause him to *suffer*, and though the Lord makes his life a guilt offering...After the *suffering* of his [Christ's] soul, he [God] will see the result of the suffering of his soul and be *satisfied*...For he bore the sin of many, and made *intercession* for the transgressors.

In his mediatorial role, Christ, living a sinless life and dying a selfless death, obtains favor from God so that he can approach and beseech Him for mercy and forgiveness on behalf of sinful man. God is not required to offer forgiveness, yet Christ's sacrifice appeals to the intrinsic love and longsuffering of God. Christ, as the obedient son who sacrifices himself, intercedes to obtain the mercy of the Father for those who are to be adopted in God's family. From his paternal qualities of pity and love, the Father grants an avenue of forgiveness for mankind.

As noted previously, just as Scripture requires man to *please* God, so Christ, as a Son, was required to *please* his Father. This was evident first at Christ's baptism in which the Father states, "This is my Son, whom I love; with him I am *well pleased*" (Matthew 3:17). Christ maintains this posture as he says in John 8:29, "...for I always do what *pleases* him" or in John 5:30, "for I seek not to *please* myself but him who sent me." Christ's ultimate pleasing of the Father in regard to salvation was, as stated in Ephesians 5:2, his "sweet-smelling sacrifice" destined to appease the Father's anger against sin and provide grace for mankind, his lost children. Christ could do this because he was holy, blameless and pure. The total effect of Christ's sacrifice, resurrection and ascension to heaven is described in Hebrews 7:25-26:

> Therefore he is able to save completely those who come to God through him, because he always lives to intercede for them. Such a high priest meets our need — one who is holy, blameless, pure, set apart from sinners, exalted above the heavens.[27]

The Old Testament provides the historical precedent for the concept of *appeasing the anger of God* against sin. First, the animal sacrifices of the Old Testament, although typically pointing to the ultimate sacrifice of Christ, were intended to appease God's anger against sin for the people of that time. God would "smell the sweet savor of the sacrifice" and in turn he would relent of his wrath and forgive the individual for his sin. This is noted, for example, in Leviticus 5:5-10, 6:21:

> When anyone is guilty in any of these ways, he must confess in what way he has sinned...and the priest shall make atonement for him for his sin...it is a sin offering...The priest shall then offer the other as a burnt offering in the prescribed way and make atonement for him for the sin he has committed, *and he will be forgiven*...and burn the memorial portion on the altar as an aroma pleasing to the Lord.[28]

The appeasement motif is also evident in many Old Testament narratives which depict a righteous individual who is looked upon with favor by God. This favored individual is able to be a mediator or intercessor who persuades God to turn away his wrath from sinful people. One of the primary examples of this intercessory role is Moses. When Moses received the Ten Commandments, he remained on the mountain with God for forty days and nights. By this time the people thought that God and Moses had abandoned them, and they proceeded to make their own god out of gold and call upon it in an effort to secure protection in the hostile desert. In observing their apostasy, God says to Moses: "I have seen this people...and they are a stiff- necked people. Now leave me alone so that my *anger* may burn against them and that I may destroy them" (Exodus 32:9-10). In an attempt to appease God's anger and persuade him that this would not be the best course of action, Moses replies in Exodus 32:11-13:

> "O Lord, why should your anger burn against your people...Why should the Egyptians say, 'It was with evil intent that he brought them out, to kill them in the mountains and to wipe them off the face of the earth'? Turn from your fierce anger; relent and do not bring disaster upon your people. Remember your servants, Abraham, Isaac and Israel, to whom you swore by your own self..."

After this impassioned and dramatic plea from Moses, Exodus 32:14 records God's astounding response: "Then the Lord relented and did not bring on his people the disaster he had threatened." This shows the virtual human-like quality of God, who can be persuaded to change his mind through the appeal of a worthy and significant person. In fact, Exodus 33:5 records that God remained so angry against the people for their sin that when he later tells Moses to lead them out of that place he says, "Tell the Israelites, 'You are a stiff-necked people. If I were to go with you even for a moment, *I might destroy you.*" Apparently, God was on the verge of destroying all of them and only Moses's plea abated that occurrence.

The appeasement of God becomes even more pronounced in the remaining section of Exodus 32:30-32:

> The next day Moses said to the people, "You have committed a great sin. But now I will go up to the Lord; perhaps I can make atonement for your sin." So Moses went back to the Lord and said, "Oh, what a great sin these people have committed! They have made them-

selves gods of gold. But now, please forgive their sin — but if not, then blot me out of the book you have written."

Even though God eventually destroyed and punished some of the people (as recorded in Exodus 32:27-35), he did not destroy all of Israel. This is similar to Christ offering himself as an atonement, appeasing the anger of God on behalf of the human race. In turn, God decides not to condemn all of mankind, yet he still punishes and destroys those within mankind that he has singled out for his retribution.

Other examples of appeasement in the Old Testament include Abraham's plea for the cities of Sodom and Gomorrah which God had intended to destroy (Genesis 18f). God's anger is temporarily stayed as Abraham, who pleads with God for mercy, attempts to find ten righteous people in those cities to satisfy God. God agreed that his anger would be appeased if ten righteous people could be found. God granted this request because he had respect for Abraham and looked with favor upon him. We could also say that the ten righteous people, if they could be found, would also have served to abate God's anger.

Another example of appeasement is Job who offered sacrifices to God for his children who perhaps may have sinned against him (Job 1:5). In light of Job's actions, the Old Testament prophets also recognize the mediatorial role of a righteous person in appeasing God's anger. At the height of Judah's apostasy, Ezekiel 14:14,20 states:

> Even if these three men — Noah, Daniel and Job — were in it, they could save only themselves by their righteousness, declares the Sovereign Lord...as surely as I live, declares the Sovereign Lord, even if Noah, Daniel and Job were in it, they could save neither son nor daughter. They would save only themselves by their own righteousness.

Here we see that after serious and continual transgression against God, none in the nation can appease God's anger. He is determined to destroy Judah because their sins have been continual and grave, without repentance. By posing the hypothetical example of appeasement from Noah, Daniel, and Job who would, under more normal circumstances, be able to appease God's anger toward the people, Scripture shows the precedent for the mediatorial role of intercession accomplished by Christ in redeeming mankind. This same truth is evident in Jeremiah 15:1, which states: "Then the Lord said to me: 'Even if Moses and Samuel were to stand before me, my heart would not go out to this people. Send them away from my presence!'" Here again we see the possibility that, under more normal circumstances, God would have allowed the intercession of a Moses or a Samuel to appease his anger against sin. We also see the intense and passionate emotion displayed by God in his anger as he speaks of his "heart" that he would not allow to "go out to his people" which results in his sending them "out of his presence!" — as an angry father or king might do. We find a similar principle in Jeremiah 5:1 where God says to Jeremiah, "Roam to and fro through the streets of Jerusalem...if you can find a man, if there is one who does justice, who seeks the truth, then I will pardon her." Or as Ezekiel 22:30 says, "I looked for a man among them who would build up the wall and stand before me in the gap on behalf of the land so I would not destroy it, but I found none."

Summary Points

1) Paul uses the word "alone" very frequently. Many usages appear in the very contexts which speak of faith and justification, but he never uses "alone" as a qualifier or description of faith. For Paul, faith carries far too much meaning to be limited by the word "alone." The only time Scripture joins "faith" with "alone" is in James 2:24 where it is specified that we are "not justified by faith alone."

2) When Paul says that man cannot be justified by works or through the law, in the larger picture, he is referring to any and all works done by man. For the Jews, works of law primarily referred to the ceremonial rites of the Old Testament, but can

also refer any work of law which attempts to put God in debt. The ceremonial rites could not justify because they were under the Law, whereas New Testament sacraments justify because they are under grace.

3) Paul teaches that because of the principle of obligation or debt, man cannot be justified by works. Doing works, outside the realm of grace, attempts to obligate God to pay the worker, as an employer pays his employee. If so, then the relationship is one based on a strict, legal contract; not on grace. God, because he is the Creator and perfect, and man, who is the creature and imperfect, cannot place God in a position of legal obligation.

4) Conversely, Paul teaches that works, performed under the auspices of God's grace, do indeed justify the individual. Paul teaches that through God's grace he can accept the faith and works of the individual for the purposes of salvation. New Testament passages that speak of works being judged with a view toward gaining eternal life are not hypothetical.

5) Paul places faith in opposition to works because faith is used to represent a personal, sincere, grace-based relationship with God, whereas works are used to represent an impersonal, contractual, non-grace relationship. Faith is the element of human volition which recognizes and acknowledges God's grace and thus it is the first element that establishes our relationship to God.

6) Paul teaches that we fulfill the law, and are justified through obedience to the law, by loving God and loving our neighbor as ourselves.

7) Although Paul tells us to model our behavior on the law, he has the intent of the law, or the higher purpose of the law, in view. On the other hand, he is adamant against legalistic obedience with the intent of merely receiving payment from God.

8) Scripture teaches that within the system of grace, the individual must please God by his faith and obedience. If he does not please God, then he cannot be saved. God is the sole judge of whether we have pleased him, for he knows our hearts.

9) Scripture teaches that God gives gracious merit to individuals who have pleased him, and he will graciously reward them with eternal life for their faith and obedience. He rewards them not from obligation but from his sheer benevolence to those who earnestly seek him.

10) All men are sinners in the eyes of God and in order to receive salvation it is necessary that all men be redeemed through the atoning work of Christ. No one is saved without the work of Christ being applied to him, since Christ is the only one who made it possible for God to give his grace to whomever he wishes.

11) Christ did not take on the guilt and sustain the full punishment required of man for sin, since hell itself is the ultimate punishment for sin. Rather, Christ became a propitiatory sacrifice in order to appease the wrath of God against sin, and in so doing, preserves God's honor, holiness and justice. In turn, he opens the doors of grace and makes it possible for every man to attain salvation.

12) God's grace, through anticipation of the atonement of Christ in the New Testament, was made available to those in the Old Testament, and thus they were saved in the same way as we are today. As regards their relationship to God, Old Testament people were to understand the ultimate purpose of the law in the same way we are to understand it today.

13) Through the measure of grace God gives each individual believer, he expects that the believer will exercise that grace by continuing to believe in God despite the circumstantial experiences of life that may cast doubt on God's integrity. In this

regard, Abraham is one of the greatest examples of faith in the Scripture and one on whom we should model our own faith in order to be justified.

14) Paul teaches that faith must express itself through love in order to effectuate justification. The qualities and requirements for genuine love are specified throughout Scripture.

ENDNOTES

[1] The difference between "salvation" and "justification" is that the former term is often used to represent the general aspects of our topic, while the latter usually refers to the particular basis or reason one can be saved. Sometimes the words are used interchangeably, depending on the context in which they are placed.

[2] Paul uses the words *only* or *alone* in the justification contexts of Rom. 3:29; 4:12; 4:16; 4:23. Gal. 2:10; 3:2; 4:18; 5:13. It is the same word James uses when he says "not by faith *alone*" (Jam. 2:24).

[3] Galatians 3:8,16.

[4] For example, the Catholic Council of Trent held that "...he is ingrafted, receives in the said justification together with the remission of sins all these [gifts] are infused at the same time: faith, hope, and charity" (Session 6, Chapter 7, DS 800).

[5] 2 Peter 3:16.

[6] God obligates himself to Abraham through a "promise" (Rom. 4:16f; Heb. 6:13-18). Since in this case God obligates himself, rather than man obligating God, there is no infringement on the principles of grace. Rather, God's self-imposed obligation is prompted and sustained by his grace.

[7] Using Paul's wording, the Catholic Council of Trent, Session 6, Chapter 8, states: "...because none of those things which precede justification, whether faith or works, merit the grace itself of justification; for, 'if it is a grace, it is not now by reason of works; otherwise (as the Apostle says) grace is no more grace.'"

[8] See also the Catholic Catechism, Sections 578-579.

[9] Ibid., Section 1963.

¹⁰ We can say, however, that God gave Adam and Eve a "suspended sentence," since he did not take their lives immediately.

¹¹ Augustine writes: "What is grace? Something given gratis. What is given gratis? That which is bestowed rather than paid as owed. If it is owed, it is wages paid, not a gift graciously given" (*Homilies on the Gospel of John*, PL 3, 9; JR 1807).

¹² The Scripture is replete with references to God's personal nature. The following are just a few of the many descriptions: sorrow and pain (Gen. 6:6; Matt. 26:38); love (Is. 43:4; Jn 3:35); hate (Ps. 5:5; 11:5; Rom. 9:13); singing for joy (Zeph. 3:17; Matt. 26:30); laughter (Ps. 2:4); jealousy (Deut. 32:21; Jam. 4:5); compassion (Ps. 86:15; Matt. 15:32); sadness and consternation (Ezk. 18:23,32; Jn. 11:35); anger (Ex. 32:10; Rev. 6:16); grief and vexation (Ps. 78:40; Eph. 4:30); pity (Ps. 103:13; Jam. 5:11); pleasure (1 Chr. 29:17; Lk. 12:32).

¹³ Cf., Acts 2:38; Rom. 6:1-4; Col. 2:11-12; 1 Pet. 3:21. Baptism is the sacrament of the New Covenant, while circumcision was a sacrament of the Old Covenant. The New Covenant was prophesied in Jer. 31:31-34 and is fulfilled in the New Testament Church, according to Heb. 8:10-12. In the New Covenant God will "put my laws in their minds and write them on their hearts." The writing of God's laws on the mind and heart is accomplished through the sanctifying grace infused into the individual at Baptism. Grace inheres to and regenerates the soul, providing the power to know and obey God's laws.

¹⁴ In the New Testament, the phrase "works of the law" is used only seven times (Rom. 3:20, 28; 9:32; Gal. 2:16; 3:1, 5, 10). Paul shifts to the singular word "work" (as opposed to "works of law") in Rom. 4:1-8 (cf., Eph. 2:8-9; Phil. 3:9; Tit. 3:5). This shows that Paul's concern is not merely with the antithesis between the Mosaic law and grace, but with the more general and timeless truth that a "works for pay" gospel, whether the works are based on the Jewish Torah, natural law, or any other earthly law, is condemned for all peoples. Thus, such Old Testament people as Abel, Enoch, Noah and Abraham, who lived before the Mosaic law was established, were nonetheless saved by grace through faith, not works of debt, just as those like David and Rahab, who lived during the Mosaic law, were saved by grace

(cf., Heb. 11:1-19; Romans 4:4-8; James 2:25). That the grace/ works distinction applies to all peoples in all times is why the Council of Trent stated in Canon 1 of the sixth session: "If anyone shall say that man can be justified before God by his own works which are done either by his own natural powers, or through the teaching of the Law, and without divine grace through Jesus Christ, let him be anathema."

[15] See also Paul's disavowing of law for justification in Rom. 3:9-20; 4:13-15; 7:6-8; 11:1-6; Gal. 3:10-12; 17-22; 5:3-4; Eph. 2:8-9; Phil. 3:9; Tit. 3:5; 1 Tim. 1:8-9; Jam. 2:10-13.

[16] Catholic Catechism, Section 1963: "According to St. Paul, its [the law's] special function is to denounce and disclose sin...However, the Law remains the first stage of the way to the kingdom. It prepares and disposes the chosen people and each Christian for conversion and faith in the Savior God. It provides a teaching which endures for ever, like the Word of God." The Council of Trent, Canon 20 states: "If anyone shall say that a man who is justified and ever so perfect is not bound to observe the commandments of God and the Church, but only to believe, as if indeed the Gospel were a mere absolute promise of eternal life, without the condition of observation of the commandments: let him be anathema."

[17] The Council of Trent made it clear that nothing good can be done by man without the grace of God: "Justification must be derived from the predisposing grace of God through Jesus Christ...whereby without any existing merits on their part...through his stimulating and assisting grace are disposed to convert...nor on the other hand can he of his own free will without the grace of God move himself to justice...we confess that we are anticipated by the grace of God" (Session 6, Chapter 5).

[18] In the New Testament, God's "kindness" and "grace" are interchangeable (e.g., Eph. 2:7; Tit. 3:4; Rom. 11:22).

[19] cf., Rom. 2:17, 23; 3:27; 4:2; Eph. 2:8-9; 1 Cor. 4:7.

[20] Ecclesiasticus 2:10-14.

[21] Ecclesiasticus 44:19-21.

[22] Of the 49 times this word is used in the Old Testament, over half of the passages refer to "faithfulness" (e.g., Ps. 89:1, 2, 5, 8, 24, 33; 119:75, 90; Pro. 28:20; Lam. 3:23, et al). Other passages refer

to "truth" or "steadfastness" (e.g., Jer. 5:1, 3). In many of these passages *emunah* is used in reference to the character of God.

[23] Council of Trent, Session 6, Chapter 11; Canon 23. We should also realize that Christ's suffering and death was not a legal payment or legal punishment for sin, since legal entities do not allow innocent people to be punished for the wrongs committed by others. Judicial entities simply have no legal basis to punish anyone other than the perpetrators. Since Christ's suffering and death is not a required legal action but a voluntary sacrifice to appease God's wrath and preserve his honor and holiness (John 10:17-18), it can be personally accepted by God, who, in turn, applies it graciously to all who wish to benefit from its results.

[24] Acts 20:28; 1 Cor. 6:20; 7:23; 1 Pet. 1:18-19.

[25] Christ is called the "offering" (Eph. 5:2; Heb. 7:27; 9:28), a "sacrifice" (1 Cor. 5:7; Eph. 5:2; Heb. 9:28; 10:12), and a "propitiation" (Rom. 3:25; 1 Jn 2:2; 4:10). In the Scriptural language "He himself *bore* our sins in his body on the tree..." in 1 Pet. 2:24, the Greek word is a sacrificial term referring to Christ as a "sin offering" to God. .

[26] The personal anger of God against sin is a major theme in the Old Testament, (cf., Ex. 4:14; Nm. 11:1,10; 22:22; 25:3-4; 32:10,13,14; Dt. 6:15; 7:4; 13:17; 29:20-28; 31:17; 32:22; Jos. 7:1,26; Jud. 2:14,20; 2 Sam. 6:7; 24:1; 2 Kgs. 13:3; 24:20; Ps. 6:1; 69:24; 85:5; Eccl. 39:28; 45:19; Is. 5:25; 63:3; 66:15; Jer. 4:8; 12:13; 25:37; Lam. 1:12; Ezk. 5:13; 20:8; Hos. 8:5; Mic. 5:15; Nah. 1:2-3; 2 Macc. 5:17; 7:33; Heb. 3:3.

[27] Christ's present and continual high priestly intercession before God is the reason why the Catholic Mass daily offers or re-presents Christ's immolation to God. The intercession continually appeases the wrath of God against sin. It is also the reason why we confess our sins at Mass and why the reception of the Eucharist forgives our sins.

[28] See also Lev. 4:20, 26, 31, 35; 6:7; 19:22; Num. 15:25-28.

HOW CAN i GET TO HEAVEN

CHAPTER 2

DOES JAMES TEACH THAT I'M JUSTIFIED BY MY WORKS?

The Catholic Council of Trent (1545-1563) frequently quoted from the Epistle of James to show the Protestant theologians that man is indeed justified by works. Since the statement in James 2:24, "a man is justified by works and not by faith alone" is clear and unambiguous, it served as one of the best proofs of the Catholic position and that of Christian history prior. In answer to James's statement, the Protestant theologian Martin Luther maintained there was a contradiction between Paul and James. He decided in favor of Paul and concluded that James was an "epistle of straw" and subsequently sought to "throw Jimmy into the stove."[1] Some time later, his contemporaries, especially Philip Melanchthon, persuaded Luther not to reject the book of James from the accepted canon of Scripture. In giving this advice, however, Melanchthon and his colleagues now had to find a new explanation to deal with the book of James. Since the Reformation, Protestant theologians have given many and varied explanations in attempts to harmonize James with Paul. Indeed, this task of explaining James becomes even more formidable for the Protestant challenger when he considers that the phrase "*faith alone*" appears only once in the New Testament — and there it is preceded by the words "*not by.*"

WHAT IS JAMES' BASIC MESSAGE TO US?

After admonishing Christians not to discriminate against the poor (James 2:1-9), and further encouraging them not to come under judgment by breaking the law (2:10-11), James warns in 2:12-13, "Speak and act as those who are going to be judged by the law that gives freedom, because judgment without mercy will be shown to anyone who has not been merciful..." Here is James's first reference to the coming judgment. It is a judgment that will show either mercy or no mercy to the one being judged; thus, the question of whether one will be saved or damned is clearly in view.

James elaborates on the context in which he is writing by the question he raises in James 2:14: "What is the profit, my brothers, if anyone says he has faith but does not have works? Can faith *save* him?" The matter James poses is one of eternal importance. "Will he indeed be saved?" is a haunting question that begins the section on faith and works. James is not making idle threats when he warns them in the previous verses not to discriminate against the poor and not to fall into the sins of adultery and murder. In light of his rhetorical question in verse 14, the consequence of such sinful actions are that one will *not* be saved. By extension, we must also understand that the one who may *not be saved* in James 2:14 is the same person who may *not be justifi*ed in James 2:21-26.

James also focuses on the same issue we have seen Paul cite so frequently in his epistles: the second greatest commandment. In James 2:8, he writes, "If you really keep the royal law found in Scripture, 'Love your neighbor as yourself,' you are doing right. But if you show favoritism, you sin and are convicted by the law as lawbreakers." "Love your neighbor as yourself" is the focal point of this section. It is significant that James appeals to the "royal law *found in Scripture*" to reinforce this point. This law of love was recorded as far back as Leviticus 19:18. Things have not changed in that respect. James takes this "royal law" and opposes it to "showing favoritism," obviously teaching that one is not loving his neighbor when he favors one person over another.

In 2:15-16, James elaborates on how a person is to love his neighbor: "Suppose a brother or sister is without clothes and daily food. If one of you says to him, 'Go, I wish you well; keep warm and well fed,' but does nothing about his physical needs, what good is it?" Not providing for another's needs is another form of the discrimination against the poor to which James had first alluded to in 2:5: "Suppose a man comes into your meeting wearing a gold ring and fine clothes, and a poor man in shabby clothes also comes in..." By the use of the word "suppose" in both 2:5 and 2:15, James is presenting two hypothetical yet highly probable cases to his audience. In both cases the situation involves one who is not financially well-off, in the first with "shabby clothes," in the second "without clothes." In both cases, if one were to abide by the "royal law of Scripture" which is to "love your neighbor as yourself," then he would treat the poor man in the first case with the same respect as the rich man, and he would give the poor man in the second case some clothes and food. Hence, when James asks the all-important question "Can faith save him?," he is directing it to the person who is not abiding by the royal law to love one's neighbor. Not only would James say that his faith will not save him, but as 2:9 says, "if you show favoritism, *you sin* and are convicted by the law as lawbreakers." The emphasis on sin is very apparent. Thus we must understand that if one sees a brother or sister in physical need and deliberately chooses not to provide for them, it is not just a lack of works, it is also *sin*. As James says in 4:17, "Anyone, then, who knows the good he ought to do and doesn't do it, sins." Or as John says in 1 John 3:17, "If anyone has material possessions and sees his brother in need but has no pity on him, how can the love of God be in him? Dear children, let us not love with words or tongue but with actions and in truth."[2]

James had mentioned previously in 1:27, "Religion that God our Father accepts as pure and faultless is this: to look after orphans and widows in their distress and to keep oneself from being polluted by the world." Orphans and widows would indeed fit into the same class of destitution as the man dressed in shabby clothes in James 2:2 or the man with no clothes and food in James 2:15. Not taking care of their needs would be classed as sins of *omission*. In addition, as James never tires of reminding his audience not to sin, he includes a command to refrain from the world's influence. These "worldly" sins, which are later specified in James 2:10-11 as murder, adultery, etc., are sins of *commission.*

James says in 2:17, "Even so, faith, if it has not works, is dead by itself." By the words, "even so," James is connecting the previous two verses (15-16) concerning taking care of someone's physical needs with the principle that faith without works is dead (verse

17). In other words, a deliberate refusal to provide for the needs of the poor and destitute shows either that one's faith is already dead or that it died at the moment of refusal.[3] The concept of "dead faith" is a major theme in the chapter since James mentions it three times (verses 17, 20, 26). In the last reference (verse 26, "the body without the spirit is dead").

James considered the people to whom he was writing as "*believers* in our Lord Jesus Christ" (James 2:1). This means that they had faith. The main question, then, is whether they will consistently add works to their faith.[4] On the one hand, if they have never chosen to add works to their faith, then they have always had a dead faith. On the other hand, if an incident occurs in which they choose not to add works to faith, then they have ruptured the relationship between faith and works at that instant. Any instance of separating works from faith is sin (e.g., not helping a brother in need is sin, as noted in James 4:17). This does not mean that faith is nonexistent, however. Just as a dead body exists by the mere fact that someone recognizes it as dead, by analogy dead faith can exist as faith. Hence, one should not misconstrue James's point in referring to "dead faith" to say that the faith is nonexistent; rather, James is referring to faith that is not formed into action even as a dead body without the spirit has no capability to act. As the spirit gives physical life to the body, so works give life to faith. Only faith alive with works — works of love and avoidance of sin — pleases God.

By adding the words "by itself" in 2:17, James is pointing out his objection is to a faith that is alone. If James was not interested in objecting to the solitude of faith he could simply have said, "Faith, if it does not have works, is dead" without the addendum of "by itself." Whatever one's conception of the relation between faith and works, James is making it clear that the best way to describe the rupture in the relationship is to say that it puts faith into a position of being "by itself" (verse 17) or that faith is "alone" (verse 24). Apparently there is no better way to describe it. It is not called "unqualified faith" or "non-justifying faith." James does not want to give the impression that as long as faith is of a sufficient quality then faith by itself can save. Faith and works are two separate entities: one believes, the other acts. Sin (bad work) does not necessarily destroy faith but it does make one ineligible for salvation. By analogy, faith that cannot be used in justification is a "dead faith." To balance this equation, one must also recognize that Scripture also speaks of "dead works."[5] Work, by itself, will not produce justification either, since, as we have learned earlier, those who do works without the proper faith-relationship with God are attempting to obligate God to pay them as an employee expects from his employer. Faith and works, being separate entities, must be joined together for justification to occur. Hence considering that James has chosen language which specifies not the quality of faith but the addition or subtraction of works to faith (e.g., 2:14: "you have faith but do not have works"; 2:17: "faith, by itself"; 2:24: "not by faith alone"), one should not understand the question "Can faith save him?" in 2:14 to read "Can *that kind* of faith save him?", but rather "Can faith *alone* save him?" or "Can faith, *by itself*, save him?" James' answer is an unequivocal no.

Protestant interpretations often claim that the works which James has in view are those that inevitably, automatically, or necessarily flow from true faith. Consequently, they claim it is not the works that determine the justification of the man but his faith, since true faith will inevitably produce good works. In this framework, works are considered merely a *by-product* or *result* of faith. Works themselves do not justify; they only prove that the faith is real. Consequently, the weight is shifted to faith and the individual need only have a "saving faith" to secure his justification.[6]

Protestant theology finds it necessary to emphasize the quality of faith, as opposed to separate categories of faith and works which must join together, because of its understanding of justification. In essence, the Protestant conception of justification is that one is saved by an initial act of faith. In that act of faith, God is said to impute the righteousness of Christ to the individual so that God can now consider him as a just person even though in reality he is not a just person intrinsically. Any works coming after the solitary act of faith must be placed in another theological category—a non salvific category called "sanctification." In other words, the act of faith seals the justification and the person is now out of the category of justification and into the category of sanctification. Since sanctification is the only category in which he can do works, then works cannot be directly connected to the category of justification. Hence, Protestants reason that James's stress on works is only for the purpose of demonstrating the authenticity of the initial faith in which one accepted Christ. If the works are not of the expected quality, then this, in many Protestant views, shows that one never had true faith and therefore was never justified originally.

In answer to this we say the following. Although we can agree that faith for justification must be genuine, this does not mean that the works which accompany faith are mere qualifiers or descriptions of faith, as though "quality faith" alone is all that James is requiring.[7] Rather, James is teaching that we must intentionally and voluntarily add works to faith in order to effectuate and complete justification. Let us examine more of James's description of faith and works to show the fallacy of Protestant thinking on this issue.

James opens up his context in 2:1 by saying, "My *brothers*, as believers in our glorious Lord Jesus Christ..." He continues with this *brotherly* address in 2:5, "Listen, my *brothers*..." and uses it again in 2:14, "What good is it, my *brothers*..." (cf., James 1:16,19). Here we see that James is not addressing some amorphous collection of people who have merely assented to Christian principles of conduct as if they possessed only a civil religion. These are people whom James knows very well, people who are in the Church, people who have been baptized, confessed their sins, and are already called "believers in our glorious Lord Jesus Christ" (2:1). James confirms this genuine state of belief by mentioning their intimate gatherings of worship in verse 2: "Suppose a man comes into your meeting (or "synagogue")." These people already have faith, but what is the problem? They are tempted to show favoritism to the rich man and to despise the poor man. Are the works of kindness and love just flowing naturally out of them? Indeed they are not. Apparently, they must be taught and trained to do good works, and they must be made aware that if they decide not do them it is sin—sin that could result in damnation. They must make a decision not to discriminate—it does not merely flow from them naturally. Granted, once they have cultivated their faith they should possess a better spiritual disposition from which to perform good works, but this does not mean that at each moment when works are required that they will see them inevitably appear. Good works will not automatically flow from them any more than refraining from overt sin happens automatically without a conscious decision to abstain from sin. The backdrop for James's teaching is the age-old battle between the spirit and the flesh. The spirit tells them to love the poor man but the flesh tells them to discriminate against him. To encourage them, James refers them to the "Royal Law found in Scripture—Love your neighbor as yourself."

WHAT DOES JAMES SAY IN THE REST OF HIS EPISTLE?

In examining the context of the chapters surrounding the Epistle of James, we find the same evidence that good works do not inevitably or necessarily flow from the Christian. Rather, James teaches that the individual must make a conscious decision not only to refrain from sin but also to do good works. James 1:4 states one of the major themes of the book: "*Perseverance* must finish its work so that you may be mature and complete, not lacking anything." He reiterates the theme in 1:12: "Blessed is the man who perseveres under trial..." In 1:20-22, James explains that man's sin, specifically his anger, does not produce the righteousness of God. He also commands them to "get rid of all moral filth and evil," demonstrating that they must make the conscious effort to attain the righteousness of God. Earlier, in 1:5-7, James had told them that if they lacked wisdom to do these good works, they should ask God, who gives generously to all. But he warns that one must ask God without doubting; otherwise, one will not receive God's divine help. Again, he places the burden on the individual to cooperate with the grace that God has given him.

In 1:21, James says that doing such things "can save you." He uses the word "save" five times in this epistle. We have already noted one of the most important in 2:14 where James asks the rhetorical question "Can faith save him?" One other instance of "to save" occurs in 4:12. Here James says, "There is only one Lawgiver and Judge, the one who is able to *save* and destroy. But you—who are you to judge your neighbor?" This warning is quite ominous. Notice that James speaks of "judging your neighbor." He further develops the theme in 4:11 with the warning, "Brothers, do not slander one another. Anyone who speaks against his brother or judges him speaks against the law and judges it." This closely resembles what James said in 2:1-13 (the passage just prior to the controversy about faith and works in 2:14-26), where he faulted them for discriminating against the poor and committing adultery and murder against their brothers. James 2:13 specified a "judgment that will be shown without mercy" for those who do such things. Similarly, 4:12 warns them that God is the one who "saves and *destroys*." Clearly, James wants to avoid giving the impression that their salvation is secure and guaranteed. He makes it clear that if they persist in sin, they will be "judged without mercy" (2:13) and "destroyed" (4:12).

We can see James's serious intent by the way he opens up chapter 4. In 4:1, he specifies their "fights and quarrels." These come from the "desires that battle within" them (i.e., their concupiscence or inclination to sin). In 4:2, he says they "murder and covet." In 4:4 he calls them "adulterous people" who are "friends of the world." In 4:8 he calls them "sinners" and "double-minded." We must keep in mind that James is not speaking to the unbelieving world; rather, to the Christians in the Church. We see this, for example, in 4:2 as he points out that they "do not ask *God*," and in 4:11 as he again calls them "brothers." Repeatedly, he places the burden on the Christian to choose right—to make a conscious decision to seek God—just as he told them in 1:2-6 to seek God's wisdom in knowing how to endure trials and not fall into sin. James emphasizes this responsibility in 4:7 when he commands them to:

> Submit yourselves, then, to God. Resist the devil and he will flee from you. Come near to God and he will come near to you. Wash your hands, you sinners, and purify your hearts...grieve, mourn, and wail. Change your laughter into mourning and your joy into gloom. Humble yourselves before the Lord, and he will lift you up.

Can anyone doubt from reading these passages, addressed specifically to Christians, that works of obedience do not just inevitably flow from believers but that they must recognize themselves to be in a constant daily struggle to resist their sinful inclinations? Indeed, James leaves them no room for doubt about this truth. The text states that they are this way because they have chosen not to do good works. If they had, God would have helped them.

Now we can see more clearly why James in 2:14 holds their salvation in abeyance with the haunting question "Can faith save him?" The issue is not merely whether or not the Christian's good works will justify him, but whether or not he has refrained from sin. "Good works" refer not only to doing something positive (e.g., feeding the hungry) but also to refraining from the negative, i.e., sin. Since sin can occur not only by commission (e.g., murder, adultery, coveting) but also by omission (e.g., James 4:17: "anyone who knows the good he ought to do and doesn't do it, sins"), then the potential for sin has a direct bearing on our understanding of whether faith alone can save him.

This is not all. In chapter 3, James again describes the bad works that will jeopardize one's salvation. James gives the most astounding treatise on the evil of the *spoken word* found in Scripture. Speaking to the same Christian audience in 3:9 (NB, the continual use of "my brothers" in 3:10, 12; cf., 1:16,19; 4:11), James points out that with the tongue they "praise the Lord and Father" but at the same time "curse men made in the likeness of God." This is the same accusation he made in 1:26, "If anyone considers himself religious and yet does not keep a *tight reign on his tongue*, he deceives himself and his religion is worthless," and in 4:11, "Brothers, do not *slander* one another..." In this pervasive context, two important points emerge. First, chapters 1, 3, and 4 of James, all of which warn against sin, especially sins of the tongue, surround chapter 2's discussion of faith and works. This positioning leads us to conclude that the potential for sin, especially sins of the tongue, is germane to the discussion of faith and works. In light of this fact, in chapter 2 James consistently stresses what a brother "says" as he discriminates against the poor (e.g., James 2:3: "but *say* to the poor man...sit on the floor by my feet"). In this instance, James concludes that they have become "*judges* with evil thoughts" (2:4), which is the same language he uses in 4:11, "Anyone who speaks against his brother or *judges* him." In 2:16 he also points out what is *said*: "one of you *says* to him, 'Go, I wish you well; keep warm and well fed.'" This person, like the one in 1:26, cannot keep a tight reign on his tongue but instead spills out spiritual platitudes that help no one. James could have taught the same truths without this hypothetical dialogue. He could simply have made a matter-of-fact statement such as "what good is it if one has faith but does not care for someone's physical needs?" The stress on the words the Christian *speaks*, however, illustrates an important theme in the book of James: *watch what you say—or you may harm someone*. The tongue can give pretense of religiosity; it can judge another; in fact, "it is a world of iniquity" (3:6).[8]

Second, after James's treatise on the tongue in 3:1-12, he follows with "Who is wise and understanding among you? Let him show it by his good life, by *deeds* done in the humility that comes from wisdom." Clearly, then, controlling one's tongue is a matter of wisdom and understanding. In 3:1, James points out that they were all wishing to be "teachers." They all had *something to say*, as it were, things they thought were full of wisdom and understanding. In their teaching they "praised God" but "cursed man made in the image of God." They would sing God's praises with the tongue but then treat men, including their Christian brothers, with contempt. They would teach faith with their tongue but curse men both by the tongue and lack of good deeds. Thus, in so many words, James says in 3:13, "Do you really want to have wisdom and understanding? Then show it by deeds done in humility." This is the same "wisdom" he told them to seek in 1:5-6. The opposite of this wisdom, as James goes on to say in 3:14-16, is "bitter envy" and "selfish ambition" and "every evil practice." Perhaps the teachers of 3:1 were prone to living by this double standard—teaching faith but doing evil. Again, we see that the contrast James develops throughout this epistle is good works versus bad works, obedience versus sin, "saying" you will do good versus actually doing good. When James says "let him show it" in 3:13, he is using the same word he used in 2:18 in the faith and works controversy, i.e., "I will show you." The mind can be deceived into thinking it has done good but it cannot know for certain, yea, it cannot know at all, until it makes a conscious and consistent effort to do good and avoid sin. Goodness will not flow naturally; in fact, the believer's inner nature will continually fight against doing good. He must control his sinful desires and discipline himself to do good works. By the grace and wisdom of God, which he must also consciously and consistently call on for help, he can be victorious. He *must* do this, for without holiness he will not see the Lord (Hebrews 12:14), or in James's words, he will not be "saved" (2:14) or "justified" (2:24).

James continues the stress on avoiding sins of the tongue in Chapter 5. In 5:1-6, the Christians are being persecuted and physically abused by the rich masters. In 5:7-12, James tells them to be patient in this trial until "the Lord's coming." Interspersed with this warning is the admonition not to sin with one's tongue. In 5:9, James warns them: "Do not *grumble* against each other, brothers, or you will be judged. The Judge is standing at the door!" Perhaps in suffering under the strain of persecution they were beginning to take it out on their Christian brothers by verbally abusing one another. James reinforces his admonition by citing an example from the Old Testament: Job, who did not curse God or his neighbors with his tongue even though he was put through a terrible test. It was Job's very wife who told him, "Curse God and die" (Job 2:9). In response, the most important statement in all of Job appears in Job 2:10: "In all this Job did not sin with his *lips*." James continues the same line of argument when in 5:12 he tells them not to *swear* by anything and to let their "yes" be "yes" and "no" be "no." Again the stress is on the possibility of sinning with the tongue. James recommends that for those who do not hold up under the persecution, either physically or spiritually, to call for the presbyters of the Church who will pray over them and seek God's grace and healing. If one has sinned, either with the lips or in any other manner, the Lord will forgive him and raise him up (5:13-18). Those who bring the wayward brother to the presbyters receive James's commendation for a good work (5:19-20).

ARE JAMES AND PAUL SAYING THE SAME THING ABOUT JUSTIFICATION?

At this point, it would be helpful to see the parallels between James and Paul. In Galatians 5:6, Paul speaks of "faith working through love." In this context, Paul includes the "Royal law" of James 2:8 in Galatians 5:14 by the statement, "The entire law is summed up in a single command, 'Love your neighbor as yourself.'" In the same context, Paul also speaks about avoiding sin by not living in the sinful nature (Galatians 5:15-26); the same theme that James takes up in James 1:13 and 2:10-11. Finally, in Galatians 5:21, Paul warns of the consequences for disobedience as "those who live like this will not inherit the kingdom of God." James warns of the same consequences in 2:13 when he says, "because judgment without mercy will be shown to anyone who has not been merciful." The similarities between Paul and James are not mere coincidence. Faith requires the addition of love towards God and one's neighbor. It is clear, then, that salvation is not by faith alone, for either Paul or James.

In the following verses of Galatians 5, Paul goes on to describe the same battle between the Spirit and the flesh that we saw James repeat so often. In Galatians 5:16 Paul says, "So I say, live by the Spirit, and you will not gratify the desires of the sinful nature. For the sinful nature desires what is contrary to the Spirit, and the Spirit what is contrary to the sinful nature." Next, Paul's warning in 5:21 is that if one lives by the sinful nature he will lose his inheritance in the kingdom of God. Likewise, James makes it clear that he is just as serious, continuing in 2:9-13 that if one discriminates against a lower social class, then he will be judged by God "without mercy."

This analysis is important because it shows that for both Paul and James works are the ultimate factor in determining the justification of the individual. If one decides not to follow the Spirit and instead to follow his sinful desires and discriminate against the poor, God will judge him. This is not just a judgment to determine how low his status will be in heaven. No, according to James 2:14 it is a judgment that allows James to ask the all important question, "Can faith *save* him?" This rhetorical question shows clearly that James is referring to whether one is saved or damned in light of his works.

LET'S LOOK CLOSER AT JAMES CHAPTER 2

We notice in James's hypothetical examples of the poor man walking into a meeting with shabby clothes in 2:1-5, and the poor man with no clothes in 2:15, that he wants his audience to think about what they would or should do if a situation like this ever presents itself to them. "What would you do if..." is the type of argumentation he is using. In this method, James forces the individual to examine himself and make a decision: "Will I discriminate or not discriminate?" "Will I help by giving clothing and food or will I not help?" The decision process is what James is trying to probe and establish here. "I say I believe in God and love God; I say I love my neighbor. Am I willing to make the physical effort to help my neighbor with whatever his needs are?" This decision process confronts any person who says he has faith in God. According to James, it is a decision to which he must say "yes," or he will not be justified. His hypothetical example of helping someone with physical needs shows by its very nature that it is a *daily* decision, a decision to which the answer must be "yes" at any moment in a person's life when he is confronted with the possibility of doing good. If he does not answer affirmatively, he sins. If he does not repent of his sin, he will not be justified.

The distinction between the Protestant concept of works that inevitably flow out of true faith and the concept of James in which a person must make a conscious decision to help a brother in need is an important one to stress. Scripture does not teach a mechanical process in which faith automatically produces good works. It is not as if once the button of faith is pushed that the conveyor belt of works will begin to produce the desired product. In fact, as the individual confronts the decision to sin or not to sin each day of his life, so he also confronts the decision to do good works or not do good works, and the two are intimately interrelated. Merely having faith, even good-quality faith, does not mean one will refrain from sin in each situation; likewise, having faith does not mean one will necessarily decide to do good works. As Paul warned the Galatians, "Those who do such things will not inherit the kingdom of God" (Galatians 5:21), so it would be equally valid to give the same warning to those who say they have faith but do not do good works—they will not inherit the kingdom of God. Again, James is crystal clear about this ultimatum when he introduces his proposition with the question, "Can faith *save* him?" To interpret otherwise would give no substantial meaning or impact to this question.

James continues this theme in 2:18 by picking up the hypothetical objector left over from 2:16: "But someone will say, You have faith; I have deeds. Show me your faith without deeds, and I will show you my faith by what I do." In this verse James is again basing his argument on what someone *says* as opposed to what he does. Behind the challenge to "Show me your faith without works" is the assumption that someone can convince another by what he *says* that he indeed has faith. He can even do so without showing any works. Conversely, his opponent says that he can show faith by his works. That this incident is put in the form of a dialogue between two opponents would mean that both individuals are dealing from a theological basis, i.e., rather than observing the whole of each other's lives, they are conversing at a moment in time about who between them has the correct understanding of faith and works. Interpreting this verse within the context that James sets up, the first opponent, confronted with the destitute man that James describes in 2:15-16, would conclude that in order to be saved he does *not* need to provide for the poor man's needs. It is simply sufficient that he have faith in God. The second individual insists that one must add to faith by caring for someone's physical needs. We must understand that James is not condemning the first opponent for giving verbal affirmation of faith. Faith is an act of the will. It puts one on the road to salvation. Faith is good. Having faith in God is much better than being an atheist. James maintains, however, that if one is to be saved, having faith in God is not enough. One must also make a conscious effort to join works with faith in order to show that he is willing to do *all* that God requires for righteousness. It is relatively easy for me to have faith in God's existence, and to believe that he may perhaps want me to do a *few* things to acknowledge him, but doing works of love for people who are lowly and despised is difficult. The world would pass the needy by without lifting a finger, just as Jesus pointed out in the parable of the Good Samaritan of Luke 10:30-32 the priest and the Levite who passed by the wounded man without helping him. Christians must rise above the mediocrity of the world and be like the Good Samaritan. That kind of love is what will justify their entrance into heaven. When the Lord asks them at judgment day if they have fed the hungry and clothed the naked, they must be able to answer in the affirmative or he will condemn them (Matthew 25:31-46). If one refuses to add works of love to faith when the opportunity arises, then the rhetorical question of James 2:14, namely, "Can faith ['by itself'] save him?", must be answered in the negative.

In order to tone down the seriousness of this issue, some Protestants turn to the statement James makes in 2:19: "You believe that there is one God. Good! Even the demons believe that—and shudder." They propose that James's only concern is that someone not have faith like that of the demons. As long as he does not have "that kind" of faith, he can be assured of having "saving faith." This kind of interpretation is a distortion of James's teaching. James has already established in his context the major tenet that faith and works must both be present in a working relationship, actively participating in caring for someone's physical needs (verses 15-17). Then why does James add the demons to the discussion? By the mere fact that demons are not often used as an example of someone who has faith, James's inclusion of them into the discussion serves as a hyperbolic example of his thesis in the face of the hypothetical objector. In other words, if one does not accept James's opening argument that in order to be saved one must consciously add works to faith by actively participating in caring for the needs of the destitute, then James will take his opponent back to a truth that he cannot deny, namely that the demons also have a belief in God, however limited it is. As we discovered in Hebrews 11:6, faith has two basic components. First, one must believe that God exists. The demons have this component.[9] However, they do not have the second component, that is, they do not aspire to God as "the rewarder of those that *diligently* seek him." Diligently seeking God requires that they work to please him—something the demons will never do.

As we noted above, James is presenting his point in the form of argumentative dialogue. This is evident in the way he refers to his hypothetical opponent in 2:18 by the clause "But someone will say..." The example of the demons is a powerful argument to convince the opponent because it takes the extreme negative case and makes it the background for the plausible positive case—like putting a white dot on a piece of black paper. That being said, however, James's main argument is not the contrast between demon faith and Christian faith, but between a Christian who takes care of his brother's needs and a Christian who does not. "Can the mere faith of the latter save him?" is the question remaining for James to answer even more completely.

In the following verses (2:21-26), James goes into the third phase of his answer. The first phase concerned the hypothetical situation in which one must decide whether to care for his brother. The second phase used a hyperbolic contrast between Christian faith and demon faith. The third phase concentrates on two real-life examples of the principles James is attempting to illustrate. In this phase, James completes his argument.

Considering that the man with whom he is arguing is not yet convinced of his point, James opens in verse 20 with the address, "You foolish man..." This kind of introduction would be intended, perhaps, for some of the more obstinate Jews of that day. Whether the Jew is the only member of James's audience is not known (James 1:1), but even if Gentiles were included, as they probably were, the church at this time contained many Jewish Christians. Ironically, James seems to be having the opposite problem from the one his brother Paul had. Paul was struggling to educate the Jew that the system of law/works could not save anyone, while James is arguing that works are necessary for salvation. The reason Paul and James have these different foci is that the Jew was clinging to his ceremonial rituals and attempting to elevate them as the works that God required, rather than performing works of love encapsulated in the command "love your neighbor as yourself." To be sure, Paul condemned the whole category of law as a means of salvation, but the primary dimension of the law used as a means of salvation for the typical Jew was the ceremonial law, e.g., circumcision, dietary ordinances, etc. For Paul, if one insists on being circumcised as a legal requirement for being a Christian, then one repudiates the system of grace and places himself in the system of law. Anyone who is places into the system of law will be condemned because then he must obey the whole law faultlessly, and for a single sin he will be held guilty (Galatians 5:6). For James, the same principle is true (James 2:10). The Jew could not cling to his ceremonial works and ignore the "royal law" of loving the Lord and his neighbor as himself. Although James does not explicitly present the argument as one of ritual law as opposed to royal law, his choice of Abraham as his prime example to prove his point implies this intent. Since the Jew sees Abraham as his godly mentor, James must attack the false notion of Abraham to which the Jew clings. As Paul argues in Romans 4, it was not mere ritual rites that justified Abraham, but a life of faith and obedience that pleased God. Later in the chapter, James presents an even stronger argument as he speaks of the Gentile harlot, Rahab, who was justified even though she knew nothing of Jewish ritual.

James begins the third phase of his argumentation in 2:21: "Was not our father Abraham justified when he offered his son Isaac on the altar." Unlike Paul's quote of Genesis 15:6 that he made in Romans 4:3, which James now references in James 2:23, James's commentary on the offering of Isaac is significant, since Genesis 22 does not explicitly say that Abraham "was justified" or "credited with righteousness" at that moment in time. Only James's interpretation of the incident tells us that the attempted sacrifice of Isaac is considered a "justification" of Abraham. This tells us that the word "justification," or its cognates, does not have to appear in the original account for the concept of justification to be in view. This will become more important later when we discuss the *process* of justification in chapter 4.

LET'S LOOK AT ABRAHAM'S FAITH AND WORKS IN GENESIS

Next, James elaborates on the example of Abraham in James 2:22: "You see that his faith and his actions were working together, and his faith was made complete by what he did." James gives us two aspects of the relationship between Abraham's faith and works: (1) faith and deeds were working together, and (2) his works completed or perfected his faith. As we noted previously, Protestant interpreters tend to separate Abraham's faith from his works in order to compensate for the disjunction they impose between the imputed justification and the ongoing sanctification. In doing so, they look upon the account in Genesis 15 as the decisive moment of faith which gives Abraham his actual justification, while they view Genesis 22 as illustrating the works that inevitably tagged along after the faith and justification of Genesis 15 were established. James, however, already concludes in 2:22, in reference to the offering of Isaac (before he addresses the account of Abraham's faith in 2:23 in reference to Genesis 15), that Abraham's faith and works were "working together." This shows that Abraham's attempted sacrifice of Isaac was also an act of faith, not merely a work following the faith he displayed in Genesis 15 a decade or so earlier. Hebrews 11:17, 19 contains this analysis: "By *faith*, Abraham, when God tested him, offered Isaac as a sacrifice...Abraham reasoned that God could raise the dead, and figuratively speaking, he did receive Isaac back from death." Abraham's faith and works were "working together" in Genesis 22. Thus we should not think of Genesis 15 as merely establishing the faith of Abraham and of Genesis 22 as demonstrating the works of Abraham. James considers the faith and works of Genesis 22 as an indivisible unit. This likewise implies that we should not attempt to understand other instances of either faith or works that are highlighted in Abraham's life without considering their respective counterpart. Just as the account of Genesis 22 assumes Abraham's *faith* without explicitly mentioning it, so Genesis 15 must assume Abraham's *works* without explicitly mentioning them. In light of this new perspective, we must again go back to the accounts of Abraham's life in Genesis 12-21 to see how his faith and works were always "working together."

In Genesis 12:1-3, God calls Abram out of Haran and Abram sets out on his way to the Promised Land of Canaan. In this command God gives Abram certain promises: "I will make you into a great nation and I will bless you...and all the peoples of the earth will be blessed through you." Genesis 12:4 records Abram's response: "So Abram left, as the Lord had told him..." This passage does not specifically mention either "faith" or "works," yet both are implicit in the account. That Abram believed God had a special land in store for him is evident in Abram's departure from Haran; likewise, his work of obedience is equally obvious by the same departure. If anything is more prominent, it is the actual work of obedience displayed specifically by Abram's departure from Haran. The faith which convinces him to leave is implicit.

Yet that faith, according to Paul, is obviously a major underlying feature of this account, as he states in Hebrews 11:8: "By *faith* Abraham, when called to go to a place he would later receive as his inheritance, obeyed and went, even though he did not know where he was going."

Paul's account has two important characteristics. First, he defines Abraham's faith primarily in terms of his obedience. This shows the intrinsic synergism between faith and works for justification. Second, he describes the cognitive aspect of Abraham's faith as "even though he did not know where he was going." As mentioned previously, the faith that God is trying to draw out of Abraham is more than an acknowledgment that God exists; rather, he is attempting to elicit a deep faith from Abraham; one that trusts implicitly in God's integrity to do what he says he will do; a faith that believes that God is looking out for Abraham's best interests even though all the circumstances at the time do not dictate such assurance. As Hebrews 11:6 states, Abraham's faith allows him to wait to see God as "the rewarder of those who diligently seek him," the word "diligently" denoting a long process in drawing out faith in Abraham. Hence, the only way for Abraham to establish his faith is actually to leave Haran at God's command not knowing where he is going or what he will confront when he gets to his destination. In fact, Abram had sufficient cause to fear as soon as he entered the land of Canaan. Genesis 12:6 records the kind of people he or his descendants would eventually encounter: "Abram traveled through the land...At that time the Canaanites were in the land." According to Numbers 13:31-14:4, some of the people who inhabited Canaan were giants who seemed much fiercer and stronger than the average man. Later in their history, the Israelites would become so frightened of them that they would rebel against Moses and complain that God had taken them out of Egypt to destroy them at the hands of these giants (Deuteronomy 2:20). Hence, Abram, having only his wife Sarai and his nephew Lot with him, must have had very great faith in God to protect him.

From the account in Genesis 13 one might conclude that Abram had a momentary lapse of faith. A famine arises in the land of Canaan. Without seeking God's advice, Abram went to Egypt for food. Arriving in Egypt, Abram fears that the Egyptians will seize his wife due to her great beauty. He tells Sarai to say she is his sister so that the Egyptians do not kill him. Rather than trusting in God at this point, Abram lets the Egyptians believe that Sarai is only his sister and not his wife. (Actually, Sarai is Abraham's sister, so what he says is not totally false but rather a half-truth and consequently deceiving.) Although it may seem that Abram has a lapse of faith, the text does not give enough information to determine whether doubt is his state of mind or not, nor does it record that God warned Abram not to go down into Egypt, as he later warned Isaac in Genesis 26:2. On the contrary, God immediately comes to Abram's rescue by inflicting "serious diseases" on Pharaoh and his household for taking Sarai. This suggests that Abram's walk with God is sufficiently in order that God acts on his behalf, which is not necessarily what God does when someone sins.

As we move on in the Genesis account, we observe in Abram a very faithful and loving man. Genesis 13 describes a conflict between the herdsmen of Abram and the herdsmen of Lot. As the peacemaker, Abram suggests that he and Lot divide the land, giving first choice to Lot. Lot takes the more fertile land of Jordan which was "watered like the garden of the Lord." Abram is left with the land of Canaan. There, he erects an altar in honor of the Lord after God reiterates the promise he first made with him when he left Haran. This account shows his generosity to man and devotion to God, works that our author, James, would certainly approve for justification.

In Genesis 14, invading armies rout the plain of Sodom and Gomorrah where Lot lives and take Lot captive. Not giving a second thought to his own life, Abram gathers 318 fighting men and pursues the kidnaping army. He rescues Lot, Lot's family, and his possessions. This shows his courage and love for his fellow man. Later in the same chapter, we read of Abram's meeting with Melchizedek, king of Salem, who is a priest of the Most High. Abram bows himself before Melchizedek and gives him a tenth of all his possessions, showing his humility and generosity. Next, the king of Sodom offers Abram possessions that were part of the spoil when they rescued Lot. Abram refuses to take the possessions, not wanting to appear as if he had benefitted by someone else's hand. This incident shows Abram's integrity and lack of greed.

The next major event in Abram's life is the encounter with God in Genesis 15. In the first verse, God tells Abram, "Do not be afraid, Abram. I am your shield, your very great reward." Abram has heard God's voice once before so it is not likely that he is fearful at this point. Living in a strange land among strange people can be very frightening, however. God assures Abram that despite these strangers he is his *shield*. Wherever Abram goes, God will be there to protect him.

Sensing the love that God is bestowing upon him, Abram perhaps wanting to save face for God politely mentions that God has not yet given him the son he had promised. God had spoken of being his reward, but there is as yet no reward of a son. Here God interjects and explains that Abram will indeed have a son by his own wife Sarai. The famous text of Genesis 15:6 states: "And Abram believed the Lord, and he credited it to him as righteousness." As we noted earlier, this was indeed a great step of faith for Abram. Although this text does not tell us explicitly, we understand from Paul's commentary in Romans 4 that Abram is one hundred years old at this time and Sarai is ninety. Sarai had proven to be barren all the years up to her ninetieth birthday, an age far beyond normal child-bearing years. Yet despite the circumstantial evidence that speaks against God's integrity, Abram believes. Abram does not believe, however, as a spur-of-the-moment decision to trust God. He has built up a life of trusting God since the moment twenty-five years earlier when he, in a similar act of faith and obedience, answered the summon of God to leave Haran. The act of believing God in Genesis 15 is just one more step in the life of faith, hope, and love that Abram has already displayed many times in the past.

Regarding Abram's obedience which joins with his faith in Genesis 15, we must remember that the two spouses were nearing a century old, and because of Sarai's known barrenness, Abram and Sarai most likely had not engaged in intimate relations for a long time prior to this event. In any case, we are obliged to recognize that the couples mere act of intimate relations in anticipation that God would produce the promised son from this union indicates both Abram's and Sarai's trust and obedience.

Second, Genesis 15 shows that Abram continued to obey in the period after God counted his belief as righteousness. In Genesis 15:7, God speaks to Abram and declares that he has called him out of Ur of the Chaldeans to give him the promised land. Abram inquires of the Lord how he can know that he will receive the promised possession. God commands Abram to bring various animals to a designated place. Abram obeys by killing the animals and separating them into halves. Through this, God makes a covenant with Abram and promises that his descendants would inherit the land. Abram's obedience in participating in the covenant ritual shows his trust and obedience in God.

As great as Abram's faith is in Genesis 15:6, later the promise of God to give him a son begins to fade in Abram's mind. Such is the case described in Genesis 16 when Abram listens to Sarai's advice to take Hagar for a wife in an effort to produce the child that God has apparently not given to Abram. Abram's complicity with Sarai is surprising since he has previously inquired of God in Genesis 15:2 whether Eliezer his servant was to be the inheritor that God promised. God had assured him that Eliezer was not the recipient but that Abram would have his *own* child. Perhaps since God has not said specifically that Sarai would be the mother of the child, Abram may have been reasoning that God's general statement "but a son coming from your own body will be your heir" in Genesis 15:4 leaves room for taking Hagar as a wife. Whatever his reasoning, Abram listens to the advice of Sarai without consulting the Lord. This shows somewhat of a retreat from the faith he exhibited in Genesis 15:6.

Genesis 17 records a dramatic instance of another retreat from faith. It is now thirteen years after Abram had first retreated from faith in Genesis 16 by taking Hagar as a wife. If Abram had doubted the promise of God in Genesis 16, we can imagine what thirteen more years of not seeing Sarai produce the promised child has done. Genesis 17:17 records Abraham's state of mind. After God promises once again that Sarah will bear the child, "Abraham fell face down and laughed and said to himself, 'Will a son be born to a man a hundred years old? Will Sarah bear a child at the age of ninety?'"[10] It is hard to believe this is the same man who a decade or so earlier had accepted God's words without question in Genesis 15:6. The nuances of language in the Hebrew version of Genesis 17:17 portray the scene as if Abraham is rolling on the floor in hysterical laughter and making snide comments under his breath about his and Sarah's old age. A decade and a half ago, the proposition of having a child had seemed at least probable. But with the passage of time, certainly a passage of time that Abraham had not expected, the prospect of having his own child becomes outright laughable, at least in human terms. Fortunately for Abraham, God does not become angry when Abraham virtually laughs in his face. Instead, God politely brings him to his senses by reiterating the promise. But God does not forget this lapse of faith, as we shall soon see.

Abraham's and Sarah's doubt produced several consequences. First, an unanticipated jealousy and hatred arises between Sarah and Hagar, causing Sarah to ask Abraham to send Hagar away. Second, the son born to Hagar, Ishmael by name, though blessed by God, eventually becomes the progenitor of the Arab nations, Israel's bitter enemies in the future (Genesis 16:12).

Abraham's next encounter with God occurs in Genesis 18:23f in the destruction of Sodom and Gomorrah. Because of the intimate relationship that Abraham has already established with the Lord, Abraham pleads with God not to destroy the city if he finds only ten righteous people living there. Perhaps Abraham is concerned about his nephew Lot and his family who have made their home in Sodom. As it turns out, God takes Lot and his family out of Sodom before he destroys the city. The point we are making here is that in God's eyes Abraham is significant enough to be able to strike a compromise with God. This again is indicative of a long and abiding relationship of trust, understanding, and obedience. It is for Abraham's righteous relationship with God that God reconsiders, if only temporarily, his original assessment of Sodom and Gomorrah. Scripture reflects a common understanding that God will graciously honor the request of one who is righteous to benefit another (cf., Deut. 9:13-29; Ezek. 14:14; James 5:17).

This dimension of Abraham's relationship with God also appears in Genesis 20 when Abraham prays for the well-being of Abimelech after the latter has mistakenly taken Sarah for his own. In Genesis 20:7 God tells Abimelech to ask Abraham to pray for him, and verse 17 states that Abraham did pray and in turn God restored the fertility of Abimelech's household. Abraham's reputation is well-known in that place, for Abimelech admits to

Abraham in Genesis 21:22 that "God is with you in everything you do." This kind of recognition comes only through an intimate walk with God in which Abraham's faith and obedience please God sufficiently that God desires to bless him in this way. Genesis 21:33 again expresses Abraham's faith and obedience to God: "...and there he called upon the name of the Lord, the Eternal God." Of course, we must not leave this incident without pointing out that Abraham has again made the same mistake he had made in Genesis 13 when he allowed Pharaoh to take Sarah under the pretense that she was only his sister, not his wife. Here we see that Abraham is an ordinary man—one with many doubts and fears in a frequently hostile world.

Finally in Genesis 21, Isaac, the long-awaited fulfillment of God's promise, is born. Some years later, God approaches Abraham for his supreme test of faith. Genesis 22 records that God commands Abraham to take Isaac and sacrifice him. Perhaps this is the third consequence of Abraham's retreat from faith noted earlier when in Genesis 16 he takes Hagar as a wife, and in Genesis 17:17 he laughs at God's promise. Those moments of doubt and lack of consultation with the Lord may be the very reason God has to test him one more time. The doubts concerning God's integrity have retarded Abraham's faith to some degree and now Abraham, with God's help, must eradicate that doubt. To do so God will now subject Abraham to the severest test of faith in God's integrity ever given to man.

As we noted previously, James has set up a context in which to answer the question "Can faith save him?" in reference to the works one must choose to do. In order to be the prime example of James's thesis, Abraham's salvation must have equal potential of being granted or of being denied, based on his works. Though Abraham had showed great faith a decade or so earlier in Genesis 15:6, God has not forgotten his lapse of faith in Genesis 16:1f and 17:17. Abraham has not only disappointed God, but has even personally insulted God by laughing at the promise. After so much time since the original promise in Genesis 15:6, his fear and respect of God has subsided to a considerable degree. Hence, Abraham has opened himself up for another test—the harshest test he will ever face—the sacrifice of his own son.

If Abraham had not come to know God as well as he now does in the thirty or so years prior to the test in Genesis 22, he might be tempted to think God was a blood-thirsty murderer who has enticed him with promises of life but has really wanted death. Instead, the life of faith and obedience Abraham has cultivated with God help him decide at this point to trust God. Abraham has finally witnessed the birth of the promised child and this has restored his faith in God. God has kept his part of the bargain. God has also prepared Abraham for the final test by a marvelous display of fearful judgment in the destruction of Sodom and Gomorrah in Genesis 18. Abraham knows that God means business. In light of this, the lingering doubt concerning Abraham's reverence and respect for God now has to be answered. There will be no more laughing. God will test Abraham's reverence by asking him to do something that seems totally absurd and, ironically, could even cause Abraham to laugh in God's face again. In more sublime moments, Abraham might be driven to say, "You mean you want me to kill the very son that I have agonized over for the last 25 years? You have got to be joking!" This would be an appropriate reply if the person addressed were not God Almighty. This time, though, Abraham, instead of laughing, raises the knife to kill Isaac, putting his complete trust in God. According to Hebrews 11:19, Abraham does not raise the knife out of blind allegiance, rather, he reasons that if Isaac dies, God would even raise him from the dead to fulfill the promise. As he raises the knife, God stops him and says, "Now I know that you *fear* God." God does not say, "Now I know that you have faith in me" or "Now I know that you are obedient to me," even though Abraham certainly possesses those virtues. At this point, God's concern is fear and reverence. No matter how foolish the circumstances have appeared, God literally wants to see the *fear* in Abraham's eyes, a fear which recognizes that God is who he says he is and knows what he is doing. In short, it is no laughing matter. As Ecclesiasticus 25:10-11 states, "How great is the one who finds wisdom! But none is superior to the one who fears the Lord. Fear of the Lord surpasses everything; to whom can we compare the one who has it?"

This final test in Genesis 22 seals and confirms the covenant between God and Abraham. Abraham will undergo no more climactic tests but may now live his life out in the simple faith and obedience he had cultivated many years before. At each encounter with God, God has reiterated the promises to Abraham concerning the land.[11] What is most important to understand in the sequence of these promises is that the promise to bless Abraham and his descendants is not ultimately confirmed until the final test of Genesis 22. This means that the stipulations of the promise given in Genesis 12-17 cannot be fulfilled unless Abraham passes the final test of offering up Isaac as a sacrifice. Genesis 22:15-16 states:

> The angel of the Lord called to Abraham from heaven a second time and said, '*I swear by myself*, declares the Lord, that *because you have done this and have not withheld your son*, your only son, I will surely bless you and make your descendants as numerous as the stars in the sky...and through your offspring all nations on earth will be blessed because you have obeyed me.'

Of all the times that God has stipulated the components of the promise to Abraham in Genesis 12-22, this is the only time that God has said "*I swear by myself.*" This language denotes that God has confirmed and sealed the covenant promises. They would not be altered for any reason. This is such an important issue that Paul refers to it in absolute terms in Hebrews 6:13-17:

> When God made his promise to Abraham, since there was no one greater for him to swear by, he swore by himself...Men swear by someone greater than themselves, and the oath confirms what is said and puts an end to all argument. Because God wanted to make the unchanging nature of his purpose very clear to the heirs of what was promised he confirmed it with an oath.

That this divine oath-swearing occurs at Genesis 22:16, (and not at Genesis 15:6), shows that without the faith and obedience of Genesis 22 the righteousness previously credited to Abraham would become null and void. Prior to Genesis 22, God would not have had to honor the covenant he made with Abraham if Abraham had subsequently disobeyed. Genesis 22:16's wording, "because you have done this and have not withheld your son, your only son" implies this because God conditions his oath on the obedience of Abraham. His obedience is of such cosmic importance that the blessing to his seed, and to the nations, rests virtually on Abraham's shoulders alone. His act in Genesis 22 is the quintessential act of faith and obedience that has reverberations for the rest of the world into eternity.

We might ask at this point that if the oath-swearing in Genesis 22:16-17 is the most important exchange between God and Abraham as regards the promises, why does Paul not mention this event in Romans 4 when he speaks of Abraham? In fact, Paul either ignores or is oblivious to the lapses of faith that Abraham exhibited in Genesis, speaking of Abraham only in glowing terms, e.g., "Without weakening in his faith...yet he did not waver through unbelief regarding the promises of God..." (Romans 4:18-21). The key to understanding Paul's perspective in Romans 4 is to realize that here he is dealing with the issue of circumcision. Since the Jews had elevated circumcision to be their rite of passage into heaven, Paul must explain the chronological relationship between the establishment of circumcision as opposed to the establishment of Abraham's faith that was credited to him as righteousness. Paul argues that since the covenant of circumcision came chronologically *after* Abraham's faith and righteousness, then his circumcision could not have begun his justification or righteousness. In other words, Abraham had to have faith in God's grace before he did any works. Trying to do works without faith would have put Abraham in a situation that Paul describes in Romans 4:4 as, "when a man works his wages are not credited to him as a gift, but as an obligation." Works done without faith put one in the system of law and obligation. Works done in faith put one in the system of grace that seeks to please God. To be sure, Abraham's obedience to the covenant of circumcision was a good work that pleased God, but that is only because Abraham had already established a grace relationship with God. Paul understands circumcision positively as, "a seal of the righteousness that he had by faith" (Romans 4:11), and thus as a good and wholesome work. But because the Jews lack a faith like Abraham's—a faith that believes "that God has power to do what he has promised" (Romans 4:21)—whatever works they do only draw them further away from God. As Paul says in Romans 9:32, "Because they pursued it not by faith but as it were by works." Paul's point, then, is not to deny that works play a primary role in the justification of the individual, but rather, to prove, by the chronological layout of the Genesis account, that through grace Abraham had genuine faith in God before he set out to work for God. One must believe in God and be in the state of grace in order to do work that is pleasing to God. If not, one is still operating in the system of law. On the other hand, as we have seen in his Galatian epistle, Paul whole heartedly agrees with James that if the works done subsequent to the establishment of faith turn out to be disobedience instead of obedience, this makes one unacceptable for justification.

At this point someone may argue that Paul's chronological distinction between Abraham's faith and his circumcision merely proves that *faith alone*, as long as it is established prior to works, causes the crediting of righteousness. This is not Paul's meaning or intent. As we saw above, Paul picks the chronological distinction between the faith of Genesis 15 and the works of Genesis 17 only to show that one must have faith in the grace of God before he can expect God to recognize and reward his works (Romans 4:12). Paul recognizes Abraham's work of circumcision as a legitimate work that pleased God. Circumcision was indeed a sign of the covenant, but the Jews misinterpreted this to make circumcision the only means of obtaining the promises of the covenant.

We must not misconstrue the understanding of Paul in Romans 4, however, to teach that Paul would have discounted any works done by Abraham prior to his expression of faith in Genesis 15:6. We have already seen from Genesis 12 that when God first commanded Abraham to leave Haran that Abraham exhibited faith and works that were pleasing to God. His faith in God had put him in a relationship of grace that allowed God to look with favor on his works. In Hebrews 11:8 Paul verified this faith and obedience: "By faith Abraham, when called to go to a place...obeyed and went." At each point in Abraham's life his faith and works were, as James says, "working together." In Romans 4, Paul is not faulting Abraham's concept of faith and works. He is faulting the Jews. He has to expose a glaring contradiction in their theology so they can see how spiritually bankrupt they are. To do this, he attacks the very practice in which they most take pride—circumcision. Works without faith will simply not pass muster with God. All in all, as James points out that faith without works is dead, Paul's point is that work without faith is dead.

We may infer that James understands a continual relationship between faith and works from the use of the plural "works" rather than the singular "work" in James 2:20-24. Although James is singling out the sacrifice of Isaac as the work of Abraham, this is only for the purpose of illustration. As we noted earlier in this chapter, James 2:15 also presents the situation where one sees a brother or sister in need of food and clothing. The individual must couple his faith with works by making a decision to help that needy person. Such situations are not isolated events in a person's life. On numerous occasions one becomes aware of another's physical needs, and, as James teaches, God expects him to answer each situation with the resources God has placed at his disposal. Hence, we speak of the plural "works" in the sense of a life of work. On the other hand, we do not speak of "faiths" since normally we cannot quantify faith, but rather, understand it as a quality or state of mind.

JAMES HAS MORE TO SAY ABOUT ABRAHAM

James continues in 2:23 with his analysis of Abraham: "And the Scripture was fulfilled that says, 'Abraham believed God, and it was credited to him as righteousness,' and he was called God's friend." The clause, "and the Scripture was fulfilled" is not a statement we would expect at this point, since the Bible normally uses such phrasing in the fulfillment of a prophecy pointing to an actual event in the future.[12] In fact, the Bible contains no instance of the clause "and the Scripture was fulfilled" which does not take into account the prophecy of a future event. The faith of Abraham, being an actual event in itself, is not really a prophecy as we normally understand the word. Nevertheless, according to James, the event of faith in Genesis 15:6 includes a prophetic element and as such the prophecy is waiting for an event in the future for its fulfillment.

Before we look more closely at how the faith of Genesis 15:6 was fulfilled, we must emphasize that James 2:23 does not imply that God had to wait a decade or more for Abraham to finally show works that fulfilled the faith of Genesis 15, or wait three decades for Abraham to fulfill the faith from Genesis 12.[13] Abraham demonstrated throughout his life the works that "work together" with faith by continually loving his neighbor, avoiding sin, worshiping God, and many other acts of obedience. We have already detailed many instances of these works that occurred prior to Genesis 15 and Genesis 22.[14] These are the same works that James requires of Christians in the chapter under discussion (James 2:8-11). Since Abraham had already accomplished works of love and obedience, there may be a much more profound reason why James is pointing to the sacrifice of Isaac in Genesis 22 as the "fulfillment" of the faith in Genesis 15:6.

Looking again at the event of faith in Genesis 15:6, we see two components to what Abraham is believing. The first is that Abraham's heir will not be Eliezer, his servant, but rather Abraham's own son. Second, God takes Abraham outside to look at the heavens and promises that his offspring will be as numerous as the stars of the sky. The first promise was fulfilled prior to Genesis 22 at the birth of Isaac recorded in Genesis 21. The second promise would not see fulfillment for many years to come, although it was potentially realized in the birth of Isaac. Thus, these events are not the direct "fulfillment of Scripture" to which James is pointing. James is more specific. He states that the Scripture of Genesis 15:6 has to be fulfilled in two ways. First, "Abraham believed God" and second, "and it was credited to him as righteousness." The sacrifice of Isaac fulfills both of these requirements. The final fulfillment of Abraham's belief in Genesis 15:6 comes when he believes again in Genesis 22. As Paul says in Hebrews 11:17, "By *faith* Abraham, when God tested him, offered Isaac as a sacrifice."

In both Genesis 15 and 22, God's integrity is on the line. Despite the circumstantial evidence, Abraham must believe that God can give him a child even though he is one hundred years old and Sarah is ninety and proven to be barren. He must also believe that God will preserve this child even if he happens to be killed by Abraham's knife. Abraham's faith is "fulfilled" because it is an enduring faith. Abraham possesses, to use Paul's phrase of Ro-

mans 1:17, "a righteousness that is revealed from faith to faith"—
one instance of faith to another instance of faith.

The second part of Genesis 15:6 (i.e., "and it was credited to
him as righteousness") is also fulfilled in Genesis 22 because one
can also understand the faith Abraham manifested in Genesis 22 as
a *crediting of righteousness*. Whenever Abraham exercises faith in
God, he is credited with righteousness. It is not a one-time event in
his life. In fact, in Genesis 22 the faith required to sacrifice Isaac is
a much more mature and stronger faith than the faith in Genesis
15, especially since Abraham had later shown some doubts about
the faith he exhibited in Genesis 15 when he laughed at God's promise in Genesis 17:17. If there is any faith that deserves the *crediting
of righteousness,* it is the faith of Genesis 22 where only an angel
from heaven stopped Abraham at the very last moment from plung-
ing the knife into Isaac. The crediting of righteousness in Genesis
22 does not infringe on the chronology Paul sets up in Romans
4:10-16, where he specifies that Abraham's crediting of righteousness in Genesis 15 came *before* his circumcision in Genesis 17.
The crediting of righteousness in Genesis 22 merely extends that
of Genesis 15.

The event of Genesis 22 is also more important than that of
Genesis 15 as regards the crediting of righteousness because, unlike Genesis 15:6, Genesis 22 includes a high-profile event that
once and for all will either establish Abraham's faith or negate his
faith. Once Abraham ties Isaac on the altar and raises the knife,
there is no turning back. If he unties him, he has lost faith in God
and God will no longer be pleased with him. Fortunately, Abraham
does not untie Isaac, and for this James says Abraham "was called
God's friend" (James 2:23).

We must understand Genesis 22 as one event in many of
Abraham's life in which he is "credited with righteousness," and
this is the very reason why James concludes his remarks on Abraham
by saying: "You see that a person is justified by what he does and
not by faith alone." James and Paul use the same word for *justified.*
In reference to men who are pursuing salvation, *justified* has no
usage other than in the sense of justification before God for righteousness. Hence, James's use of the word *justification* in reference to the faith and works of Genesis 22 means that James is

borrowing the phrasing of Genesis 15:6 ("and it was credited to him as righteousness") and applying it to Genesis 22 by his conclusion, "a person is justified by what he does and not by faith alone." If righteousness was not credited to Abraham in Genesis 22, James could not have used the word *justified* in reference to that event. Supporting this analogy, James in James 2:23 understands the noun "righteousness" in the same way that Paul does, which then requires that he understand the verb "justified" that he uses in James 2:24 in the same way that Paul does.[15] Thus, Abraham was truly and salvifically justified in Genesis 22.

The unique way James has crafted his language prohibits any misconstruing of what he wrote. James says two things in James 2:24 which reinforce each other: (1) that a person is justified by works, and (2) that he is not justified by faith alone. James is using the clearest form of argumentation: making an affirmation of his case and at the same time asserting a negation of the most important opposing case. If he had said only that a person was justified by works, one might possibly think that James is merely making an addendum to the teaching that faith justifies. But in adding the negation, James tells us the focus and reason for his affirmation. It is not only to advance the truth that works justify an individual, but it is to obliterate the opposite idea that one can be saved by faith alone. The negative statement is how we know James is using *justified* in the same sense that Paul used it, for if James was not concerned that someone would be misled by thinking that Abraham was justified by merely having faith, then he would have had no cause to add "*justified...not by faith alone.*" We see that James is quite aware of the possible interpretations of Abraham's faith precisely because he quotes Genesis 15:6, the very passage that Paul uses. It is also likely that James knew of Paul's use of Genesis 15:6, having been the bishop of Jerusalem in full purview of church doctrine at the time (cf., Acts 15:13). Hence, it is only logical to assume that in giving his affirmation and negation about justification, James has taken into account that some would misconstrue Paul's teaching on Genesis 15:6 and say that one is justified by faith alone. James will simply not allow that option.

Many Protestants try to dismiss James's teaching by claiming that he is using a different sense of the word "justified" than Paul uses. They refer to James's use of justification as a "vindication." In other words, they claim James is not concerned whether one is saved, but only with the proof that the person was already justified sometime in the past. But the context of James 2 does not support such reasoning. First, it would certainly be illogical for James to use a non-salvific sense of the word *justified* when he is trying to make a case that one is "not justified by faith alone." In other words, if James were teaching a concept of *vindication* he could have chosen a word that solely and clearly refers to vindication, rather than a word that is commonly understood to refer to salvific justification. Second, if James had vindication in mind he could have simply said, "you see, a person is *vindicated* by works" without the addendum "and not by faith alone." The addition of "and not by faith alone" introduces a specific element and direction to his argument, for it clearly shows that James is attempting to correct a false notion about the solitude of faith in justification, not suggest that Abraham was merely vindicated by his works. Third, if James was arguing for the vindication of Abraham, this line of argumentation would only make sense if one of James's hypothetical opponents had claimed that Abraham was "*vindicated* by his faith alone." If so, James would have easily refuted the argument by saying, "you see, a person is vindicated by what he does and not by faith alone." Such refutation would have required James to use "vindicated" in the first part of his argument (verses 20-21) in order for him to use it in the latter part (verse 24); otherwise, the concept of vindication simply would have no referent in the context. If James meant to teach only vindication in verse 24, the syntactical structure of the sentence would require that the phrase "not by faith alone" have its referent in "is vindicated," and thus the text would have to read as "you see, a man is vindicated by works and not vindicated by faith alone." It would assert that one is vindicated not only by faith but also by works. We see, then, that by injecting the concept of *vindication* into James 2:24, Protestantism has actually done more damage to its case than would have otherwise occurred, for the concept of vindication must then apply to both faith and works, which then destroys faith itself as being salvific.

We can also attack this line of argumentation by examining the way the New Testament uses the word "justified." Although it may be *possible* to construe the Greek word as referring to a vindication, this is neither the normal sense of the word, nor is such a sense ever used in a salvation context in the New Testament. This is significant, because if the meaning of *justified* as referring to a vindication is not used elsewhere in the New Testament in the context of salvation, then there is no precedent for using it as such in the epistle of James. James makes it clear when he opens the discussion in James 2:14 that he is setting up a salvation context by asking the rhetorical questions, "What good is it, my brothers, if a man claims to have faith but has no deeds? Can faith save him?"

Four, perhaps five, authors of the New Testament use the word *justified:* Matthew, Luke, Paul, James, and John. Matthew uses it in 12:37 ("for by your words you will be justified, and by your words you will be condemned"). It is clear that Matthew's context is one of salvation/damnation. Luke uses the word in his gospel and in the book of Acts. In Acts 13:39 he writes, "Through him everyone who believes is justified from everything you could not be justified from by the law of Moses." Obviously, Luke is using *justified* in reference to salvation. Paul uses *justified* 27 times in his epistles but in only one place does he use it outside a salvation context. However, in this single instance he is referring exclusively to God (i.e., Romans 3:4, "so that you may be justified in your sayings"). God is justified because he has the *quality* of justice within him, or because he is the subsisting source of all goodness and thus of all justice. Finally, James uses *justified* three times, twice in reference to Abraham and once in reference to Rahab, both, as noted above, within the context of salvation or damnation. Hence, we must conclude from this evidence that in the New Testament, *justified*, when used in reference to man, deals exclusively with man's justification before God and its outcome of salvation or damnation. To claim, then, that James is using the word *justified* differently from Paul is simply unsupportable.

Advocates of the vindication theory commonly refer to one New Testament usage of *justified* to support their contention that James may not be using the word "justified" in the same sense as Paul. John Calvin used this single example and many modern evangelicals continue to use it. In Matthew 11:19, Jesus says, "And wisdom is justified by her works." Similarly, Luke 7:35 reads, "And wisdom is justified by all her children." The proposed argument is that these passages are using *justified* in the sense of vindication or demonstration, not as a salvific justification. We respond to this argument as follows: Matthew 11:19 and Luke 7:35 are not using *justified* in a context that discusses the technical aspects of justification or the general category of salvation. In fact, it is only because the context of these verses does not concern itself with justification and salvation, not because *justified* can normally be understood as a vindication, that the meaning of *justified* can be given a different nuance in these passages. A similar thing happens in poetry. Words that have a technical meaning in everyday speech suddenly take on a different nuance when put in a metaphorical or symbolic context. In such a case we should not misconstrue the metaphorical usage of a word with the technical or lexical meaning of the same word.[16] Obviously, "wisdom" cannot be justified in the salvation sense because it is an abstract virtue, not a man who needs to be saved from sin. Hence, when the word "justified" refers to "wisdom," its meaning must change to accommodate the poetic context in which it is placed. Matthew 11:19 and Luke 7:35 are purely metaphorical contexts and thus they change the technical meaning of the word "justified." James 2:14-26 is not metaphorical. All in all, when James and Paul use the term "justified," they are referring to an *active* event, not a passive demonstration.

As noted above, we should understand the faith and works of Genesis 22 as the quintessential event that justifies and credits Abraham with righteousness, but not the only event that does so. James has chosen Genesis 22 because of its intimate connection with the promised seed and the multiplication of progeny from that seed. Abraham lived a whole life of faith and works stemming from his first walk of faith in Genesis 12, (or even prior), when God called him out of his own country. As we have seen earlier with Enoch and Noah, Abraham *walked with God.* James's final remark, "and he was called God's friend," suggests such a life of faith in intimacy with God. The phrase is not a direct quote from Genesis but alludes to historical and prophetic writings dated more than a thousand years after Abraham. The two passages in view are 2 Chronicles 20:7 ("of Abraham your friend") and Isaiah 41:8 ("Abraham my friend"). These passages could be reiterating what was already known of the relationship between God and Abraham during the latter's lifetime. We have already seen a suggestion of this reputation in Abimelech's remark about Abraham in Genesis 21:22. Most likely, a tradition arose citing the patriarch as God's friend and was later put into writing by the Chronicler and Isaiah. The contexts of 2 Chronicles 20:7 and Isaiah 41:8 appeal to the faithful relationship established between good king Jehoshaphat and the Lord, as God helps him defeat Moab and Ammon, as well as a reaffirmation of God's help in destroying other enemies. As noted earlier, these kinds of relationships speak of *lifelong* commitments to God. The closest thing in Scripture to being the "friend of God" is David's being called "a man after God's own heart" (cf., 1 Samuel 13:14; Acts 13:22). God had said this about David after he had observed him for some time. It was because of David's character that God chose him to replace Saul as king, passing up his seven brothers on the basis that "God looks into the heart" of those he chooses (1 Samuel 16:7-13). Once again, it is not just the beginning of faith or of works, but the whole life of faith and works, that God views in the individual.

WHO IS RAHAB? AND HOW WAS SHE JUSTIFIED?

To cap off his argument that faith and works "work together" in justification, James appeals to a very remote case—a case of justification that would really rub against a Jew's pride. James chooses Rahab, the Gentile prostitute, who showed faith in God by believing that he would destroy her city, and displayed works by hiding the Israelite soldiers who came to spy out the land (Joshua 1-2). James's use of the word *even* in the statement, "was not *even* Rahab...considered righteous" is akin to saying, "yes, even Rahab, who you would think could not obtain righteousness, did." Hebrews 11:31, in the statement "By *faith*, the prostitute Rahab..." confirms that Rahab's faith is necessary for God to accept her works. James may have used the example of Rahab for several reasons. First, the immediacy of her faith and works contrast sharply with the unbelief and disobedience characteristic of the Jews prior to the conquest of Canaan. As noted in Deuteronomy 9:5f, the taking of Canaan was due not to the righteousness of Israel but to the wickedness of the Canaanites and the promise by oath that God made to Abraham in Genesis 22. Second, that she was a prostitute who made it to the kingdom of heaven hearkens back to the statement of Jesus in Matthew 21:31, "I tell you the truth...the prostitutes are entering the kingdom of God ahead of you." Third, that a Gentile understood the reign of God and her own sin adds another person to the class of Gentiles who, as Paul says in Romans 2:26, "are not circumcised but keep the law's requirements," and in Romans 2:10, "but glory, honor, and peace for everyone who does good...first for the Jew, then for the Gentile. For God does not show favoritism." As we will see in chapter 4 with the case of Cornelius, Rahab is one who, prompted by the drawing grace of God, cooperates with that grace and seeks him for salvation.

The most significant aspect of Rahab's story in the discussion of justification is that there is no categorical or chronological distinction between her faith and her works. James considers them as one unit. Perhaps anticipating that someone might try to divide the faith of Abraham recorded in Genesis 15:6 from his work recorded in Genesis 22 in order to make a case that the works were only fruits of Abraham's faith and not an integral part of his justification, James adds the story of Rahab which has no such possible distinction. We see this first in the way Paul explains the faith of Rahab: "By faith the prostitute Rahab, because she welcomed the spies, was not killed with those who were disobedient."[17] Paul does not describe Rahab's faith as merely a state of mind, but in language which specifies her actions, i.e., "she welcomed the spies." Her faith is related in terms of her works, or her faith and works were "working together" for her justification. As Paul did, James elaborates on the same actions of Rahab as he says in James 2:25, "she gave lodging to the spies" and "sent them off in a different direction." The addition of "sent them off..." shows that this was a deliberate plan of action, in two successive steps, devised by Rahab. James does not specifically mention the faith of Rahab as Paul does, rather, he cites only the two phases of her works. In comparison to Paul's description, James's description leaves Rahab's faith implicit. When James mentions someone's good works, we must remember that faith is also included. As far as the New Testament writers are concerned, faith and works are inseparable in regard to justification.

In the account of Rahab in Joshua 2:9-11, Rahab's faith in God was prompted by her fear in his judgments. Rahab says to the Israelite soldiers:

> I know that the Lord has given this land to you and that a great fear of you has fallen on us...We have heard how the Lord dried up the water of the Red Sea for you when you came out of Egypt, and what you did to Sihon and Og...whom you completely destroyed...for the Lord your God is God in heaven above and earth below.

Though this description of Rahab's state of mind shows a great fear of God and an acknowledgment of his Lordship over the universe, one could not propose that Rahab was already justified by this fear. It is only when she pleads for mercy and barters to protect the spies in exchange for her and her family's lives that the New Testament writers consider her justified. This is why they describe her faith only from the vantage point of her works, not as her mental state of fear concerning God's judgments prior to meeting the spies. Rahab proves this when in Joshua 2:10-11 she acknowledges, by using the plural "we," that *everyone* in the city of Jericho is in a state of fear of God's destruction. All of them, however, were destroyed.

As we noted earlier, as James opens up the discussion of Rahab's justification, he introduces her account by the phrase, "*In the same way...*" By this wording, James is intimately connecting the justification of Abraham with the justification of Rahab. He is teaching that there is no difference in the way these two people were justified. If there were, then God would have two systems of justification, one for the Jews and one for the Gentiles, which according to Romans 2:10 cited above is impossible—God shows no favoritism between Jew and Gentile, and there is no name under heaven by which men can be saved other than that of Jesus Christ (Acts 4:12). We can conclude, then, that the inseparability of the faith and works that justified Rahab speaks of the same inseparable nature of the faith and works that justified Abraham. In Rahab, faith alone cannot justify because faith is only and specifically brought to the fore by her works of obedience. In addition, James's use of the word *justified* in reference to both Rahab and Abraham shows that he sees the justification of each as identical.

We must also reiterate that one cannot say that Rahab's justification was merely a *vindication* (as some have tried to say of Abraham's justification in James 2:24), since she was not justified prior to her meeting with the Israelite spies. Rahab was a prostitute who lived an immoral life until she encountered God through the Israelites. We may assume, although Scripture does not explicitly state it, that once Israel destroyed Jericho, Rahab and her family became part of the Israelite community and continued to obey the laws of God. It is for her abiding faith and works that the New Testament writers can hold her up as an example of justifying faith and works. Hence, if Rahab is not merely vindicated but is truly justified, then James's use of the phrase "*in the same way*" in reference to Abraham proves once again that James's use of the word *justify* does not convey a mere vindication but a true justification in righteousness of Abraham. It can work no other way.

James concludes this section by appealing in 2:26 to a simple biological fact: "As the body without the spirit is dead, so faith without deeds is dead." In other words, without adding works, faith cannot be used for justification. Since everyone knows that a body without the spirit means the body is dead and cannot come back to life unless the spirit is restored, so faith cannot be included in justification unless it is infused with works. The works, then, become just as much a salvific part of the individual's justification as his faith. As James says in 3:13: "Who is wise and understanding among you? Let him show it by his good life, by deeds done in the humility that comes from wisdom."

SUMMARY POINTS

1) Protestants have devised many and varied explanations to neutralize the clear and unambiguous statement in James 2:24 that "man is justified by works and not by faith alone." Each of these explanations concludes that James is not teaching that

man is salvifically justified by works, and that James does not have the same sense of justification as Paul. Puzzled by James's language, Martin Luther concluded that the epistle of James was a spurious book and should not be canonically authoritative for New Testament teaching.

2) Countering the Protestant explanation of the epistle of James which states that James means that "men" witness Abraham's works, the Genesis text (Genesis 22) does not include any men as witnesses to Abraham's works, but only God himself.

3) Countering the Protestant explanation of James which holds that the word "justified" as James uses the term refers to a "vindication," rather than to a salvific justification, as Paul uses the term, are the following arguments:

a) If James were teaching a concept of "vindication," he would have said, with the proper Greek word, "you see, a person is *vindicated* by works." Moreover, since James adds the clause "and not by faith alone" we know that he is correcting a false notion concerning the solitude of faith in justification, not suggesting that Abraham was vindicated by works.

b) If James were attempting to teach a vindication of Abraham, the specific argumentation he used would make sense only if James's opponents had claimed that Abraham was "vindicated by faith alone." In other words, if the vindication hypothesis were true, syntactical requirements would have forced James to use the meaning of "vindicated" in the first part of his argument (2:20- 21) in order also to use it in the latter part (2:24). Since the grammatical structure of the verse would then require that the phrase "not by faith alone" have its referent in the phrase "is vindicated," this would force the meaning of the verse to be, "a person is vindicated...not by faith alone" — a meaning that has no relevance to James's discussion.

c) The New Testament does not use the word "*justified*" in the sense of vindicated in contexts which are soteriological, i.e., contexts which discuss salvation or damnation. Moreover, such passages as Matthew 11:19 where one could plausibly interpret the Greek word as referring to a vindication do so only in a metaphorical sense; therefore they do not use *justified* in the same sense that James, and even Paul, use the term, which is historical and literal.

d) James's discussion of the events surrounding the justification of Rahab preclude assigning the meaning of "vindicated" to the word justified. Rahab's justification, as described in James 2:25, is a salvific justification, not a vindication. Moreover, James specifies that Rahab was justified "in the same way" that Abraham was justified. Therefore, one cannot understand Abraham's justification as a vindication.

e) Since James and Paul use the same Greek noun ("righteous") in reference to Abraham, and interpret the word in the same way (cf., Genesis 15:6, Romans 4:3, James 2:23), it would be totally incongruous for one of them to use a different meaning of its verbal cognate *justified* in reference to Abraham.

f) The Protestant position assumes that Abraham's justification is a once-for-all event. James's all important question "Can faith save him?" (2:14), however, includes Abraham within its purview. Hence we must conclude that if Abraham's works were not of the quality that James prescribes in the context (2:15), then Abraham would not be justified. Abraham could not be justified in a "once-for-all" event in Genesis 15:6 and at the same time have that justification put in jeopardy by disobedience to James's requirement of works for justification. If this could happen, the question in 2:14 would have no meaning.

4) Abraham's acts in Genesis 12, 15, and 22 were acts of faith *and* works. We should not misconstrue Paul's stress on Abraham's faith in his view of Genesis 15:6 to say that Abraham performed no works of loving obedience to God at this time or prior, nor should we misconstrue James's view of works in Genesis 22 to say that Abraham's attempted sacrifice of Isaac was not a supreme act of faith. Similarly, Abraham's departure from his homeland in Genesis 12 also couples his faith and works in regard to justification. Throughout his life, in the periods recorded in Genesis 13-14, 16-21, and 23-25 which are between the times of his recorded faith and obedience in the New Testament, Abraham continued to live in faith and obedience, with only minor lapses along the way. Genesis 22's importance is its detailing of Abraham's quintessential act of the faith-and-works which allowed God to swear an oath of blessing to him and for all his future descendants. Abraham's act in Genesis 22, not Genesis 15:6, was the most important act in Abraham's life. Moreover, the act in Genesis 22 was just as much a crediting of righteousness to Abraham as that in Genesis 15:6.

5) The entire context of the book of James concerns what one must do to be saved. He concentrates on obedience to the law as the means of salvation, and eternal judgment for those who disobey that law.

6) James includes sins of commission as well as omission in his warning against disobedience to the law. The supreme law, or "royal law," that James has in view is the law of love.

7) By calling them "believers in the Lord Jesus Christ," James assumes that the audience to whom he writes already has faith in God. The main question, then, that James poses to them is whether they have added works to their faith. James does not suggest that works will immediately or inevitably flow from one who has faith, in spite of the fact that he may have a greater disposition towards good works once he has faith. James teaches that one who has faith must make a daily, conscious decision

to do good works, just as he must decide each day to refrain from sin. In fact, if he chooses not to do good works when the opportunity arises, he has sinned (James 4:17).

8) James does not support the Protestant concept that one can be saved as long as he has "saving faith." James is not so much attempting to qualify the faith needed for justification as he is saying that one must consciously add works to faith in order to be justified. A person, to be justified, must persevere to his last breath in this conscious decision to add works to faith.

9) One of the most heinous in the catalogue of sins that James specifies is sin of the tongue. What is "said" to God and man is of the utmost importance to James and a major criterion on how the individual will be judged.

10) Both Paul and James speak of the works of love that one must add to his faith in order to be justified.

11) Like Paul, James concludes that if one chooses the system of law and desires God to evaluate him on that basis without the benefit of grace, he must then obey the whole law without fault. For one fault, the law will utterly condemn him.

END NOTES

[1] Luther stated: "Therefore St. James' epistle is really an epistle of straw, compared to these others, for it has nothing of the nature of the gospel about it" (LW 35, 362); and "The epistle of James gives us much trouble, for the papists embrace it alone and leave out all the rest ... Accordingly, if they will not admit my interpretations, then I shall make rubble also of it. I almost feel like throwing Jimmy into the stove, as the priest in Kalenberg did" (LW 34, 317).

[2] "Even though incorporated into the Church, one who does not however persevere in charity is not saved. He remains indeed in the bosom of the Church, but 'in body' not 'in heart'" (Vatican Council II, *Lumen Gentium,* 14...); "therefore the first and most

necessary gift is charity, by which we love God above all things and our neighbor because of him..." (*Lumen Gentium*, 42).

3 Catholic Catechism, Section 1033: "Our Lord warns us that we shall be separated from him if we fail to meet the serious needs of the poor and the little ones who are his brethren." (See also Sections 2443-2449).

4 The New Testament speaks directly to the aspect of "adding" to faith, e.g., "For this reason, make every effort to add to your faith goodness ... knowledge ... self-control ... perseverance ... godliness ... brotherly kindness ...love" (2 Peter 2:5-8). This is said in a context of striving to complete one's salvation, as noted in the final exhortation of the passage, "Therefore, my brothers, be all the more eager to make your calling and election sure. For if you do these things you will never fall and you will receive a rich welcome into the eternal kingdom..." See also Col. 1:4-5; 1 Tim. 1:14; 2 Tim. 1:13; 3:10; Tit. 2:2; Philem. 5; Rev. 2:19.

5 cf., Hebrews 6:1: "repentance from dead works"; Hebrews 9:14: "will cleanse the conscience from dead works"; Rom. 9:32: "they sought it not by faith but as it were by works."

6 Although "saving faith" has become a very popular phrase in Evangelical teaching on justification, Scripture never uses such terminology. Of the 125 times the Greek word "Save" is used in the New Testament, it is never used as an adjectival participle in conjunction with the noun faith, or any other noun. It is only used in noun and verb form. On the other hand, faith is described in various ways, e.g., "I...delight to see how firm your faith in Christ is" (Col. 2:5); "a sincere faith" (1 Tim. 1:5; 2 Tim. 1:5); "rich in faith" (James 2:5); "standing firm in the faith" (1 Peter 5:9); "your most holy faith" (Jude 20).

7 It is important to note here that Catholic theology distinguishes among three states: (1) one who has faith united with hope and love and thereby procures salvation (Council of Trent, Session 6, Chapter 7); (2) one who retains faith but has fallen into mortal sin and thereby loses the grace of salvation; (3) one who loses his faith, e.g., by heresy or apostasy, and thus loses the grace of justification (Council of Trent, Session 6, Chapter 15). In light of perspective #2, we should note that the distinction that is often made between "intellectual faith" and "heart faith," which

concludes that the former is *not* salvific and the latter *is* salvific (i.e., what is commonly termed as "saving faith"), presents a false dichotomy within the total picture of justification. Although one who has "intellectual faith" is usually a callous, unrepentant person, by the same token, a person who has "heart faith" may fall into mortal sin and end up under eternal judgment. His faith may still be strong after he sins but if he were to die at that moment, his mortal sin would bring him under condemnation. Hence, whether it is "intellectual faith" or "heart faith," it still remains that faith alone cannot save. Defining faith in terms of "saving faith," then, merely begs the question.

A more illustrative way to see that James is not concerned with mere intellectual faith is to replace each reference to "faith" in James 2 with "intellectual faith." One will soon see that "intellectual faith" does not fit in the context.

8 "If you blow on a spark, it will glow; if you spit on it, it will be put out; yet both come out of your mouth. Curse the gossips and the double-tongued, for they destroy the peace of many...Those who pay heed to slander will not find rest...Many have fallen by the edge of the sword, but not as many as have fallen because of the tongue" (Ecclesiasticus 28:12-18).

9 Catholic theology holds that just as a demon can believe in God's existence and power yet still be condemned, so a person in mortal sin can still believe in God and yet still be under eternal condemnation. In this sense, then, James's use of the demons is not strictly hyperbolic. The sins James mentions in James 2:11, e.g., murder and adultery, are mortal sins. If a Christian fell into such sin he would essentially be in the same situation as the demons in regard to faith, i.e., believing yet condemned. Unlike the demons, however, he still has time to repent and be restored to grace. In order to be restored to grace, and thus justified, the person must have the mortal sin forgiven. Sins of such serious nature must be forgiven by God through the instrumentality of the Church. Hence this is another reason why *faith alone* cannot justify. One must add repentance to his faith, along with works of penance (prayers and good works) and restitution (restoring or repairing the damage done by sin). Passages teaching both the Church's mediatorial role in the forgiveness of sins, and the dis-

tinction between mortal and venial sin, are plentiful. For the former, cf., Matt. 16:19; 18:18; John 20:23; 2 Cor. 2:7; 5:18; James 5:14-15; for the latter, cf., Matt. 12:39; 23:14-15; Luke 10:12; 12:47-48 (1 Tim. 1:13; Luke 23:34; 2 Pt. 2:21); John 5:14; 19:11; Acts 2:38; 5:3-5; 19:18; 1 Cor. 3:14-17; 6:9; Gal. 5:19-21; Eph. 5:5; 1 Thess. 2:16; 2 Tim. 3:5-6; Heb. 10:26-29; James 3:1; 1 John 5:16-17; Num. 15:27-36; Deut. 22:22; 29:19-21; Lam. 4:6. In the Old Testament, generally, sins punishable by death were mortal sins. See also Council of Trent, Canons on the Sacrament of Penance, e.g., Canons 4, 7, 9, 12-14; Catholic Catechism, Sections 980, 1395, 1440-1460, 1854-1864; as supported by the Church Fathers: Clement, Ignatius, Irenaeus, Tertullian, Cyprian, Lactantius, Hilary, Aphraates, Ambrose, Jerome, Augustine, Cyril, et al.)

[10] Genesis 17:5 is the point at which God changes Abram's name from "Abram" (meaning "exalted father") to "Abraham" (meaning "father of a multitude"). In Genesis 17:15 God changes Sarai's names from Sarai ("Jah is prince") to "Sarah" (meaning "princess").

[11] Genesis 12:2-3,7; 13:14-17; 15:16-21; 17:3-8; 22:17-18.

[12] e.g., Mark 15:28; John 17:12.

[13] Since Ishmael, who was born after God came to Abraham in Genesis 15, was thirteen years old when Abraham circumcised him in Genesis 17:25, at least thirteen years must have elapsed between the Genesis 15 encounter and the covenant of circumcision in Genesis 17. Abraham was ninety-nine at the circumcision. Isaac was born in Genesis 21, and since he was of a mature talking age in Genesis 22:7, this would make him about 5-10 years old at the time, which would thus be approximately two decades from Genesis 15. Since Abraham was 75 years old when he left Haran, this would make the time from Genesis 12 to Genesis 22 about thirty years or more.

[14] Genesis 17:3, 23; 18:2, 32; 20:17; 21:11-14, 22, 27, 33.

[15] "Righteousness" and "Justified" derive from the same Greek root word.

[16] For example, in the metaphorical expression "you are the apple of my eye," we certainly should not understand "apple" as a person who was transformed into a piece of fruit in someone's eye.

The technical understanding of an apple is a piece of fruit, but the poetic context changes the connotation of *apple* to a term of endearment. In any case, we cannot define the technical meaning of words by appealing to their use in poetic contexts.

[17] Council of Trent, Session 6, Canon 24: "If anyone shall say, that justice received is not preserved and also not increased in the sight of God through good works but that those same works are only the fruits and signs of justification received, but not a cause of its increase: let him be anathema."

HOW CAN I GET TO HEAVEN

CHAPTER 3

HOW DID JESUS TEACH ME TO GET TO THE KINGDOM OF HEAVEN?

Jesus has much to say on how one is justified and attains salvation. Unfortunately, many non-Catholic faiths often neglect to give Jesus's teaching its proper place in the study of justification. Instead, they make Paul's teaching the ultimate authority while Jesus's teaching is used merely as a supplement.[1] In reality, such artificial elevation of Paul's teaching reveals not only an improper regard for Jesus's teaching, but a misunderstanding of Paul's teaching as well. Let's investigate why this is so.

THE STORY OF THE RICH YOUNG MAN

In the story of the Rich Young Man, faith is not the issue. He believes God exists and that he has a duty to God. As the scene begins, when Jesus refers to the "One who is good" (i.e., God), the Rich Young man does not disagree or argue. In the clearest language possible, Jesus teaches that the central issue involves whether he has combined his faith with works of love sufficiently to gain eternal life. To a certain degree, he has obeyed and Jesus acknowledges that prior obedience. In fact, after acknowledging his obedience, Mark 10:21 adds, "And looking at him, Jesus felt a *love* for him..." Jesus does not ridicule or shun his prior acquiescence to God's law. He feels a loving affinity toward this man for his previous obedience. The man is not the typical Pharisee who says one thing and does another; who takes advantage of widows and then for a pretense stands on the street corner praying (Matthew 23:14). No, the Rich Young Man was close to the kingdom of God, but he had not yet arrived. There was at least one more work he had to do.

A similar discussion of the nature of the law arises in Mark 12:28-34. One of the teachers of the law had heard Jesus give a remarkable answer to the Sadducees concerning the resurrection and felt inclined to inquire about something on his own heart. The text does not say he came to trap Jesus, as was so often true of the Pharisees. Perhaps this man, like Nicodemus the Pharisee in John 3, was a sincere inquirer who was intrigued by the teaching of Jesus. He asked Jesus which commandment was the most important. Jesus answered that he is to love the Lord with all his heart, mind, and strength, and to love his neighbor as himself. The teacher of the law agrees with Jesus. He even adds the remark that obeying these two commands is better "than all burnt offerings and sacrifices," showing his understanding that God is looking inwardly at men not outwardly, a clear teaching from the Old Testament (cf., 1 Samuel 15:22; Hosea 6:6; Micah 6:6- 8; Hebrews 10:8). Jesus agrees with him and says, "You are *not far* from the kingdom of God." This statement shows us in Jesus's view, the more one acknowledges and obeys the commandments of God, the *closer* he is to the kingdom of God. There is no discussion here about faith. Faith is presumed. The question is: has this man developed his faith into love? If he loves, then he has either entered into the kingdom or is *not far* from it. All this teacher of the law has to do is to practice continually what he already believes, and he too will enter the kingdom. As we summed up the teaching of Paul in chapter 1 from the statement he made in Romans 11:35 ("Who has ever given to God that God should repay him?"), we can likewise sum up the teaching of Jesus from one of his most succinct and penetrating teachings. In Matthew 12:7, Jesus quotes from Hosea 6:6 in the Old Testament and says, "I desire mercy, not sacrifice."

As for the Rich Young Man, he will now receive his greatest test, a test even like that of Abraham who was asked to offer his son Isaac, a test to see if he has cultivated his faith into a real love of God and neighbor. As Paul says, he can have faith great enough to move mountains or live by a written code of ethics, but if he does not have love from his heart, he is nothing. Faith works in love and love is the supreme work.

We notice that Jesus says to him in Matthew 19:21, "If you want to be *perfect*..." This is the same word Jesus used in the Sermon on the Mount in Matthew 5:48: "Be *perfect*, therefore, as your heavenly Father is *perfect*." Jesus says this in a context about the nature of love. We must "love our enemies" and "bless those who persecute." We are not to love only those who love us; otherwise, we are no different from pagan people. Hence, we are perfect in God's eyes if we can love the unlovable. This is not an impossibility since God would not give us moral commands that we cannot not keep.[2] Granted, we will fall from our ideal on many occasions, but we repent, pick ourselves back up through the power of God's grace, and try again.

The final command to the Rich Young Man is, "...go, sell your possessions and give to the poor, and you will have treasure in heaven. Then come, follow me." This confirms Jesus's lifting up of the interior law as the very means of salvation,[3] not the system of law, or life by a written code, but the principle of God's laws expressed from the heart in the spirit of love and compassion. Essentially, Jesus is saying that if you want to enter the kingdom of heaven then you must act like those in the kingdom of heaven. In short, you must know how to love. This is not just a teaching tool to draw out a resignation to *faith alone* theology from the Rich Man. No, he must go beyond faith into a realm of being to which he probably had never given much thought. The way Jesus wants him to love his neighbor is not just by refraining from the negative, e.g., not stealing from him or not killing him, but by doing something positive, that is, taking care of all his needs. As James says, when we see a brother or sister in physical need, we must take care of those needs (James 2:15). One must go beyond the written code of, "don't do this, don't do that." One must live a selfless life. James also says, "Anyone, then, who knows the good he ought to do and doesn't do it, sins" (James 4:17). As to who the recipients of our love should be, Jesus answered that question in the parable of the Good Samaritan; it is anyone who is in need that crosses our path (Luke 10:25-37). If we don't do these things, then we are not fit for the kingdom of heaven.

HOW DID THE GOOD THIEF
ON THE CROSS GET TO HEAVEN?

In discussions between Catholics and Protestants on how one is saved, the latter will invariably point to the good thief on the cross as the perfect example of salvation by faith alone. Because of the thief's apparently sudden expression of faith, and Jesus' immediate acceptance of him into paradise, they make a general rule and conclude that only faith is necessary for all those desirous of salvation. In turn, everything from baptism, to repentance, to works, to holiness are said to be unnecessary in order to be saved.

Since few passages in the Gospels can even remotely support *faith alone* theology, we can understand why some Protestants feel so drawn to the thief on the cross. But even if we were to grant that the good thief presents one instance of salvation by faith without works, the exception does not make the rule. In such instances where the normal circumstances of life prohibit one from doing what is ordinarily required, God allows exceptions.[4] Such, for example, was the case of David and his men in the Old Testament who, out of hunger, ate the consecrated bread that was only lawful for priests to eat (cf., Lev. 24:5,9; 1 Sam. 21:6; Matt. 12:1-12). Jesus uses this incident to admonish the Pharisees who had accused the disciples of working on the Sabbath as they picked grains to eat. Jesus concludes that the Sabbath was made for man, not man for the Sabbath. Of course, if David had gone in every day and eaten the showbread, making it into the rule of his life rather than the exception, he would have been in sin and condemned by Jesus. But such was not the case. Likewise, neither Jesus nor the thief, with their hands, so to speak, "tied behind their backs," are expected to follow normal procedures. Just as Jesus would not deny salvation to a person unable to do works because he was without arms and legs, so he would not deny it to the man dying on the cross next to him because the man, though contrite, was no longer able to amend his life. A handicapped person can express faith, hope, and love in Jesus and he will be saved, even though someone else must care for him. Such was the case of the good thief. He expressed his faith, hope, and love in Jesus and received salvation in return. That being said, we can now look more closely at the incident.

We notice first that although both thieves reproach Jesus in some measure (Matthew 27:44), eventually the good thief rebukes the unrepentant thief (Luke 23:40). He does this in the face of the others gathered at the cross who are jeering at Jesus and telling him to "save himself" (Luke 23:35-37). Jesus had taught long before: "Whoever acknowledges me before men, I will also acknowledge him before my Father in heaven" (cf., Matt. 10:32; Rom. 10:9). Next, the good thief asks the other, "Don't you fear God?" (Luke 23:40). We must assume that the good thief had an acute and personal fear of God in order to demand it from the other thief. He is like many who the New Testament says fear God and are blessed with salvation (Acts 10:1-4; 17:4,17, 25-26; Rom. 2:6-8). Perhaps this thief had feared God for some time before his sentencing for theft. We are not certain when the good thief committed his crime, nor do we know whether or not he had reconciled with God before his civil punishment on the cross. We cannot just assume he continued wicked and unrepentant up to the very last moment he met Jesus on the cross.

Next, the good thief tells the unrepentant thief that both of them are "punished justly" (Luke 23:41). This shows his inner sense of justice in that he is able to convict himself of sin before God. He also says of Jesus, "this man has done nothing wrong," realizing the goodness of Jesus (Luke 23:41). This implies that he knew something of Jesus prior to their meeting at the cross. He was perhaps familiar with Jesus's life and knew that he had not committed any crimes. Next, he says, "Remember me when you come into your kingdom" (Luke 23:42). We wonder where this man obtained such knowledge if this was the first time he had heard of Jesus. There is no recorded conversation about the kingdom of God during the crucifixion. Jesus was virtually silent during the whole event, speaking only seven short times. The thief might have known about the kingdom prior to the cross. This lowly thief understood Jesus's mission and purpose which even many of the apostles had a hard time understanding (Luke 24:25-26). Hence, everything in this story points to this thief having been prepared for this final moment with Jesus.[5] Finally he hears Jesus say, "Today you will be with me in paradise." Since this statement is an answer to the question about entering the kingdom, we may assume that "paradise" is the kingdom. Taking the man's statement as the thief's admission of guilt, Jesus's invitation into paradise implies the forgiveness that accompanies repentance. The man acts, and Jesus responds. The thief, not Jesus, initiates the conversation. As God had blessed Cornelius in Acts 10 for his fear and devotion, so Jesus blesses the thief. All in all, there is no warrant for imposing a *faith alone* theology in this unusual incident. The thief apparently already had faith in God as demonstrated by his "fear of God" that he expressed to the other thief. He now had to put that faith into action by reaching out to Jesus in perfect contrition, however limited he was in doing so. Had he not reached out, he would have been condemned just like the unrepentant thief who remained silent. As we will see in Jesus's remaining encounters with people of faith, they each had to come to him in repentance, seeking to be forgiven; hence, their faith was not alone.[6]

JOHN 5:24: "WHOEVER HEARS MY WORD AND BELIEVES"

According to one Evangelical, "...it is easy to demonstrate from Jesus' evangelistic ministry that He taught *sola fide*."[7] One would think after reading this statement that the gospels are just filled with references to *faith alone*. We are surprised to find, however, that this commentator cites only four passages in all of Jesus's teaching to support his claim — but none of them use the phrase "faith alone."[8] Of John 5:24, he says, "That verse clearly states that on the basis of faith alone, sinners pass out of death and into eternal life." Let's examine this very closely. John 5:24 reads, "I tell you the truth, whoever hears my word and believes him who sent me has eternal life and will not be condemned; he has crossed over from death to life." Obviously, John 5:24 does not use the word *alone,* but the reader is pre-conditioned to believe that such is Jesus's meaning. Moreover, because the word *works* is absent from John 5:24, this is further proof that Jesus taught *faith alone* justification. But this is argumentation from silence and ignores all Jesus's other teachings that include works as the measure of one's acceptance with God. Not the least of these teachings appears right in the very context under discussion just four verses later in John 5:28-29 where Jesus says, "Do not be amazed at this, for a time is coming when

all who are in their graves will hear his voice and come out —
those who have *done good* will rise to live, and those who have
done evil will rise to be condemned." We see that in using such
language Jesus is certainly not shy about referring to faith in one
breath and works in the next. Apparently he feels it is not a contradiction to say that the one who *believes* has eternal life but that the
same person will be evaluated for his *deeds* to determine whether,
in the end, he will be saved or not. This is not a novel teaching of
Jesus nor of the rest of Scripture.[9]

Other Evangelicals make similar claims of Jesus's teaching.
One team writes: "In the Gospel of John only one condition is laid
down for obtaining eternal life: belief (e.g., John 3:16, 36; 5:24;
20:31)."[10] Unfortunately, they make the same mistake as the previous Evangelical by not addressing the rest of the context. For example, though they are correct in stating that John 3:16 refers to
belief, they fail to recognize that this aspect of justification is followed in John 3:21 with the words, "But whoever lives by the truth
comes into the light, so that it may be seen plainly that what he has
done has been done through God." Here Jesus does not emphasize
those who believe but "whoever lives by the truth." In fact, Jesus
implies that they come to the light of faith precisely because they
have been living in the truth. Jesus is not divorcing faith from works.
He is intimately connecting one with the other for the purposes of
salvation. These, as we have learned earlier, are not boastful, self-
righteous works done under the system of obligation, but works
that have "been done through God." Again, we see the unfortunate
tendency of Protestants to interpret Scripture's use of *faith* to be
faith alone, yet Scripture never uses such terminology; rather, it
invariably couples faith with works in the realm of grace for the
purposes of justification.

HOW DOES JESUS USE THE WORD "JUSTIFIED"?

In Jesus's use of the word *justification* there is always a clear
indication that he is not using it in the sense of a one-time forensic
act of God. For example, in Matthew 12:36-37 Jesus says, "But I
tell you that men will have to give an account on the day of judg-

ment for every careless word they have spoken. For by your words you will be *justified* and by your words you will be condemned." Here Jesus mentions the judgment that each man must face at the end of time for the works he did on earth. This in itself is a problem for Protestant theology since a salvation based on *faith alone* should have no room for a final judgment based on works.

To understand this verse completely we must address each of its four components: (1) a judgment for works, (2) the use of the term *justified*, (3) the ultimatum of salvation or condemnation, and, (4) the reference to the final judgment. There is no clearer language from the lips of Jesus other than that of Matthew 12:36-37, which uses the word *justified* in a salvation/damnation context. In Matthew 12:36-37 Jesus is not using the word *justified* any differently from Paul who also uses the word in similar contexts concerning the final judgment (cf., Rom. 2:13; 1 Cor. 4:4). Although Jesus's words imply the requirement of faith, his focal point is the individual's works that justify or condemn him. Not only that, but no bad work escapes his scrutiny, since the verse specifies that he will judge "*every* careless word." Hence, Jesus, like James, teaches that our works play a primary role in determining our justification.

One of Matthew 12:36-37's most important features is that in it Jesus speaks of the "day of judgment." Whether this is the general judgment when all souls will stand before God, or the particular judgment when individuals will stand for judgment at death, Jesus does not specify.[11] Nevertheless, he does specify that the ultimate justification takes place at the final judgment of that individual. An end-time judgment that alone determines whether the individual is ultimately justified puts the concept of the one-time, imputed act of justification into an acute contradiction. When a Protestant theologian applies justification, he speaks of it as a past event never to be repeated. But Jesus is using the word justification far beyond the initial stage of becoming a Christian, making it continue until the end of the person's life at which time it will be determined whether he will be ultimately justified or not. Hence, justification is not a one-time event never to be repeated but is a continual process with its final outcome reserved for judgment day. In addition, the individual's works will be the controlling criterion for the final justification.

THE PROUD PHARISEE AND THE HUMBLE TAX COLLECTOR

In accord with its general use in Scripture, Jesus also uses the word *justified* in reference to the *present* justified state of the individual. In the parable of the Pharisee and the tax collector of Luke 18:9-14, Jesus makes this final remark concerning the latter, "I tell you that this man went home *justified* before God. For everyone who exalts himself will be humbled and he who humbles himself will be exalted."

Before Jesus tells the parable, Luke gives the reason for its telling: "To some who were confident of their own righteousness and looked down on everybody else, Jesus told this parable..." Jesus develops the contrast wherein one party thinks he is living in a justified state, yet despises others who do not have the same social or spiritual status he thinks he has attained. Jesus goes on to describe this hypothetical Pharisee as one who prays and thanks God he is not like other sinful people, especially the despised tax collector he is standing next to. Not only does this Pharisee think he is free from sin, but he goes the extra mile, as it were, by fasting and giving tithes. Meanwhile, the tax collector recognizes his sin and pleads to God for mercy. For that repentance, Jesus says he is justified before God.

Jesus makes a similar judgment in Luke 16:15. Speaking of the Pharisees again, he says: "You are the ones who justify yourselves in the eyes of men, but God knows your hearts. What is highly valued among men is detestable in God's sight." It is obvious that Jesus is interested in the heart of the individual, not what he can puff up on the outside to make himself appear righteous before men. Such hypocritical behavior is even more odious to God than other sins. What is significant in this teaching is its remarkable similarity to the teaching of the apostle Paul. Paul was just as concerned about living from the heart as opposed to living merely from a written code of law. We will recall that Paul said in Romans 2:29, "No, a man is a Jew if he is one inwardly; and circumcision is circumcision of the *heart*, by the *Spirit*, not by the *written code*. Such a man's praise is *not from men, but from God*."

It is no surprise that Jesus's and Paul's teaching are identical. Life by the *written code* only breeds pride and arrogance like that displayed by the Pharisee. Instead, God is pleased with one who loves him from his heart, by the Spirit of life, who seeks divine praise, not human praise. It is no coincidence that this principle of Paul's introduces his teaching on justification proper that is followed in Romans 3-4. The Jews thought they could be justified by keeping the outward commands of the law but didn't realize the corruption of their hearts. Paul also spoke about being forgiven of sin within this justification context just as Jesus did of the tax collector (cf. Luke 18:9f; Rom. 3:23-25; 4:5-8; 2:4). The forgiveness of sins is what brings justification. Those who humble themselves before God and admit their sin will be justified. Those who do not admit their sin will not be justified.

One of the assumptions Protestants make when they interpret Luke 18:14 is that the justification of the tax collector is the single point in his life that he was justified. In contemporary understanding, it is as if the tax collector were walking up the aisle after saying the sinner's prayer and finally receives the grace of God into his life and now he is a Christian. Once justified, the tax collector will now go home and lead a life of sanctification.[12] The context of the passage does not support such an interpretation, nor is it consistent with the rest of Jesus's teaching. Granted that, regarding works, the parable does not refer to works specifically, but then neither does it specify the word *faith*. Rather, the emphasis is on *repentance,* which implies both faith and works. The very next chapter in Luke 19:1-9 provides a shining example of how Jesus responds to such repentance in an incident with a real-life tax collector, Zacchaeus. In responding to Jesus's invitation, Zacchaeus says, "Look, Lord! Here and now I give half of my possessions to the poor, and if I have cheated anybody out of anything, I will pay back four times the amount." Here is true repentance. Zacchaeus is not just believing that Jesus is his personal Savior, but he is seeking to make a work of restitution for his sins. The very law of Israel required such a work of repentance and Zacchaeus is going above and beyond that law by offering to give as much as *half* his possessions (cf., Exodus 22:1-3; Leviticus 6:4-5; Numbers 5:7; 2 Samuel 12:6). This is just what Jesus had told the Rich Young Man of Luke 18:22 in order to obtain eternal life, "Sell everything you have and give to the poor, and you will have treasure in heaven." Although the account does not state this, we might say that the Rich Young Man stole from the poor indirectly and thus needed to make "restitution."

Notice Jesus's response to this repentant tax collector after he volunteers to pay back the money he stole: "Jesus said to him, 'Today *salvation* has come to this house, because this man, too, is a son of Abraham...'" It is the faith in Jesus coupled with the works of restitution, amounting to a sincere repentance on Zacchaeus' part, which in turn prompts Jesus to grant him salvation. We notice also that Jesus designates Zacchaeus as a "son of Abraham." This does not merely mean that Zacchaeus was a Jew but that he was a "Jew inwardly" who "walked in the footsteps of the faith of Abraham" who was also justified by his "faith" and "works" (cf., Romans 2:29; 4:12,16; James 2:24).

Simply put, this parable of Jesus illustrates a proud man and a humble man. The Pharisee is the proud man who, as Paul says, lives by a "written code," not by the "heart" and the "Spirit" (Romans 2:29). He is a man who, because he does certain works, expects and even obligates God to favor him. He is one who wishes to receive justification as something owed for his work. He is operating in the system of law. On the other hand, the tax collector is the humble man who recognizes that God owes him nothing. Unlike the Pharisee, he brings his works before God with sincere faith and love. He repents, and in doing so, comes under God's system of grace rather than law. Under grace, his works are accepted, not because he is obligating God to do so, but because God does so purely from his mercy. Moreover, God expects the tax collector, if he has stolen any money (probably a tax collector's most prominent sin) will cease to do so and give back what he has stolen. Such is the ongoing work of repentance which he initiated in confessing his sin. If he sins again by stealing money, he will have to return to the temple and confess his sin, lest his justification be nullified. Moreover, no one will argue that faith and repentance are the beginning of salvation. Whether the respective tax collectors will continue to be faithful and endure to the end is a matter not addressed by Jesus. All in all, nothing in the passage proves a once-for-all imputed justification by *faith alone*.

THE SERMON ON THE MOUNT: HOW DOES IT TEACH US TO GET TO HEAVEN?

Jesus frequently uses the person of the Pharisee when he is illustrating the nature of hypocrisy and specifying behavior that will prohibit one from entering the kingdom of heaven. Matthew 23 records Jesus's most famous attack against the Pharisees, commonly known as "the Seven Woes." Each woe begins with the same refrain, "Woe to you, teachers of the law and Pharisees, you hypocrites!" and in each case Jesus points out an action in which the Pharisees and teachers of law give a show of religiosity to men but in their hearts are full of pride and hatred. It is religion based strictly on a written code, without sincere faith and love. Matthew 23 is Jesus's description of those who attempt to be made righteous by law without grace.

In making the Pharisees an example of those who will not enter the kingdom of heaven, Jesus warns others that they must be better than the Pharisees in order to enter the kingdom. In Matthew 5:20, Jesus says, "For I tell you that unless your righteousness *surpasses* that of the Pharisees and the teachers of the law, you will certainly not enter the kingdom of heaven." This saying is included in the Sermon on the Mount. Just prior to this, Jesus had given the nine beatitudes in which he praised the righteous conduct of certain people (Matthew 5:3-12). With each blessing he includes a promise, and each promise points to the final reward of the heavenly kingdom, e.g., "Blessed are those who are persecuted because of righteousness, for theirs is the kingdom of heaven."

Following this, Jesus gives six statements beginning with the refrain, "You have heard it was said, but I say unto you..." regarding murder, adultery, divorce, oaths, personal vengeance, and love for enemies (Matthew 5:21-48). In each case, Jesus explains that men must go beyond mere outward obedience to the law and to look at the motives of their actions. For example, Jesus teaches that a man sins not just by physically committing adultery with a woman but also by looking at her lustfully. Jesus wants them to go beyond the rudimentary written code of law that people observe on the outside, (a law in which people do what is basically required and no more) and to embrace a higher law that seeks to examine every thought and action from the perspective of whether it pleases God and truly benefits our neighbor. We must obey, knowing that God judges the heart, not merely the outward actions.[13]

Again, in Matthew 6:1-18, Jesus admonishes us to give to the poor, pray, and fast, in each case telling us not to do these things in front of others in order to be noticed by them but to do them in secret where only the Father sees them. Thus we see that the Sermon on the Mount is basically a sermon on living from one's heart in order to please God, not from mere outward actions in order merely to please men. The Pharisees were of the latter variety, always doing things with an eye toward impressing men while inside they were full of hate for both God and man. Knowing their hearts, Jesus says that our *righteousness* must surpass that of the Pharisees in order to enter the kingdom of heaven (Matthew 5:20). As we have shown above, the whole tenor of the Sermon on the Mount, both before and after this saying, is to teach the inner obedience of the heart, thus it is obvious that the righteousness Jesus wants us to attain is not merely a product of some kind of theological imputation but a personal striving of the individual whose desire is to please God with all of his thoughts and actions. Moreover, that the attainment of this type of righteousness is directly related to whether one is ultimately saved is clear from Jesus's warning in Matthew 5:20 that if one does not attain such righteousness: "you will certainly not enter the kingdom of heaven." Jesus does not place the challenge of high obedience merely in the realm of *sanctification*, as many Protestants categorize works subsequent to justification; rather, he places these high-order works in the realm of salvation, i.e., as determining whether one will be saved or not.

There isn't one word in the Sermon on the Mount about *faith alone* as the measurement for entering the kingdom of heaven. Rather, the Sermon is completely and wholly saturated with admonitions concerning obedience from the heart. Jesus's language is clear. Our righteousness must "surpass" that of the Pharisees. According to the *context*, this can happen only when we make the conscious decision to love God and our neighbor from the heart, performing not as men-pleasers but as God-pleasers. As with Paul's and James's writings, Jesus's focus in the Sermon on the Mount is on pleasing God sufficiently to enter the kingdom.

While in the parable of the tax collector the penitent simply goes to the temple admitting that he is a sinner and is subsequently justified, in the Sermon on the Mount Jesus makes quite an issue about the contingencies surrounding God's forgiveness. Jesus begins by specifying one of the petitions of the Lord's prayer as "Forgive us our trespasses as we forgive those who trespass against us" (Matthew 6:12). The comparative word "as" shows that God's forgiveness of our sins depends on our forgiveness of other's sins. Jesus immediately clarifies that this is indeed his meaning in Matthew 6:14-15, "For if you forgive men when they sin against you, your heavenly Father will also forgive you. But if you do not forgive men their sins, your Father will not forgive your sins."

Jesus also teaches this principle in the parable of the Unmerciful Servant, Matthew 18:21-35, where the master forgives his servant, but the servant does not forgive his subordinate. Jesus concludes in verse 34-35, "In anger his master turned him over to the jailers to be tortured, until he should pay back all he owed. This is how my heavenly Father will treat each of you unless you forgive your brother from your heart."

The message is clear. We obtain forgiveness of our sins not through accepting an alien righteousness of Christ but by the works of forgiving our neighbors who sin against us. By forgiving them, God forgives us and views us as righteous in his sight. The mere fact that Jesus includes the stipulation that God must forgive our sins shows that Jesus is not speaking of an absolutely perfect righteousness that God expects from us. He knows we will sin, perhaps in some cases by not forgiving our brother as we should. But as long as we humbly recognize and confess of our sins from our heart, and as long as we follow through with the works of repentance, we are working in the realm of grace and God is pleased with us and will grant us the kingdom of heaven. This is not a teaching reserved for a "millennial kingdom," nor is it a mere hypothetical means to show us the purpose of the law to reveal sin. Jesus makes his intention clear in Matthew 5:18-19:

> I tell you the truth, until heaven and earth disappear, not the smallest letter, not the least stroke of a pen, will by any means disappear from the Law until everything is

accomplished. Anyone who breaks one of the least of these commandments and teaches others to do the same will be called least in the kingdom of heaven, but whoever practices and teaches these commands will be called great in the kingdom of heaven.

Not only is Jesus upholding the precepts of the Law, he is reinforcing them by saying that God will notice our breaking the *least* commandment. The principle of Law will last until "everything is accomplished," or, as Jesus earlier taught, when "heaven and earth disappear." We have already seen this principle in Jesus's use of the word *justified* in Matthew 12:36-37 to teach that God will judge "*every*" idle word." Jesus teaches in Matthew 5:18 that the progressive fulfillment of the Law does not abolish the Law. Those who do not place themselves in God's grace will be subject to the requirements of the Law till the end of time. In addition, those who are in God's grace must obey the Law from their heart to please God as a child seeks to please his father.

WE SHOULD COME TO JESUS LIKE THE REPENTANT WOMAN

The setting in Luke 7:36-50 portrays Jesus dining at a Pharisee's house. A woman comes in and, crying, begins wiping Jesus's feet with her hair and pouring perfume on them. The Pharisee is indignant because the woman is a known sinner. He thinks that Jesus should have known better than to associate with her. To explain these impromptu actions, Jesus tells the Pharisee a parable about two men who had their debts forgiven, one a large debt, the other small. At Jesus's prompting, the Pharisee concludes that the one who was forgiven the larger amount would love his master more. Jesus applies this to the sinful woman who is now seeking forgiveness. Jesus further admonishes the Pharisee for not having greeted him with the customary kiss and anointing. These were common customs of greeting and affection for friends and guests in those times. Thus, Jesus is pointing out that Simon did not show Jesus even the least amount of love. The woman, on the other hand, showed her love by doing the very things Simon ought to have done. Perhaps she noticed that Simon had not given the customary greetings and may have felt it her responsibility to do so. Her greeting, however, is filled with emotion, sorrow and love. It is after, not before, this exercise of love by the woman that Jesus remarks about her forgiveness. He then concludes, "Therefore, I tell you, her many sins have been forgiven— for she loved much. But he who has been forgiven little loves little."

Here Jesus is tying in the forgiveness of the woman's sins with the love she showed to Jesus. It is not simply that she believes in Jesus. Faith, of course, prompted her to come. It is what the Council of Trent calls "the beginning of salvation."[14] The real focus, however, is on her humbling herself, coming to a stranger's house in front of many guests and washing Jesus's feet and applying perfume, all in an effort to show her love for him. At the least, the woman's faith is, as Paul says in Galatians 5:6, a "faith working through love," but it is certainly not a faith alone. Jesus would not have specified her love to such a degree if he did not mean to combine her love with her faith as the cause for her forgiveness and salvation. Luke makes it clear that the woman is a known sinner, and thus in sin when she comes to Jesus, by his statement, "who had lived a sinful life" (verse 37). That Luke says these sins are forgiven only *after* she shows the three signs of love to Jesus (verse 48) is confirmation that her love was an integral cause of her forgiveness and justification. For *faith alone* to be the cause of her forgiveness the story line would have concentrated on her faith as opposed to her love, and Jesus would have forgiven her sins *before* the acts of love. If her faith alone had obtained her forgiveness, Jesus would not have confused the issue by making it appear that her love was the turning point in her spiritual cure. Moreover, if faith had been the only criterion for her forgiveness, Jesus would have said thus before elaborating on Simon's lack of love and the woman's contrasting love. She comes to Jesus doing acts of love because she is seeking forgiveness, not doing acts of love because she has already been forgiven. Jesus never met this woman before, so he could not have forgiven her sins prior to this incident. Luke does not record that the woman says anything to Jesus, that is, she does not verbally ask for forgiveness. Her actions of love alone speak of her desire and need for forgiveness.

If God had forgiven the woman of her sins privately before she ever came to Jesus, there would be cause to say that the love she showed to Jesus was a result of that previous forgiveness. The perfect passive verb in the statement of verse 47, "her many sins have been forgiven" may imply such prior forgiveness. It is more likely, however, that the subsequent statement in verse 48, which uses the same perfect passive tense ("your sins have been forgiven"), and which places the reference point for the past action at the beginning of the time Jesus is speaking to her, acts as a commentary on the verb tense of verse 47 and implies that this was the first time the woman was formally forgiven and the first time she became conscious of her forgiveness. Since nothing else in the context would indicate a forgiveness prior to her meeting of Jesus, we must assume that the woman was not forgiven until after her show of love, as Luke 7:48 suggests. Hence, the love of the woman is both the cause and the result of the forgiveness. The parable shows that as the woman seeks forgiveness, love simultaneously flows from her. It is the love of the woman which allows Jesus to know she is truly repenting. The Pharisee, on the other hand, doesn't seek forgiveness of sin (because he does not recognize his own sin) and thus he does not express any sorrow or love for Jesus. In fact, he even distrusts Jesus to the point that he secretly accuses him of being a fraud, as verse 39 indicates.

Although love is an integral part of the forgiveness, there still remains some question as to why Jesus tells her in verse 50, "Your *faith* has saved you, go in peace." If love is the key to the passage why didn't Jesus say, "Your love has saved you"? There are several reasons for this. First, as noted above, faith is the beginning of salvation. Without faith it is impossible to please God. Verse 37 tells us that the woman "learned that Jesus was eating at the Pharisee's house," which prompted her to come. Thus, she must have known something about Jesus and had some rudiments of faith in Jesus and a knowledge of her own sinfulness. The text does not tell us if for some time she had already stopped sinning prior to meeting Jesus. It simply calls her "a sinner." But she needed to act on her faith. Jesus was not simply going to read her mind in her house and forgive her of sin. Thus the love that moved her to act brought her faith to fruition, and it was on this basis that the faith saved her.

Second, Jesus is accomplishing two things regarding Simon the Pharisee. The first is to show how little he loves. The key is that Simon does not recognize his own sinfulness but looks down on the woman who is a known sinner, just as in Luke 18:9 of the Pharisee who looks down on the tax collector who is a known sinner. Jesus, by his parable of the two men who owed money, desires to teach Simon that his capacity to love, whether God or man, can be no greater than his sense of his own sin. The second thing Jesus accomplishes is to show Simon and his guests that *none* of them has any faith in Jesus. Simon first raises doubts about Jesus in verse 39 when he says, "If this man were a prophet he would know who is touching him and what kind of woman she is — that she is a sinner." Thus, Simon not only despises the woman but, more importantly, he even questions the character and veracity of Jesus. This lack of faith in Jesus is also evident among the guests, as verse 49 records: "Who is this man who even forgives sins?" Ingeniously, without remarking directly on their lack of faith, Jesus does so *indirectly* by telling the repentant woman that her faith has saved her. No doubt the guests heard Jesus say this and correctly understood it as an indictment against them for their own lack of faith. Thus we should not take the addition of "your faith has saved you" as a dogmatic statement to promote a *faith alone* theology. Rather, we should understand the statement within the whole context of the passage, a passage that speaks of the great faith and love of the woman, as opposed to the lack of faith and love in Simon and his guests.

THE FAITH OF THE BLEEDING WOMAN

Another instance in which faith features prominently is the story of the woman who had an issue of blood for twelve years. Luke's version of this story begins at Luke 8:40 when Jairus, a ruler of the synagogue, came to Jesus begging him to cure his sick daughter. On the way to Jairus's house, the woman with the issue of blood came through the crowd and touched Jesus's clothing, and immediately she was healed. Matthew's version tells us that the woman had thought to herself that touching the garment would bring her healing (Matthew 9:21). As he cures her, Jesus responds with: "Daughter, your faith has healed you." Here is a simple story to illustrate the humble, child-like faith that Jesus wants from us. Among many doubters, the woman stands out as the example par excellence of pure faith in God. She has a faith which recognizes that God is much more powerful than she, a God who has the power to cure a disease that up until this time seemed hopelessly incurable.

Though we must be careful not to minimize the importance of faith, we must also point out a number of factors that militate against extracting a *faith alone* theology out of this simple story. First, it is immediately apparent that the woman *acted* on her faith by reaching out to touch the clothing of Jesus. She did not sit in her home just believing she could be cured. She put her faith into action, and it is the combination of faith and action that cured her. Second, the passage is not speaking about salvation, per se. The woman may later have become a true child of God, but the story does not say so, nor is it the point of the story. Many people who Jesus cured of diseases and who saw other miracles of Jesus did not end up believing in him for salvation. The feeding of the five thousand in the next chapter of Luke, or the healing of the ten lepers in Luke 17:11-19 in which only one came back praising God and thanking Jesus, are cases in point. John's version of the feeding of the five thousand indicates that after participating in the miracle, most of the people walked away in unbelief when Jesus revealed the true nature of the bread from heaven (John 6:1-65). This is not to say that the woman who was cured of her bleeding did not become a Christian, but only that the story does not mention this dimension and thus cannot be used as an illustration of salvation nor prove a *faith alone* theology.

THE FAITH OF THE PARALYZED MAN

The Synoptic gospels record a scene in which the friends of a man with paralysis cut a hole in the roof of a house and lower the man in front of Jesus.[15] As Jesus watches this unusual effort, he acknowledges their faith and subsequently tells the paralytic that his sins are forgiven. The question arises why Jesus did not immediately cure the man, since that seemed to be the concern of his friends. In actuality, the paralytic is not cured until after a confrontation with the Pharisees concerning Jesus's initial act of forgiving the man's sins.

As we compare and contrast this story with the account of the woman with an issue of blood, a question arises concerning the relationship between healing and the forgiveness of sins. In the account of the bleeding woman we concluded that the physical healing of an individual did not necessitate that the sins of the same were forgiven, nor that salvation is necessarily involved at all. This coincides with the many times Jesus performed miraculous works in the midst of various people without any indication that they received salvation.[16] However, in the story of the healing of the paralytic, we have an occasion in which not only is a person healed but is also forgiven of sin because of an act of faith in Jesus. In fact, the paralytic's sins are forgiven first, even though it seems from the story that he came only to be physically healed. This would seem to contradict our earlier proposition that healing does not necessarily involve the matter of sin and salvation. In order to answer this question, we must examine the context of the passage.

As noted above, alongside the healing of the paralytic is the confrontation between Jesus and the Pharisees. The Pharisees, who consistently challenge the motives and integrity of Jesus, are going to be taught a great lesson by Jesus. In fact, Jesus does not cure the paralytic until the discussion with the Pharisees is over, showing that Jesus deliberately refrained from initially healing the man to provoke an objection from the Pharisees. As he usually does in situations like this, Jesus accomplishes his primary task of helping the individual in need, and at the same time, he silences the murmurings of his critics. Colloquially speaking, we could say that Jesus 'kills two birds with one stone.' The Pharisees want to trap Jesus and accuse him of being a fraud. As Jesus forgives the paralytic's sins, the Pharisees immediately accuse him of blasphemy by reminding everyone in the room that only God can forgive sins. Jesus, knowing their thoughts, says, "Which is easier: to say, 'Your sins are forgiven,' or to say, 'Get up and walk'?" Although it is not stated in the text, the answer to this question is that it is easier to say, 'Your sins are forgiven.' Jesus had just begun his ministry and this incident is recorded in only the second chapter of Mark's gospel. For a person, like Jesus, who is attempting to establish his identity and credibility as divine, it is easier to claim to forgive sin. Since they cannot see spiritual things, no one can either prove or disprove whether the sins have been forgiven, or whether Jesus really is God and has the power to forgive. Conversely, it is much harder or riskier to establish one's credibility by attempting to heal someone, since if the person is not healed then that failure would immediately suggest that the healer is a fraud. Assuming that the Pharisees understand his logic, Jesus continues with, "But that you may know that the Son of Man has authority on earth to forgive sins," and then turning to the paralytic, says, "I tell you, get up, take your mat and go home." Here Jesus is coupling the healing of the paralytic with his power to forgive sins. In the people's minds, no one could perform such miraculous feats unless God was with the healer.[17] If God is with the healer to heal, then it is not too much a stretch of the imagination to reason that he is indeed the Son of God who can forgive sins.

The account of the paralytic has some unique characteristics that are not found in other passages. First, as noted above, the friends expect the paralytic to be cured, but Jesus first forgives his sins. The paralytic did not show any signs that he was in overt sin, nor is there any specific history of him being in sin (as opposed to the sinful woman of Luke 7). Second, by the statement, "When Jesus saw *their* faith, he said, 'Friend, your sins are forgiven'" we see that Jesus recognizes the faith of his four companions, and possibly the faith of the paralytic, but only forgives the sins of the paralytic, rather than the paralytic *and* the four friends. Third, it is because of the faith of the men as a group that Jesus forgives the paralytic's sins, not just the faith of the paralytic. In fact, the faith of the paralytic is not explicit in the passage except for the fact that he is said to "praise God" when he was finally cured some moments later (Luke 5:25). Perhaps the friends thought that the reason the man was paralyzed was that there was some sin in his life. This was a common belief in those times, as suggested by the account in John 9:1-2 of the man born blind who was thought to be in that condition because of his or his parent's sins. The friends of the paralytic may have reasoned that the healing of the paralytic was conditioned on first having Jesus forgive his sins.

The anomalies surrounding the forgiveness of the paralytic's sins, as well as the precise relationship between healing and salvation, are more easily answered when it is noticed in Mark's account that Jesus's main activity prior to the entrance of the paralytic was that he "preached the word to them" that were gathered in the house (Mark 2:2). We can imagine that Jesus had given the same message to this crowd that he had previously given to many others when he preached the word of God. The people were taught to recognize their sins and repent. In Mark 1:15, for example, John the Baptist had introduced the mission of Jesus with the words, "The kingdom of God is near, Repent and believe the good news." After this introduction, Jesus says in Mark 1:38, "Let us go somewhere else — to the nearby villages — so I can preach there also. That is why I have come." Capernaum, where the incident with the paralytic took place, is one of those "nearby villages." In fact, as recorded in Mark 1:21, Jesus had previously lived at Capernaum and had preached the word to the people in their synagogue and they were amazed at his authority. He also cast out a demon at that visit. Thus, the mission of Jesus was well known by the people in Capernaum before the curing of the paralytic.

Although much of Jesus's encounters with people involved physical healing, this did not diminish his primary role of preaching the gospel of repentance from sin. Thus when he "preached the word" to these people in the house at Capernaum, we understand that Jesus taught them about sin. Before the arrival of the paralytic, we can assume that Jesus had already told the crowd of his mission from God to bring people to repentance, and possibly, that he himself had the power to forgive their sins, or at the least, he was ready to make his debut that he indeed was God and had power to do such things. In any case, his forgiving of the paralytic's sins was prompted by his teaching to the crowd about sin and the necessity of forgiveness. It is not unlikely that Jesus's preaching of the word was also heard and understood by the four friends and the paralytic. This is suggested by the fact that the four men had first gone to the door before they decided to cut a hole in the roof. No doubt they would have heard Jesus through the door teaching the people about the gospel.

We see in this account that the four men, including the paralytic, had great faith in the person of Jesus. Most likely they knew something about Jesus because already by this time word of his fame had spread abroad (cf., Mark 1:28, 37, 45). This is very similar to the story concerning the woman with an issue of blood. She apparently had heard of Jesus and knew she could be healed by his power. However, whereas the woman with an issue of blood is not said to be forgiven of sin, (from which it can be concluded that faith in Jesus for healing does not necessarily forgive one of sin), the paralytic is specifically forgiven of sin as he is being healed. The difference is explained in that the context of the healing of the paralytic includes the "preaching of the word" by Jesus prior to the healing, whereas the account of the bleeding woman does not. Because his message would have included the teaching of repentance from sin, it is only then that forgiveness of sin is coupled with physical healing.

WHAT ELSE DOES JESUS TEACH ME ABOUT GETTING TO HEAVEN?

In the gospels, Jesus consistently makes our salvation dependent upon our obedience. There is a marked theme in his teachings regarding people who say they believe, or who believe only for a little while, but whose works are false, missing, or incomplete. It is these who are lost. These teachings warn us that people are damned not merely for lack of faith, per se, but for not following through with their faith, i.e., for not doing works of obedience. But most importantly, not once does Jesus say or teach that someone can be eternally saved by a one-time act of faith. Rather, Jesus's teaching encompasses the whole life of the individual — a life that starts in faith and good works and continues until the end. Only when the individual has reached the end of life in the same fervor with which he started does Jesus consider the individual completely justified. From the many passages that illustrate this point, let us select a few of the most prominent.

We find Jesus laying much stress on the requirement of continuing in faith and good works toward the latter end of his public ministry, right before he went to the cross. Most of these teachings concern the judgment he will administer at his Second Coming. No verse better expresses this theme than Matthew 24:13: "...but he who stands firm to the end will be saved." This same saying appears a bit earlier in Matthew 10:22: "All men will hate you because of me, but he who stands firm to the end will be saved." The former verse (24:13) deals specifically with the destruction of Jerusalem and thus is written to a wide audience, i.e., not only to those who would be victims during the destruction of the city, but also to all future Christians, through the metaphorical telescoping of this event into the Second Coming of Christ in which he will judge the whole world (24:29-31). In the latter verse (10:22) Jesus deals mainly with the ministry of the apostles, warning that as they go to preach the gospel they will be persecuted, but that they must endure to the end, i.e., the end of their life. Hence, these warnings that one must endure to the end to be saved encompass the whole Church age, beginning with the apostles in the first century and ending with the last century at the Second Coming. Each generation of Christians, then, must "endure to the end" in order to be saved.

In these teachings, Jesus constantly reinforces the theme of *enduring to the end* by adding the refrain, "Therefore, keep watch, because you do not know on what day your Lord will come" (Matthew 24:44). He repeats this warning with emphasis in Matthew 24:36, 24:50 and 25:13. In the story of the faithful and unfaithful servants of Matthew 24:45-51, Jesus specifically warns against the kind of thinking exemplified in the unfaithful servant who reasons that his master has stayed away a long time and will not return very soon. The servant then uses this reasoning to engage in evil behavior, thinking that his master will not catch him. But Jesus warns that he will come upon that man at a time that he did not expect and subsequently judge him for his evil deeds. He will be assigned a place in the outer darkness with the hypocrites — people who say one thing but do another.

These teachings of Jesus echo teachings in other Scriptures. Long ago, the prophet Ezekiel wrote a very similar warning in Ezekiel 18:24:

> But if a righteous man turns from his righteousness and commits sin and does the same detestable things the wicked man does, will be live? None of the righteous things he had done will be remembered. Because of the

unfaithfulness he is guilty of and because of the sins he
has committed, he will die.

Here we see the same teaching, that one must endure to the
end in order to be saved. The passage describes a man who has
lived righteously for a long time, perhaps all his life, but who then
decides to do evil. Naturally, the question would arise: what about
all the good that he had done in the past? Will this not be taken into
account? The answer is a firm no. God will not judge him on how
well he lived his life in the beginning but on how his life turns out
in the end. This is why Catholic teaching puts such stress on avoiding mortal sin at all costs and preparing one's soul for death. It is
the disposition of the soul at the end of one's life that matters.
Although the punishment in eternity may be more or less, depending on mitigating factors in the man's earthly life, the point of the
teaching is that the unrighteousness he has done at the end of his
life will prevent him from entering the bliss of heaven.

The remaining teachings of Jesus in Matthew 25 all illustrate
the same point, but from slightly different angles. The parable of
the ten virgins in Matthew 25:1-13 is very pointed in its teaching
of enduring to the end. The parable opposes the five wise virgins
who were ready with oil in their lamps for the coming of the bride-
groom to the five foolish virgins who did not have oil. Jesus concludes with the saying, "Therefore, keep watch, because you do
not know the day or the hour." The teaching is clear. Salvation is
not based merely on an act of faith at the beginning of one's life but
on the continual faith and obedience throughout one's life.

The parable of the Talents in Matthew 25:14-30 reaches the
same conclusion but from a different angle. Three men receive
money to invest for their master. The master goes on a long journey with the proviso that each of the men are to invest his money in
order to gain interest. The emphasis on the "long journey" borrows
the same theme that was evident in Jesus's earlier teaching in this
discourse, i.e., that servants will take advantage of the seemingly
extended time that the master will be away so that they can do evil
and not get caught. As it turns out, one of the servants does not
invest the master's money, and even accuses the master of being a
dishonest man. The master senses his deception and banishes him

to outer darkness for punishment. Here again the story illustrates the responsibility each of us has to continue in faith and good works while the Lord is away, for he will come at a time we least expect and demand to see the results of his investment in us. If they are not present, he will condemn us.

The last story in this section, the account of the Sheep and Goats in Matthew 25:31-46, is probably the most pertinent for this discussion concerning the significance of works as the determining factor in our salvation. Separating people at the general judgment as a shepherd would divide sheep from goats in his pasture, the Lord will reward the sheep specifically because they, (1) fed the hungry, (2) gave drink to the thirsty, (3) invited the stranger, (4) clothed the naked, (5) took care of the sick, and (6) visited those in prison. These items are not just filler for the story. The whole parable centers around the doing of these virtuous acts in order to gain entrance into heaven. The parable reinforces this point by means of a double exchange. In verses 34-36, Jesus spells out all the virtuous deeds the righteous have done in order to inherit the kingdom of heaven. In verses 37-39, the wicked reiterate each of the virtuous acts and challenge the Lord as to when they ever saw him in such a destitute state that they could feed, clothe, or do any other good work to him. In verse 40, Jesus explains that doing these things to one's neighbor is just like doing them to Jesus. Apparently, the intimate connection between loving a neighbor and loving the Lord is something that they knew intuitively and therefore have no excuse (cf. 1 John 2:7-11). The doubling of this exchange then occurs in verses 41-45 with the same reiteration of each of the six virtuous acts. The only difference between the two sections is from positive to negative, i.e., "whatever you did do" as opposed to "whatever you didn't do." The reiteration of these items shows us the prominence that they hold in the teaching of Jesus.

We have already seen that Jesus's teaching is permeated with the principle that God will judge us based on our works at the end of time. Jesus makes this clear in Matthew 16:27: "For the Son of Man is going to come in his Father's glory with his angels, and then he will reward each person according to what he has done." The apostle John records the same words of Jesus in Revelation 22:11-12: "Let him who does wrong continue to do wrong...let him who does right continue to do right...Behold, I am coming soon! My reward is with me, and I will give to everyone according to what he has done." And previously in John 5:28-29: "Do not be amazed at this, for a time is coming when all who are in their graves will hear his voice and come out— those who have done good will rise to live, and those who have done evil will rise to be condemned."

These warnings show that Jesus is concerned with the whole life of the individual, not with a mere act of faith he professed a long time ago. Granted, there is certainly an intimate connection between the faith of the sheep and their works in the story of Matthew 25. We must also understand, however, that Jesus specifically uses the doing of good works as the final criterion of the value of the faith and works an individual claims to have. We must take the story at its face value and not force it through the grid of a theology of our liking. If Jesus had a *faith alone* theology in mind, he had ample opportunity to teach it. As it stands in the gospels, however, there is not one specific teaching of Jesus that would lean us in such a direction. The whole tenor of his teaching is just the opposite—works play a most significant part in determining whether we will be saved or not. If this is indeed the theme of the gospels, then there is absolutely no reason to reinterpret the works required in the story of the sheep and goats to be mere symbols or results of faith. We should understand them precisely as they are presented, as the ultimate criterion to determine our final status with God.

SUMMARY POINTS

1) Jesus never says that a person is justified by faith alone.

2) Attempts to deal with Jesus' teaching on works range by saying that Jesus taught obedience to the law (a) merely to show that man could not be justified by keeping the commandments, (b) that his teachings were merely hypothetical, or (c) that his teachings are not for the present time but are reserved for a future millennial kingdom. These are all false.

3) In the story of the Rich Man in Matthew 19:16-26 (Mark 10:17-21), Jesus commends the man for his faith and obedience to

the commandments and teaches that such efforts are the very means of salvation. Communicating to him in love, Jesus calls him to a higher level of obedience, e.g., giving his riches to the poor, in order to finally attain the kingdom of God. Jesus concludes that if he does not do so he cannot be saved; thus, works pleasing to God must be added to faith for justification.

4) Some attempt to support *faith alone* theology from Jesus's statement in John 5:24. They do this, however, without admitting that Jesus does not use the word alone, or any other qualifier, in reference to faith, and they also ignore the context which specifies just four verses later that Jesus will judge individuals based on their works.

5) Some attempt to support *faith alone* theology by citing the salvation of the thief on the cross. Even if we considered this incident an exception to the necessity of works, such exceptions do not make the rule. That being said, the story of the thief is not an exception. In actuality, the thief showed remarkable knowledge of Jesus and his mission, implying that he was familiar with Jesus's teachings prior to the crucifixion. Because the thief, though his hands were literally tied, acted on his belief in Jesus and reached out in defense of Jesus and his mission, this shows his willingness to be obedient to God. He had a sincere desire to do the works of obedience, had it not been too late to do so. This sincere willingness to obey God, and his reaching out to act in the limited capacity still available to him, were sufficient to please God and for Jesus to accept him into heaven.

6) Jesus uses the same word "justified" that Paul does. As in Paul's usage in Romans 2:13, Jesus, in Matthew 12:36-37, uses the word "justified" in reference to judging the individual's works, showing that God grants or denies justification based on one's works. Jesus indicates the kind of works he has in mind with the words, "every careless word," showing that works as slight as mere words are subject to judgment and can cause the loss of justification.

7) Some attempt to prove *faith alone* theology from the parable of the Pharisee and the tax collector in Luke 18:9-14. They base their attempt on the theory that justification is a one-time forensic event. First, there is no proof in the context that, in Jesus's mind, this was the first time the tax collector pleaded for forgiveness of his sins, especially since going to the temple to pray was a daily ritual in Judaism. Second, the subsequent account of Zacchaeus, a real-life tax collector, reveals that works of repentance are a necessary requirement in Jesus's mind, since Jesus accepts Zacchaeus' promise to pay back half of his possessions to those he cheated before he grants him salvation.

8) When Jesus teaches that in order to enter the kingdom of heaven our righteousness must exceed that of the scribes and Pharisees, the context will not allow the concept of the "alien righteousness of Christ" to be imposed on the passage. Rather, the context shows quite clearly that Jesus views works of obedience performed by the individual as the means to righteousness that will allow him to enter heaven.

9) Some attempt to support the *faith alone* theory by appealing to the story of the repentant woman in Luke 7:36-50. Although it is true that faith prompted her to come to Jesus, it was her actual coming to Jesus in a humble act of repentance, coupled with her love of Jesus, that moved Jesus to forgive her sins. This shows that love was added to her faith for justification.

10) The incident of the woman with an issue of blood in Luke 8:43-50 also denies the *faith alone* model. It is clear from the passage that the woman *acted* on her faith by coming to Jesus and touching his garment, and only then was she healed. Moreover, there is no proof that salvation was involved in this, and similar incidents of healing.

11) Various sayings of Jesus are antithetical to a *faith alone* theology. For example, Jesus's statement in Matthew 24:13 ("but he who stands firm to the end will be saved") shows that both faith and works are required up until the very end of a person's life; otherwise he will not be saved.

12) Other teachings of Jesus, e.g., the parables of unfaithful servants, the ten virgins, the talents, and the sheep and the goats, all demonstrate that we must continually add works to faith in order to be saved.

END NOTES

1 An example of such interpretation is noted in the following approach: "Instead, we must allow the primary expositor of this issue, in this case, the Apostle Paul, to speak first; his epistles to the Romans and the Galatians must define the issues, for it is in them that we have direct discussions of exactly how justification takes place. Once we have consulted these sources, we can then move on to garner other elements of the biblical revelation that are found in *tangential* ways elsewhere" (James R. White, *The Romans Catholic Controversy*, p. 147, emphasis his). Of Jesus's teaching on justification, White adds: "But he did not deem it proper to discuss the specifics of the issues prior to Calvary. In His sovereign will He left that to the Apostle Paul..." (Ibid, p. 148).

2 Council of Trent, Session 6, Chapter 11.

3 Catholic Catechism, Sections 1965-1974; 2052-2074; 2084-2550.

4 Catholic theology also allows exceptions to its requirements for salvation. For example, as firm as the Church is on the necessity of baptism to be saved (Catholic Catechism, Sections 1214-1284; Council of Trent, Decree on Original Sin), it makes exceptions (e.g., the baptism of desire) for those who cannot possibly be administered this sacrament before death. See also Council of Trent, Session 7, Canon 4; and the Catechism, Section 1257: "God has bound salvation to the sacrament of Baptism, but he himself is not bound by his sacraments." The Church also allows for "deathbed" conversion in conjunction with the Sacrament of the Sick (Catholic Catechism, Sections 1499-1525).

5 Council of Orange, 529 AD, Canon 25: "So very clearly we should believe that the faith — so admirable— both of that famous thief, whom the Lord restored to his native land of paradise, and of Cornelius the centurion, to whom the angel of the Lord was sent, and of Zachaeus, who deserved to receive the Lord Himself, was not from nature, but a gift of God's bounty."

[6] "To faith must be added: fear of Divine justice, hope in the mercy of God; love of God; hate of sin; cleansing of baptism" (Ott., *Fundamentals of Catholic Dogma*, p. 253; also Council of Trent, Session 6, Chapter 7). The good thief possessed all of these except baptism, which was not formally required until after Pentecost.

[7] John MacArthur, *Justification By Faith Alone*, p. 15.

[8] John 5:24; Luke 23:43; Matthew 9:22 (and its Synoptic parallels in Mark 5:34; 10:52; Luke 8:48; 17:19; 18:42); and Luke 18:9-14 (*Justification By Faith Alone*, pp. 15-17).

[9] cf., Matthew 16:27; 12:36-39; Rom. 2:6-8; Rev. 20:12; 1 Cor. 3:13-17; 2 Cor. 5:10; Eph. 6:8; et al. In other publications, MacArthur attempts to relegate some of these judgment passages only to the time when Christians receive personal rewards, thus eliminating any possibility of eternal condemnation. Obviously, this does not apply to John 5:28-29, since the phrases "rise to live" and "rise to be condemned" can only refer to eternal life or eternal condemnation (cf., Matthew 25:46; John 6:40;12:48; Acts 24:15; Daniel 12:2). The Protestant misapplication of the other verses mentioned will be covered in more detail in chapter 9.

[10] N. Geisler and R. MacKenzie, *Roman Catholics and Evangelicals*, p. 231.

[11] See Catholic Catechism, Section 1021-1023.

[12] R. C. Sproul, *Faith Alone*, p. 102.

[13] Catholic Catechism, Sections 1949-1986

[14] Council of Trent, Session 6, Chapter 8.

[15] Luke 5:17-26; Matthew 9:2-8; Mark 2:3-12.

[16] E.g., Matthew 11:20; Luke 17:11-19; John 6:26, 66; 10:31-32.

[17] cf., John 3:2; 9:16, 33.

HOW CAN i GET TO HEAVEN

CHAPTER 4

IS MY JUSTIFICATION A ONE-TIME EVENT OR AN ONGOING PROCESS?

The Protestant understanding of when justification occurs and how it progresses is different than the Catholic understanding. Most Protestant denominations view justification as a solitary legal act in which God designates or classifies an individual as righteous — an act which, once performed, is never repeated again. It occurs at the time the individual accepts, by faith alone, Jesus Christ and his work of redemption. More specifically, the theory says that the individual is "credited" with the righteousness of Christ. The theory takes the word *credited* to mean that the person has no righteousness within himself that God is taking into account, but only the righteousness accomplished by the sinless life, death, and resurrection of Christ. God credits the righteousness attained by Christ to the account of the individual as when an accountant makes a credit entry into a ledger book. In himself, the individual is still the same being. Nothing but his legal status with God changes in this single moment of justification. It is simply a legal declaration that God makes, designating the person to be in a justified state. The justified state means that God has forgiven his sins because Christ took the guilt and paid the penalty for his sins. Acceptance by faith means that, though undeserving, the individual receives the righteousness of Christ if he simply acknowledges its availability and efficacy by believing that he can receive it. Once this is done, the theological category of justification is complete and secure and the now justified Christian immediately passes into another theological category called *sanctification*. Within the area of sanctification, the Christian begins to live a holy life by refraining from sin, doing good works, praying, etc. The theory stresses that, although related, the area of sanctification is not to be confused with justification. In Protestant theology, justification is a one-time legal act administered by God, while sanctification is the ongoing process of personal holiness.

In Catholic theology, justification is not a one-time act of God. Although for New Testament believers justification begins at a specific point in time, (i.e., baptism), justification continues as a process throughout the individual's life. God gives his grace to the individual at baptism, but he also gives grace continually throughout the course of life. A person gains grace as he lives out his Christian life in obedience. As grace increases, justification increases, and the individual becomes more and more righteous in the eyes of God.[1] If God removes justifying grace from the individual, then justification ceases. This occurs when the individual commits serious sin. When God restores grace, he restores justification. He does not give grace in equal measure to everyone. One person can possess more than another depending both on how God wishes to distribute grace, as well as the degree to which the person cooperates with God in obedience. In the final analysis, if the justifying grace begun at baptism is not present at the end of a person's life, then he will remain unjustified and be condemned for eternity.

In regard to sanctification, there is no appreciable difference between it and justification in Catholic theology. In fact, the grace received at baptism is called *sanctifying* grace. This is the grace that sets the individual apart for God and makes him holy, and it is because of this "holiness" that he becomes *just* or *justified* in the eyes of God, that is, because he is now intrinsically holy. Paul shows the inseparable and simultaneous application of justification and sanctification very clearly in 1 Corinthians 6:10-11:

> ...nor thieves not the greedy nor drunkards nor slanderers nor swindlers will inherit the kingdom of God. And that is what some of you were. But you were *washed*, you were *sanctified*, you were *justified* in the name of the Lord Jesus Christ and by the Spirit of our God.

Here Paul speaks of being "sanctified" and "justified" as a simultaneous event, an event that occurred when the person was "washed." The New Testament uses the word "washed" in only one other place. In that passage it refers to the act of baptism.[2] Hence, as noted above, it is baptism that provides the grace of God. Paul treats both "sanctification" and "justification" as a past event that began at baptism. The terms are virtually interchangeable. The context of the passage supports this interchange, since it deals exclusively with the Corinthian's conduct, not the appropriation of an alien righteousness.

THE JUSTIFICATIONS OF ABRAHAM

The commentary on Abraham's life of faith in the book of Hebrews is an invaluable aid in understanding the concept of ongoing justification. In Hebrews 11:8 Paul states categorically, in reference to Abraham's faith in Genesis 12, where at God's command he left his homeland in Ur of the Chaldees, that Abraham already possessed justifying faith — the same faith that the Protestant view requires for justification. Paul makes explicit in several ways that Abraham's faith of Genesis 12:1-8 is the same kind of faith as displayed in Genesis 15:1-6. First, he introduces the faith both in Genesis 12 and Genesis 15 under the general heading of faith that "pleases God." This is noted in Hebrews 11:6: "And without faith it is impossible to please God, because anyone who comes to him must believe that he exists and that he rewards those who earnestly seek him." Then, prior to dealing with Abraham, Paul gives three examples of people who had demonstrated such "God-pleasing" faith, i.e., Abel, Enoch, and Noah (Hebrews 11:4-7). The language makes clear in these three examples that they all had faith that justified them before God. Hence when Paul comes to Abraham and speaks in the same glowing terms in reference to his faith in Genesis 12, we can reach no other conclusion than that Abraham had faith that justified him in Genesis 12 long before his next encounter with God in Genesis 15. It would be totally incongruous for Paul to attribute justifying faith to the three personages prior to Abraham but not attribute it to Abraham in Genesis 12.

To reinforce the above facts, Paul gives another description of Abraham's faith in the Genesis 12 period. He remarks in Hebrews 11:10 that Abraham's faith in leaving his homeland and subsequently sojourning in tents in the promised land was in reality a faith which believed that the earthly land upon which he walked was not what God had in store for him; rather, Abraham believed that God had prepared for him a "city with foundations and whose architect and builder was God." In other words, the faith Abraham possessed in Genesis 12 was already a faith that comprehended the essence of salvation, i.e., living in heaven with God forever. It is not surprising that Paul then describes Abraham's faith in the Genesis 15:6 period in precisely the same way. Paul states in Hebrews 11:16, after remarking about Abraham's faith in believing that God would give him a son, that such people show that they are not looking for an earthly city in which to dwell but a "heavenly one," acknowledging that "God has prepared a city for them." Since here he describes Abraham's mental disposition in Genesis 15 the precise way he describes Abraham's faith in Genesis 12, this forces us to conclude again that Abraham was already justified in Genesis 12. It was a faith that "pleased" God, understood that he "existed," was the "rewarder of those that earnestly seek him," and looked for a "heavenly city" built by God.

WHEN WAS DAVID JUSTIFIED?

The reader will recall from Romans 4 that in giving his principles for justification by faith, Paul quotes from David in Psalm 32:1: "Blessed is he whose transgressions are forgiven, whose sins are covered. Blessed is the man whose sin the Lord does not count against him." David is proclaiming God's forgiveness for his sins of adultery with Bathsheba and the murder of Uriah the Hittite recorded in 2 Samuel 11-12. Obviously, David is rejoicing over the fact that God has forgiven his sins. God sent Nathan the prophet to convict David, forcing him to admit his sin. Nathan's parable of the little ewe lamb brought David to his knees in repentance. This was such a monumental event in the life of David that he remarks again about the same sin and forgiveness in Psalm 51.

The most intriguing aspect of Psalm 32 as regards the discussion on justification is that Paul is using this experience of forgiveness in David's life in order to make David a primary example of a person who is justified before God. Paul's connection between justification and David's own repentance is unmistakable. He says in Romans 4:5-6:

> However, to the man who does not work but trusts God who justifies the wicked, his faith is credited as righteousness. David says the same thing when he speaks of the blessedness of the man to whom God credits righteousness apart from works...

By the phrase "David says the same thing..." Paul is indicating that David agrees with Paul's teaching that a wicked man is credited with righteousness by faith without works that attempt to obligate God. For example, David does not go to the priest and offer burnt offerings for his sin in an attempt to cover them up, or depend on his circumcision to keep him in favor with God despite his sin. Rather, David relies on God to justify him, knowing that any works he might do without true repentance to God would be pure hypocrisy. Thus, we must conclude that David is saying in Psalm 32 nothing different than Paul is teaching in Romans 4.

The most important aspect of the corresponding doctrine between David and Paul is that David is speaking not only of everyone else's sin, but more specifically of his own. This gives us the reference point we need to understand just what kind of justification Paul has in view, since he and David are, in Paul's words, *"saying the same thing."* Using David as a reference point, we are obliged to look at the circumstances surrounding David which led him to the point of his repentance in Psalm 32. The crucial question is this: Was Psalm 32 the first time David was forgiven his sins? The answer must be an unequivocal no. Yet, according to Paul, the forgiveness David received in Psalm 32 is a "justification" or "crediting with righteousness." Since this was not the first time God forgave David for his sins, we must conclude that neither was it the first time God justified or credited David with righteousness. Moreover, since Paul, in the same context, treats Abraham as the very one who was justified, then it is only natural to conclude that Paul understands David as the very one who was justified. Although David's experience may also represent how others after him are justified, our starting point for interpretation should be this passage's "face value" fact that Paul is speaking of David himself as the one who is justified at the precise moment in time that Nathan confronted him and David repented.

Reinforcing this interpretation is Scripture's clearly expressed view of David's life prior to the incident with Bathsheba as a very intimate relationship with God. In his youth David called on the Lord to defeat the mighty Goliath (1 Samuel 17). David is so close to God that 1 Samuel 13:14 and Acts 13:22 call David a "man after God's own heart," a distinction given to no one else in the Bible, which shows how close was the relationship David had developed with God long before he committed his heinous sin with Bathsheba. The Psalms, and the corresponding historical accounts in the books of 1 and 2 Samuel, prior to his incident with Bathsheba are filled with the most beautiful tributes of one who was utterly dependent upon and in love with the Lord. By all respectable standards, we must conclude that David was a true child of God many years prior to his sin with Bathsheba. Thus we would have to conclude as well that David was justified in God's sight many years prior. If he was not justified, then he was not a man of God, and he had lived his life prior to Psalm 32, and had written earlier Psalms before his encounter with Bathsheba, as a hypocrite, one who spoke intimately about God but really had no personal relationship with him.

We cannot escape the fact that Paul, in using the example of David in the context of justification, is saying not merely that David's sins were forgiven, but also that David was actually justified at this point. Paul, in Romans 4:5, underscores this fact both by speaking of "crediting righteousness" to David when he confessed his sin in Psalm 32, and by calling him a "wicked" person whom God must justify in order to return him to righteousness. We must understand, then, that a "crediting of righteousness" occurs at each point that one confesses his sins. Since this was not the first time David confessed sin before the Lord (which other Psalms verify, cf., Psalms 25:7,18; 51:5), he must have been "credited with righteousness" on each occasion of repentance. Since he was credited with righteousness upon repentance in Psalm 32, and since it is an established fact that he was a man of God prior to his sin with Bathsheba, we must therefore consider all previous acts of repentance a "crediting of righteousness."

As Paul speaks in Romans 4:5 of "God justifying the *wicked,*" and then follows with David's experience of being justified upon his repentance in Psalm 32, we must also conclude that David was considered a "wicked" man once he committed his heinous sin with Bathsheba. This is precisely the reason why David needed to be credited with righteousness, for he had lost his righteousness before God and had become a vile, wicked person in God's sight. Adultery and murder are despicable sins, sins that Paul elsewhere speaks of as sufficient to relinquish one's inheritance in the kingdom of heaven (Gal. 5:21; 1 Cor. 6:9). In Catholic theology, David, after his sexual escapade with Bathsheba and murder of Uriah, was in a state of "mortal" sin, i.e., sin that leads to eternal death. Mortal sin is that state of wickedness in which one loses the grace of salvation. At *that* point one is "ungodly" and "wicked." Unless God forgives the sin and restores the grace, such a sinner is under eternal damnation.

We should also add, as Catholic theology teaches, that in confessing his sin, David must still do penance and undergo the temporal punishment for that sin.[3] The subsequent account in the second book of Samuel records very severe punishments given to David for his mortal sin. The first was to witness God taking the life of the child born to Bathsheba, a punishment of which David was extremely sorrowful (2 Samuel 12:15-23). The second was to witness the rape and pillage of his other wives (2 Samuel 12:11-12). Although God forgave his sin, afterwards David's life was never quite the same.

Catholic theology also teaches that even though one in mortal sin has lost the grace of salvation, he does not necessarily lose his faith.[4] This was the case with David. When Nathan approached him, David still believed in God. It was this belief in God that led him to acknowledge he had sinned against God. As he says in Psalm 51:5, "Against you, you only, have I sinned and done what is evil in your sight." Hence, his sin did not destroy his belief, although it did nullify his works of obedience that had previously justified him. Only the work of repentance, through the faith he retained, would restore the grace of God to his soul. Here we see another reason why Catholicism teaches that faith alone cannot save. David still had faith after he sinned with Bathsheba, but that faith by itself could not save him. The faith could bring him only to acknowledge his sin and then allow him to know that if he repented and sought God's forgiveness it would be granted to him. How could this happen? Because God had replaced the system of law with the system of grace, in anticipation of Christ's atonement and resurrection, which allowed him to look with mercy at David's repentance. If David had been under the system of law, then no work could have brought him God's forgiveness, let alone restore David to a right relationship with God. Any work done in an attempt to appease God before grace was restored would have been repugnant in the eyes of God. Repentance is a work under the system of grace, not law, and thus Paul could say in Romans 4:6 that David was justified "apart from works." This is why Paul includes David in the New Testament teaching of justification, since as we learned previously in Romans 3:25, God had "left the sins committed beforehand unpunished," in anticipation of Christ who set aside the power of the law to condemn the sinner for those who repent.

As we proved with an exhaustive study of the life of Abraham as recorded in the books of Romans, Galatians, Hebrews and James, so we have proved with the life of David. The Scripture shows that each person's justification is an *ongoing* one. To be sure, justification begins at a certain point in one's life, but it can be lost, restored or reinforced depending on one's response to God's prompting grace. In the accounts of Abraham, David, and Rahab, there is simply nothing to dissuade us of the truth that justification is not merely a single point-in-time event but a progressive, on-going process.

THE CASE OF PHINEHAS: JUSTIFIED BY WORKS

Psalm 106:30-31 records, "But Phinehas stood up and intervened, and the plague was checked. This was *credited to him as righteousness* for endless generations to come." This passage is referring to the incident recorded in Numbers 25 in which some of the men of Israel engaged in cultic sexual intercourse with Moabite and Midianite women. For this sin, the Lord ordered Moses to kill them. In defiance, an Israelite man brought a Midianite woman into his tent, most likely to engage in sexual intercourse. Phinehas, the priest, saw this happen, grabbed a spear, and went into the tent and killed both the man and the woman. For this act, God praises Phinehas very highly and stops the plague he had inflicted on the people, which had by this time already killed 24,000. God tells Moses that Phinehas was zealous for God's honor, and that as a result of his act Phinehas had turned God's wrath away from killing even more people. God makes a "covenant of peace" and a "lasting priesthood" with Phinehas and his descendants. It is obvious that Phinehas's act of vengeance was of extreme importance to God.

In the Psalmist's evaluation of Phinehas's deed, he uses language that those of a Protestant mindset find quite puzzling. The Psalmist uses the identical phrase for Phinehas that Genesis 15:6 used for Abraham, i.e., "was credited to him as righteousness." Protestants are trained to think of the word *credited* as something that one is *considered* as having but not something inherent within the person. Thus, they say that Abraham is credited with Christ's righteousness by the "non working" instrument of faith, and that Abraham has no intrinsic righteousness worthy of God's acceptance for justification. A severe problem arises in this formulation, however, since Psalm 106:31 attributes the "crediting of righteousness" to a work. The Psalm presupposes Phinehas's faith in God, and its stress on Phinehas's work becomes all the more significant when we realize that in all of Scripture only Abraham and Phinehas are individually assigned the designation "credited with righteousness." Because it is applied to a concrete act, one cannot understand the "crediting" as a mere *considering* of righteousness that does not in reality exist, but only as a recognition of an inherent quality of the individual. In other words, one must *consider* him righteous because he *is* righteous.

THE CASE OF CORNELIUS: A GOOD MAN WHO BECAME JUSTIFIED

Scripture often portrays God's drawing, calling, and justification of the individual as very fluid, a quality in justification which again speaks of an ongoing process, not a static imputation. At the enlightenment of Peter in Acts 10:34-35 on learning that God will accept all men for salvation, he says, "I realize how true it is that God does not show favoritism but accepts men from every nation who fear him and do what is right." The Acts 10 account opens up a whole new dimension in our discussion of the righteousness God seeks in men. At the time Luke wrote Acts, specifically the incident with Cornelius he recorded in Acts 10, the gospel had not spread far beyond the borders of Judea. Cornelius was one of the first Gentiles to hear the Christian gospel formally proclaimed. Peter's understanding is that God is coming to Cornelius with the gospel because Cornelius had shown that he "feared" God and was "doing what was right" (Acts 10:2, 35). Since God does not play favorites, he will bless anyone from any nation who fears him and does good.

This portrayal of God's dealing with man is quite different from Paul's description in Romans 3:11 which says, "there is no one who understands; no one seeks for God." Apparently, many outside the orb of the formalized gospel *do* seek God and in turn God seeks them as well. How can this be if Romans 3:11 seems so adamant that none seek God? We can answer in two ways. First, in Romans 3:10, Paul sets up the context from the perspective of the system of law. We know this is true because Paul concludes this section in Romans 3:19 with the words, "Now we know that whatever the law says, it says to those who are under the law, so that every mouth may be silenced and the whole world held accountable to God." From the perspective of the system of law, no one who does good or seeks after God. God is perfect and not one can measure up to his perfect standards. Paul, in the context of Romans 2-4, applied this principle especially to those Jews who "boasted" in God's face with their legalistic works. Second, as a logical corollary, Paul paints a picture describing the condition of the whole human race without the grace of God. Without the grace of God to prompt them, no one would ever seek God on his own. God must make the first move. Once he sheds his grace upon men, then men have the responsibility to respond to God. Some do, as the case of Cornelius proves.[5]

The very psalm that Paul quotes in Romans 3:11 shows that some do respond. To begin, Paul quotes from the first three verses of Psalm 14. These verses make it clear that no one does good or seeks God. As noted above, no one who bases his actions on the system of law, can please God or seek him. Again, Paul specifies this perspective in Romans 3:19, "Now we know that whatever the law says, it says to those who are under the law..." Being "under the law" is being in the system of law — the system from which God previously viewed the human race. But in the system of grace are some who seek God and do his will. Like Cornelius, they "do what is right" — a righteousness that God can and does accept. The latter part of Psalm 14, which Paul does not quote in Romans 3, speaks of those who do respond under God's grace. The Psalmist writes in Psalm 14:4-6:

> Will evildoers never learn, those who devour *my people* as men eat bread and *who do not call on the Lord?* There they are overwhelmed with dread, for God is present in the *company of the righteous.* You evildoers frustrate the plans of the *poor* but the Lord is their refuge.

Here the Psalmist contrasts "my people" with those "who do not call on the Lord," clear testimony to a distinction between those who do seek God and those who do not. These evil people that "do not call on the Lord" *remain* the ones of whom Paul speaks in Romans 3:11 as "no one who understands, no one who seeks God." Typical of this description are the Jews to whom Paul is primarily directing his message in Romans 3. God has offered them the grace to respond but have spurned God's advances. Yet Psalm 14:5 is clear that there is a "company of the righteous," in contradistinction to "there is none righteous" in Romans 3:10. Under law there is none righteous; under grace as many as desire can be righteous before God. As Paul says in Romans 3:19, "Whatever the law says it says to those who are under the law..." If one comes out from under the system of law, the law cannot condemn him. So it is with those who seek God. They are no longer under law but are now under grace. As Paul says in Romans 7:6, we have been "released from the law."

God expects men to seek after him within the grace he has spread abroad to the whole world. Scripture states this no better than in Acts 17:26-27:

> From one man he made every nation of men, that they should inhabit the whole earth; and he determined the times set for them and the exact places where they should live. God did this *so that men would seek him* and perhaps reach out for him and find him, though he is not far from each one of us.

We notice here that when Paul is specifying that God desired men to seek him he starts by referring to "one man," namely Adam. It is not surprising, then, to find in close proximity to Adam in one of the earliest chapters of the Bible that "men began to call on the name of the Lord" (Genesis 4:26). This "calling on the Lord" occurs thousands of years before the Jews existed. It was occurring long before the flood of Noah's day. Paul states that God subsequently made all the nations (i.e., the table of nations in Genesis 10) with their specific "times and locations" for the express purpose that these men would *"seek him and find him."* As history records, some found him; some did not. But the point is clear that God created a dynamic relationship for himself and man right from the beginning. God has been seeking faithful and obedient men since the dawn of time. Although he formalized this relationship at various points, (e.g., Noah, Abraham, Israel, the Church), God was always and everywhere looking for anyone who would "do what is right" as Cornelius had done. As the prophet Zechariah records (Zechariah 1:3), "This is what the Lord Almighty says: 'Return to me,' declares the Lord Almighty, 'and I will return to you,' says the Lord Almighty." God found one such seeker in Cornelius.

What exactly did God see in Cornelius? Acts 10 gives us a vivid description. Acts 10:2 says that Cornelius and his whole family are "devout and God-fearing." Several references in Acts address non-Jews who seek God as "God-fearers," "God-fearing Greeks" or "God-fearing Gentiles."[6] Cornelius is a centurion of the "Italian regiment." He is most likely a Roman, not a Greek. There is no evidence that he is a Jewish convert; on the contrary, he is "uncircumcised" (Acts 10:45), a Gentile, according to Peter's previous thought, with whom a Jew could not associate or even visit (Acts 10:28), whereas a Jewish convert would enjoy some fellowship with Jews. Cornelius is simply a God-fearing Gentile such as Romans 2:14-15 describes, one who seeks God based on the law written on the heart. Moreover, Cornelius's entire household is "devout" and "God-fearing;" clearly he understands and acknowledges God to an extent that it has filtered down to all those with whom he is intimately associated. In Acts 10:2 Luke begins to describe Cornelius's good works: "He gave generously to those in need and prayed to God regularly." Here we have a man of faith who loves and communicates with God, and who loves his neighbor as himself. Although we know that Cornelius is responding to the grace that God has given him, Acts 10:4 shows us the perspective from which God views Cornelius: he is one who has pleased God by working righteousness. It records: "Cornelius stared at him in fear. 'What is it Lord?' he asked. The angel answered, 'Your prayers and gifts to the poor have come up as a memorial offering before God.'"

This incident makes it clear that God is responding to the faith and good works of Cornelius. According to Acts 10:35, he is one who "fears God and does what is right." It is Cornelius's righteousness upon which God looks, not an alien righteousness. In the language of Acts 17:25-26 already cited, Cornelius is one who God places in a certain 'time and location' so that he will seek God and find him, and find him he does. Cornelius seeks God through the grace God gives him and God, in turn, blesses Cornelius with the full gospel.[7] At Peter's direction, Cornelius is baptized and received as a member of the Church. The full blessings of the Christian life now flow to him and his family, and they will be witnesses to others of God's tremendous grace. Granted, Cornelius's sins are formally forgiven at his baptism, and thus the righteous work of Christ is applied to him. But one cannot miss the point of the story: clearly Cornelius is a recipient of this formal grace as a result of God's response to his works of righteousness done under the auspices of grace. Before Peter comes to visit, God has seen Cornelius through his gracious viewing, thus allowing Cornelius to please God with his "prayer and gifts to the poor." Thus one does not have to be a formal member of the Church in order to be viewed or included in the grace of God. As Peter says, "God is no respecter of persons; he accepts anyone who fears him and does what is right." Unlike so many of the Jews of his day, Cornelius is a humble man who does not demand that God pay him for his good works. As Paul says in Romans 4:3-4, God is not obligated to reward anyone because all are sinners under law, and so was Cornelius. But from the perspective of the system of grace which stems from the atonement of Christ, God can view Cornelius, and any man from any nation who fears him and does what is right, as seeking righteousness and a candidate for God's salvation.

The case of Cornelius also shows us the reality of the Catholic concept of *gracious* merit. Cornelius is a man like that of Acts 17:25-27 who is placed by God in a certain time and place for the precise reason that he should seek God. Prompted by the grace and knowledge of God, he acts upon this grace by prayer and good works, e.g., giving to the poor.[8] On a strict basis, Cornelius is a sinner like everyone else in the human race and from that perspective he does not deserve God's favor. On the basis of gracious merit, however, Cornelius can acknowledge God with the power God has placed in him, and God in turn can bless him for his efforts. In Cornelius's case God blesses him with salvation. The reward of salvation is much greater in value than the devotion and work that Cornelius performs. This is precisely how the concept of merit works in Catholic theology. God's reward of salvation far outweighs our gracious merit of it.

THE CASE OF PAUL: JUSTIFIED FROM IGNORANCE

Another case of the interplay between God's grace and the concept of gracious merit appears in how Paul speaks of his own conversion to Christianity. In 1 Timothy 1:13-16, Paul writes:

> Even though I was once a blasphemer and a persecutor and a violent man, I was shown mercy *because I acted in ignorance and unbelief.* The grace of our Lord was poured out on me abundantly, along with the faith and love that are in Christ Jesus. Here is a trustworthy saying that deserves full acceptance: Christ Jesus came into the world to save sinners — of whom I am the worst. *But for that very reason I was shown mercy so that in*

me, the worst of sinners, Christ Jesus might display his unlimited patience as an example for those who would believe on him and receive eternal life.

Here we see a connection between the mercy that God showed Paul for his sins and Paul's ignorance and unbelief in committing such things. Although he calls himself "the worst of sinners," mainly because of his utter hatred and persecution of the first Christians, Paul also tells us that it was in his zeal for the faith of his Judaistic fathers that he blasphemed and persecuted, because he simply did not know Jesus and his mission. In the accounts of Paul's conversion in the book of Acts 9:1-19; 22:1-16; 26:9-23, we find that Paul was not the worst of sinners in the sense of living a malicious life of reckless abandon or having totally disregarding the commandments of God. He says of himself in Philippians 3:6 that he was "faultless" in the righteousness of the law. Let us make clear that this is not to say that Paul gained any merit with God because of his law-keeping. Surely if Paul had died in this unconverted state he would have come under God's judgment. Jesus, however, appearing to Paul on the Damascus road, is coming not as the vengeful God who wants to destroy Paul for his sins but as a gentle inquisitor asking, "Saul, Saul, why do you persecute me?" Jesus speaks to Paul almost as if he had known him previously. Paul answers, "Who are you, Lord?" As soon as Paul hears Jesus's answer, "I am Jesus whom you are persecuting...now get up and go into the city and you will be told what you must do," Paul obeys. He has finally found the answer he was looking for and responds immediately. We must notice, however, that there is something about Paul that Jesus seeks. Paul has misdirected his godly energies out of ignorance. Paul's zeal and honesty for what he believes can now be pressed into service by Jesus for Christianity. While Paul was persecuting the Church in his zeal for God, Jesus had "patience" with him because Paul was acting in ignorance. All he needed was a push in the right direction and he would become the greatest missionary for Christianity the world had ever known. As God led Cornelius to Christianity, he likewise led Paul to Christianity — by a direct communication. As Cornelius was baptized, so Paul was baptized, that

God's grace could wash away his past sins. Acts 22:16 records God's command to Paul: "Get up, be baptized and wash your sins away, calling on his name."[9]

SUMMARY POINTS

1) Protestant denominations have differing, and sometimes diametrically opposed views, of the relationship between justification and sanctification.

2) Most Protestants view justification as a one-time, unrepeatable event, yet at the same time hold that works of obedience must qualify the faith required for justification. This view presents a very difficult theological problem because it leaves no room for works to qualify the condition of the faith before justification.

   a) Some Protestants attempt to deal with this dilemma by claiming that although works are required in order to qualify the faith of justification, it is not necessary to perform the work since God can read the individual's heart. In response, we insist that Scripture argues the case for personal justification not by appealing to God's omniscience, but from a temporal vantage point, as noted, for example, in Paul's contention in Romans 4 that Abraham was justified *chronologically* prior to his circumcision.

   b) In the Genesis 22 account of Abraham's sacrifice of Isaac, God acknowledges Abraham's faith and works only at the precise time that Abraham raises the knife to slay Isaac. To prove Abraham's faith and obedience, God insists on being an actual witness to this event. Nothing in this text suggests that God can or will view this test from his omniscience.

3) As regards the Catholic teaching that justification is not a one-time event but an ongoing process, the following points are in order:

a) New Testament writers interpret Abraham's justification as a sequence of events or a progressive justification, culminating in his willingness in Genesis 22 to sacrifice Isaac. Expressing his view, Paul equates the faith of Abraham in Genesis 12 (when he left his homeland at God's command) with the faith of Genesis 15 (when he believed that God would give him a son). Both of these instances of faith fall under the Hebrews 11:6 description of faith that "pleases God" for salvation, and therefore both must be salvific, as is the faith of Abel, Enoch, and Noah mentioned in the same context.

b) The Hebrew writer reinforces his view that the faith of Abraham in Genesis 12 is the same salvific faith in Genesis 15 by describing the former as Abraham "looking forward to the city and foundations, whose architect and builder is God" and the latter in precisely the same terms as "...instead, they were longing for a better country—a heavenly one. Therefore God...has prepared a city for them." Since the faith described in both passages share the same vision of the future, Abraham's faith in Genesis 12 was therefore salvific, and he was thus also justified at that time.

c) Paul, extending his explanation of Abraham's justification as ongoing process, follows the same pattern in his description of David. Paul quotes David's gratitude to God in Psalm 32 for forgiving his sin of adultery with Bathsheba and murder of Uriah. Paul includes this incident within his description of justification in Romans 4, which means that David was actually justified at the event recorded in Psalm 32. Moreover, since the earlier Psalms, as well as the historical record in 1 and 2 Samuel, record that David was a man of God long before the forgiveness he received in Psalm 32, the forgiveness recorded in Psalm 32 is not the only time David was justified in his life. This agrees with Catholic theology that one who commits adultery and murder is in *mortal sin* — a sin that removes sanctifying grace from the soul and puts one in an unjustified state before God. When sanctifying grace is restored, the individual is again justified in the sight of God, as Paul claims of David in Romans 4:5-8.

d) The case of Phinehas, in which Psalm 106:31 uses "crediting of righteousness" (the exact phrase used to describe Abraham in Genesis 15:6, and the only other time it is used in the Old Testament) to describe God's response to Phinehas's act in executing the apostates of Israel, shows that the Old Testament writers understand works as that which produce salvific justification, the same understanding James expresses in his New Testament epistle.

e) The case of Cornelius, whom Acts 10 describes as a man who knows and seeks for God, and whom God blesses with salvation in recognition of Cornelius's faith and works, shows the Catholic concept of the individual responding to grace and God's rewarding the individual by bestowing gracious merit for his response.

f) The case of Paul — who in 1 Timothy 1:13-16 states that God had mercy on him, a mercy in which Paul receives forgiveness of sins, because of Paul's prior ignorance of the gospel, and in order to save others by this example of Christ's patience — shows again that God is waiting for men to respond to his impulses of grace and views their response accordingly.

END NOTES

[1] The Council of Trent, Session 6, Chapter 10 states: "Having, therefore, been thus justified and having been made the 'friends of God' and 'his domestics,' 'advancing from virtue to virtue,' 'they are renewed' (as the Apostle says) 'from day to day,' that is, by mortifying the members of their flesh, and by 'presenting them as instruments of justice,' unto sanctification through the observance of the commandments of God and of the Church; in this justice received through the grace of Christ 'faith cooperat-

ing with good works,' they increase and are further justified, as it is written: 'He that is just, let him be justified still,' and again: 'Be not afraid to be justified even to death,' and again: 'You see, that by works a man is justified and not by faith only.'"

2 At the baptism of Paul in Acts 22:16, Luke records the event as "Get up, be baptized and wash away your sins."

3 Catholic Catechism, Sections 1472-1473

4 Council of Trent, Session 6, Chapters 14-15; Canons 27, 29.

5 Council of Orange, 529 AD, Canon 25: "So very clearly we should believe that the faith— so admirable— both of that famous thief, whom the Lord restored to his native land of paradise, and of Cornelius the centurion, to whom the angel of the Lord was sent, and of Zachaeus, who deserved to receive the Lord himself, was not from nature, but a gift of God's bounty."

6 Acts 13:16, 26; 16:14; 17:4, 17.

7 Catholic Catechism, Sections 1996-2004; "For he wishes to give eternal life to all those who seek salvation by patience in well-doing" (CC, Section 55). "At all times and in every race, anyone who fears God and does what is right has been acceptable to him" (CC, Sections, 761, 781). "...and you overlook people's sins, so that they may repent" (Wisdom 11:23).

8 As noted in chapter 1, God prompts to salvation by *actual* grace. Once one responds to actual grace, God provides the *sanctifying* grace of salvation. Council of Trent, Session 6, Canon 7: "If anyone says that all works performed before justification, no matter how they were performed, are truly sins or deserve God's hatred; or that the more earnestly one tries to dispose oneself for grace, the more grievously one sins, anathema sit" (JD 1557).

9 The concept of gracious merit — in which God does something good to the individual based either on the goodness God sees in the individual's intentions or on his actual obedience — permeates Scripture, especially the Old Testament (cf., 1 Kings 14:13; 2 Kings 20:1-6; 2 Chronicles 12:12; 19:3; 24:16; 30:18-20; Psalm 37:4-9; 84:11; Proverbs 12:2; 13:21; Ecclesiastes 2:26; Jeremiah 5:25; 18:10; Ezekiel 18:21; 33:14-16; Luke 8:15; Romans 2:10).

HOW CAN i GET TO HEAVEN

CHAPTER 5

CAN i LOSE MY SALVATION?

There are many who teach that a person cannot lose his salvation. They believe that once a person accepts Jesus as Savior, he is on his way to heaven, no matter what sin he may commit. A popular phrase used for this notion is "once saved, always saved." It is also known as "eternal security." In evangelization, many of these denominations begin the process by asking the person, "If you died tonight, do you know for sure that you will go to heaven?" The way this question is asked, the person is made to feel that if he doesn't know absolutely sure he is going to heaven, then he really doesn't have true faith and therefore will not go to heaven. Unfortunately, the concept of eternal security is one of the most horrendous falsifications of biblical teaching ever perpetrated on the Church.

1 JOHN 2:19

WERE THOSE WHO FALL AWAY NEVER JUSTIFIED?

Those that believe a person cannot lose his salvation are forced to answer why some practicing Christians often turn from their faith never to return again. To answer this problem, they conclude that if a person seems to fall from salvation, in reality, it only appears that way, because the person was never saved in the first place. In order to support this notion, many use a particular passage of Scripture, 1 John 2:19, as a proof text:

> They went out from us but they did not really belong to
> us. For if they had belonged to us, they would have re-
> mained with us; but their going showed that none of
> them belonged to us.

Many claim that in the above passage the apostle John is teaching that if one leaves Christianity it must be concluded that one
never belonged to Christianity. From this understanding, they pos-
tulate as a corollary that *any* individual who falls away from the
Christian faith does so because he was never a true Christian.

The main problem with this kind of interpretation is that it
takes a specific truth concerning *some* who fall away and makes
it into a general truth applicable to *everyone* who falls away. Certainly a large amount of people who leave the church never genuinely embraced the Christian faith. Jesus teaches very clearly in
Matthew 7:22-23, "Many will say to me on that day, 'Lord, Lord,
did we not prophesy in your name, and in your name drive out
demons, and perform many miracles?' Then I will tell them plainly,
'I never knew you. Away from me, you evildoers!'" The phrase,
"I never knew you" implies that they were never true Christians
but only appear to be through manifesting various miracles. This
condition of hypocrisy was perhaps true of many of the Jews in
Jesus's day. The parables Jesus tells both before and after this
teaching, (e.g., concerning trees that bear good or bad fruit and
those who build on either rock or sand), confirm Jesus's intent to
point out their false faith and works. Passages like this, however,
do not prove that a true Christian cannot fall from his Christian
faith and lose a salvation that he once possessed. They only prove
that *some* people who leave the faith were never true believers.
John already implies this condition within the context of his epistle
when he writes in 1 John 2:18: "Dear children, this is the last
hour; and as you have heard that the Antichrist is coming, even
now many antichrists have come. This is how we know it is the
last hour." Since verse 18 precedes the verse in question (verse
19), we understand that the people to whom John refers in verse
19 are the "antichrists" of verse 18. We know that John, in using
the word "antichrists," is not referring to the run-of-the-mill Christian but to treacherous *antichrists* whose sole purpose in life is to

thwart the cause of Christianity and upset the faith of the average church-going Christian. John does not hesitate to equate them with the supreme Antichrist, Satan, for after referring to him in the words, "*the* Antichrist is coming," John adds, "*even now* many antichrists have come," showing that they are of the same breed as Satan.

In 2 Corinthians 11:13-15 Paul spoke about these same "antichrists" as present within the Corinthian church: "For such men are false apostles, deceitful workmen, masquerading as apostles of Christ. And no wonder, for Satan himself masquerades as an angel of light. It is not surprising, then, if his servants masquerade as servants of righteousness..." Paul's reference to both Satan and the false apostles "masquerading" as angels of light shows that their intent is to deceive. They come into the church by stealth for the sole purpose of upsetting the faith of sincere believers. Paul also expresses this concern in verse 3 of the same chapter: "But I am afraid that just as Eve was deceived by the serpents's cunning, your minds may somehow be led astray from your sincere and pure devotion to Christ." It is these whom Paul considers as sincere believers in Christ, not the false apostles and antichrists masquerading as angels of light.

We can conclude that though 1 John 2:19 certainly makes clear that some will leave the church who were never sincere believers originally, in context this principle applies primarily to the antichrists whose purpose is to destroy Christianity. Satan, the supreme Antichrist, was never a Christian, and it follows that the antichrists who follow in his footsteps were never Christians either. Thus, 1 John 2:19 proves that *some* groups of people who were never true Christians may defect but it by no means proves that *all* people who lose their faith were never true Christians.

DOES THE BIBLE TEACH ETERNAL SECURITY?

In light of the foregoing passages which indicate that some people who were once justified could fall from that state, we must now investigate other passages that various groups use to teach that the Christian cannot fall from salvation once he is justified.

Afterward, we will analyze other New Testament passages that indeed teach that a Christian can fall from justification.

ROMANS 8:38-39

In Romans 8:38-39, Paul writes:

> For I am convinced that neither death nor life, neither angels nor demons, neither the present nor the future, nor any powers, neither height nor depth, not anything else in all creation, will be able to separate us from the love of God that is in Christ Jesus our Lord.

First, of the ten items Paul says cannot separate us from the love of God, all of them, without exception, are forces external to the individual. Death and life, angels and demons, present and future, powers, height and depth, nor any creature, are things that God has created and over which the individual has no control. He cannot control whether he is born or whether he will die; he cannot control the acts of the angelic world; he cannot control time nor the cosmos; he cannot control any other created thing or being external to himself. In Romans 8:35 Paul adds seven other items: trouble, hardship, persecution, famine, nakedness, danger, and sword. These also are external forces, and since Paul suffered most of them himself, thus he can testify that none of them stopped Christ from loving him. In other words, God has made the process of salvation so secure that he will allow no external force to disrupt its progress and completion. The individual has the guarantee, speaking colloquially, that God will not "pull the rug out from under him" by failing to provide the grace of salvation. God is not a capricious tyrant who offers salvation one day, but out of a whim decides the next day to withdraw his offer, nor will he allow anything in the universe to curtail his plan. The God of the Old and New Testament is not like the gods of Roman or Greek mythology who are fickle and fight amongst themselves. He is a solid rock that cannot be moved.

Yet Paul, while portraying God as immovable, does not include *internal* forces — forces within the individual — among those things that cannot separate the individual from the love of God. Nowhere does Paul teach that the individual cannot choose to take himself out of the salvation plan of God. Moreover, Paul does not include things such as fornication, adultery, idolatry, and stealing, in the list of Romans 8:38-39 (i.e., Paul does not say, "Neither fornication, nor adultery, neither idolatry nor stealing...can separate us from the love of God") simply because he has stated previously in passages like 1 Corinthians 6:9-10, Galatians 5:21, and Ephesians 5:5 that these sins are the very reason one could lose his salvation. God is faithful and will let no external force disrupt the salvation process, but whether the individual who claims to follow God will himself continue to be faithful is not a question Paul addresses in Romans 8:38-39.

It is clear from surrounding passages that Paul does not believe that the individual is immune from falling away. For example, two chapters earlier, addressing baptized Christians in Romans 6:12-13 he says, "Therefore, brothers, we have an obligation — but it is not to the sinful nature, to live according to it. For if you live according to the sinful nature, you will *die*; but if by the Spirit you put to death the misdeeds of the body, you will live." The *dying* Paul has in view here is the same as that in Romans 6:23: "for the wages of sin is death." Later, in Romans 11:22, Paul writes to the Gentile Christians: "Consider, therefore, the kindness and sternness of God: sternness to those who fell, but kindness to you, provided that you continue in his kindness. Otherwise, you also will be cut off."

Second, Paul's choice of language in Romans 8:31-39 de-emphasizes the individual and emphasizes the community of believers. We see this in his use of "we," "us," and "ours" throughout the text. For example, in Romans 8:31 Paul says, "What, then, shall *we* say in response to this? If God is for *us*, who can be against *us*." Similarly, in verse 32 he says, "...but gave him up for *us* all...graciously give *us* all things"; and in verse 34, "...and is also interceding for *us*. Who shall separate *us* from the love of Christ"; and in verse 37, "...*we* are more than conquerors through him who loved *us*." This is typical of New Testament language that categorizes the security of salvation within the confines of the universal community of Christians, e.g., the Church, which is conscious of both its relationship with the Lord and that the Lord will not disown his Church. God does not, however, guarantee salvation to groups and individuals within the ecclesial community should they fall into serious and unrepentant sin.

Third, in Romans 8:38-39 Paul does not speak specifically of individual salvation, rather, he specifies the "love of God." We also see this in verse 35 where Paul says, "Who shall separate us from the *love of Christ.*" The focus is on the "love of God" or "love of Christ" as that which issues forth from the Godhead to the community of believers. In other words, since God will fulfill his eternal plan dependably and with integrity, we can always depend on having the love of God. God does not love us one day and then hate us the next day. As Paul says succinctly in 2 Timothy 2:13, "If we are faithless, he will remain faithful, for he cannot disown himself." God is always faithful to his plan of salvation. He always continues to love us, so much so that he gave his only begotten Son that whoever believes in him should not perish but have eternal life (John 3:16). Wisdom 1:24 records, "For you love all things that exist, and detest none of the things that you have made, for you would not have made anything if you had hated it." By the same token, however, Paul warns us in 2 Timothy 2:12, "If we disown him, he will also disown us." Paul clearly puts the onus on the individual, who God has let free to take himself out of God's grace and love, yet Paul makes it equally clear that God will never capriciously withhold his love and grace from those who seek it.

JOHN 10:28-29

In John 10:28-29 Jesus says, "I give them eternal life, and they shall never perish; no one can snatch them out of my hand. My Father, who has given them to me, is greater than all, no one can snatch them out of my Father's hand. I and the Father are one."

Since Jesus opened the context by speaking in John 10:1-10 of the robber who enters the sheepgate by stealth to steal away the sheep, and in John 10:14-16 of the hired hand who does not protect the sheep when the wolf appears, it is obvious that Jesus is emphasizing *his* faithfulness to the sheep in contrast to the evil intent and carelessness of others. He is not attempting to teach that the individual sheep know absolutely that they themselves will remain in the fold. As Paul taught in Romans 8:38-39, John teaches in John 10:1-16 that Jesus will allow no outside force to snatch these sheep out of his hand.[1] This passage, however, does not deny the possibility of internal forces within the sheep themselves that could eventually turn them away. Many other passages in the teaching of Jesus *do* entertain the question of internal forces that draw one away from God and make it quite clear that such a falling away is a real possibility.

We must also realize that Jesus is speaking to Jews who consistently showed their stubbornness and hardness of heart. Other passages make it clear that Jesus, experiencing repeated rejection from the Jews to God's message, knew that God had blinded them so that they could not understand the gospel (Matthew 13:11-17). Hence, they were not sheep of his "fold" and could not understand his voice. Jesus remarks about the inability of certain sheep to understand him and the ability of others to understand (John 10:1-5, 16, 26). Though some Jews did understand and follow Jesus (Matthew 13:11), the nation as a whole had rejected Jesus, and Jesus in turn is rejecting the Jewish nation. He will turn to "other sheep that are not of this sheep pen" and "bring them also." Jesus is referring, of course, to the Gentile nations (Matthew 8:11-12). Hence, we see that in John 10 Jesus is speaking in very general categories. He is not teaching that any one individual can be certain that he will be saved. The individual can be certain of God's plan of salvation, and that if he is faithful to God that God will allow no one to snatch him out of it, but he cannot be certain that he himself will remain faithful. If he could be certain, then Paul's warning in 2 Timothy 2:12-13, and many other passages, simply have no relevant meaning.

DOES THE BIBLE TEACH WE CAN FALL FROM SALVATION?

Next to the person of Christ, Scripture attends to no topic more than the warning to Christians not to fall away from the faith and lose their salvation. In fact, every book in the New Testament, with the possible exception of Philemon, in some way or other suspends the outcome of our eternal destiny based on the duration and degree of our faith and obedience. Scripture offers absolutely overwhelming evidence that a believer can fall from the salvation he once possessed.

The Scriptural passages which teach that a Christian can fall from the salvation he once possessed are so clear they hardly need explanation. Their impact is greatest when we see them amassed together. To prove the point made above, i.e., that our salvation is not certain until our last breath, we will now demonstrate this teaching with a representative sample from each book of the New Testament so that the reader can see this consistent and overwhelming message in Scripture. (This is not to say, however, that the Old Testament does not contain just as much or more evidence on the same topic). Other chapters of this book also reference and discuss some of these passages.

MATTHEW

7:21-23 — "Not everyone who says to me, 'Lord, Lord,' will enter the kingdom of heaven, but only he who does the will of my Father who is in heaven. Many will say to me on that day, 'Lord, Lord, did we not prophesy in your name, and in your name drive our demons and perform many miracles? Then I will tell them plainly, I never knew you. Away from me, you evildoers."

10:22, 28, 33 — "All men will hate you because of me, but he who stands firm to the end will be saved...Do not be afraid of those who kill the body but cannot kill the soul. Rather, be afraid of the one who can destroy both soul and body in hell...But whoever disowns me before men I will disown him before my Father in heaven."

24:12-13 — "Because of the increase of wickedness, the love of most will grow cold, but he who stands firm to the end will be saved."

MARK

9:43 — "If your hand causes you to sin, cut it off. It is better for you to enter life maimed than with two hands to go into hell, where the fire never goes out."

10:21-23 — "'One thing you lack,' he said. 'Go, sell everything you have and give to the poor, and you will have treasure in heaven. Then come, follow me.' At this the man's face fell. He went away sad because he had great wealth. Jesus looked around and said to his disciples, 'How hard it is for the rich to enter the kingdom of God!'"

13:22 — "For false Christs and false prophets will appear and perform signs and miracles to deceive the elect — if that were possible."

LUKE

8:13 — "Those on the rock are the ones who receive the word with joy when they hear it, but they have no root. They believe for a while, but in time of testing they fall away."

12:43-46 — "It will be good for that servant to whom the master finds doing so...But suppose the servant says to him, My master is taking a long time in coming and he begins to beat the men servants and maid servants, and eat and drink and get drunk. The master of that servant will come on a day when he does not expect him and an hour he is not aware. He will cut him to pieces and assign him a place with the unbelievers."

JOHN

12:47-48 — "As for the person who hears my words but does not keep them...there is a judge for the one who rejects me and does not accept my words; the very word I spoke will condemn him at the last day."

15:6 — "If anyone does not remain in me, he is like a branch that is thrown away and withers; such branches are picked up, thrown into the fire and burned."

ACTS

13:43, 46 — "...Paul and Barnabas, who talked with them and urged them to continue in the grace of God...Since you reject it and do not consider yourselves worthy of eternal life, we now turn to the Gentiles."

20:29-30 — "I know that after I leave, savage wolves will come in among you and will not spare the flock. Even from your own number men will arise and distort the truth in order to draw away disciples after them. So be on your guard. Remember that for three years I never stopped warning each of you night and day with tears."

ROMANS

2:6 — "God will give to each person according to what he has done. To those who by persistence in doing good seek glory, honor and immortality, he will give eternal life. But for those who are self-seeking and who reject the truth and follow evil, there will be wrath and indignation."

8:12-13 — "Therefore, brothers, we have an obligation— but it is not to the sinful nature, to live according to it. For if you live according to the sinful nature, you will die..."

11:20-22 — "But they were broken off because of unbelief, and you stand by faith. Do not be arrogant but be afraid. For if God did not spare the natural branches, he will not spare you either. Consider therefore the kindness and sternness of God; sternness to those who fell, but kindness to you, provided that you continue in his kindness. Otherwise you also will be cut off."

1 CORINTHIANS

3:17 — "If anyone destroys God's temple, God will destroy him."

4:5 — "My conscience is clear, but that does not make me innocent. It is the Lord who judges me. Therefore, judge nothing before the appointed time; wait till the Lord comes. He will bring to light what is hidden in darkness and will expose the motives of men's hearts."

6:8-9 — "You yourselves cheat and do wrong, and you do this to your brothers. Do you not know that the wicked will not inherit the kingdom of God?"

9:27-10:6 — "No, I beat my body and make it my slave so that after I have preached to others, I myself will not be disqualified. For I do not want you to be ignorant of the fact, brothers, that our forefathers were all under the cloud and that they all passed through the sea. They were all baptized into Moses in the cloud and in the sea. They all ate the same spiritual food and drank the same spiritual drink; for they drank from the spiritual rock that accompanied them, and that rock was Christ. Nevertheless, God was not pleased with most of them; their bodies were scattered over the desert. Now these things occurred as examples to keep us from setting our hearts on evil things as they did."

10:11-12 — "These things happened to them as examples and were written down as warnings for us, on whom the fulfillment of the ages has come. So, if you think you are standing firm, be careful that you don't fall!"

15:1-2 — "Now, brothers, I want to remind you of the gospel I preached to you, which you received and on which you have taken your stand. By this gospel you are saved, if you hold firmly to the word I preached to you. Otherwise, you have believed in vain."

2 CORINTHIANS

5:20- 6:2 — "...We implore you on Christ's behalf: Be reconciled to God...As God's fellow workers we urge you not to receive God's grace in vain. For he says, 'In the time of my favor I heard you, and in the day of salvation I helped you.' I tell you, now is the time of God's favor, now is the day of salvation."

11:3 — "But I am afraid that just as Eve was deceived by the serpent's cunning, your minds may somehow be led astray from your sincere and pure devotion to Christ."

12:21-13:5 — "I am afraid that when I come again my God will humble me before you, and I will be grieved over many who have sinned earlier and have not repented of the impurity, sexual sin and debauchery in which they have indulged...Examine yourselves to see whether you are in the faith; test yourselves. Do you not realize that Christ Jesus is in you — unless of course, you fail the test?"

GALATIANS

5:19-21 — "The acts of the sinful nature are obvious...I warn you, as I did before, that those who live like this will not inherit the kingdom of God."

6:7-9 — "Do not be deceived: God cannot be mocked. A man reaps what he sows. The one who sows to please his sinful nature, from that nature will reap destruction; the one who sows to please the Spirit, from the Spirit will reap eternal life."

EPHESIANS

5:5-6 — "For of this you can be sure: No immoral, impure or greedy person— such a man is an idolator — has any inheritance in the kingdom of Christ and of God. Let no one deceive you with empty words, for because of such things God's wrath comes on those who are disobedient. Therefore do not be partners with them."

PHILIPPIANS

3:10-16 — "I want to know Christ and the power of his resurrection...and so, somehow, to attain to the resurrection from the dead. Not that I have already obtained all this, or have already been made perfect, but I press on to take hold of that for which Christ Jesus took hold of me. Brothers, I do not consider myself yet to have taken hold of it...all of us who are mature should take such a view of things...Only let us live up to what we have already attained."

COLOSSIANS

1:21-23 — "Once you were alienated from God and were enemies in your minds because of your evil behavior. But now he has reconciled you by Christ's physical body through death to present you holy in his sight, without blemish and free from accusation — if you continue in your faith, established and firm, not moved from the hope held out in the gospel."

1 THESSALONIANS

4:1-8 — "Finally, brothers, we instructed you how to live in order to please God, as in fact you are living...it is God's will that you should be sanctified: that you should avoid sexual immorality...the Lord will punish men for all such sins, as we have already told you and warned you...Therefore, he who rejects this instruction does not reject man but God, who gives you his Holy Spirit."

2 THESSALONIANS

2:13-15 — "...because from the beginning God chose you to be saved through the sanctifying work of the Spirit and through belief in the truth...So then, brothers, stand firm and hold to the teachings we passed on to you, whether by word of mouth or by letter."

3:6,14 — "In the name of the Lord Jesus Christ, we command you, brothers, to keep away from every brother who is idle and does not live according to the teaching you received from us...If anyone does not obey our instruction in this letter, take special note of him. Do not associate with him in order that he may feel ashamed."

1 TIMOTHY

4:1 — "The Spirit clearly says that in later times some will abandon the faith and follow deceiving spirits and things taught by demons."

5:15 — "Some have in fact already turned away to follow Satan."

6:10-19 — "For the love of money is the root of all kinds of evil. Some people, eager for money, have wandered from the faith and pierced themselves with many griefs....Take hold of the eternal life to which you were called when you made your good confession...command those who are rich in this present world not to be arrogant nor to put their hope in wealth, which is so uncertain, but to put their hope in God...in this way they will lay up treasure for themselves as a firm foundation for the coming age, so that they may take hold of the life that is truly life."

6:20-21 — "Turn away from godless chatter and the opposing ideas of what is falsely called knowledge, which some have professed and in so doing have wandered from the faith."

2 TIMOTHY

1:15 — "You know that everyone in the province of Asia has deserted me, including Phygelus and Hermogenes."

2:12 — "If we endure we will also reign with him. If we disown him he will also disown us."

2:17 — "Their teaching will spread like gangrene. Among them are Hymenaeus and Philetus, who have wandered away from the truth. They say that the resurrection has already taken place and destroy the faith of some."

4:10 — "for Demas, because he loved this present world, has deserted me and has gone to Thessalonica...Alexander the metal worker did me a great deal of harm. The Lord will repay him for what he has done."

4:16 — "At my first defense, no one came to my support, but everyone deserted me."

TITUS

1:16 — "They claim to know God, but by their actions they deny him."

3:10 — "Warn a divisive person once, and then warn him a second time. After that, have nothing to do with him. You may be sure that such a man is warped and sinful; he is self-condemned."

HEBREWS

2:1 — "We must pay more careful attention, therefore, to what we have heard, so that we do not drift away. For if the message spoken by angels was binding, and every violation and disobedience received its just punishment, how shall we escape if we ignore such a great salvation."

3:1, 6 — "Therefore, holy brothers, who share in the heavenly calling, fix your thoughts on Jesus, the apostle and high priest whom we confess...And we are his house, if we hold on to our courage and the hope of which we boast."

3:12-14 — "See to it, brothers, that none of you has a sinful, unbelieving heart that turns away from the living God. But encourage one another daily, as long as it is called Today so that none of you may be hardened by sin's deceitfulness. We have come to share in Christ if we hold firmly till the end the confidence we had at first.

4:1 — "Therefore, since the promise of entering his rest still stands, let us be careful that none of you be found to have fallen short of it."

4:11-13 — "Let us, therefore, make every effort to enter that rest, so that no one will fall by following their example of disobedience...Nothing in all creation is hidden from God's sight. Everything is uncovered and laid bare before the eyes of him to whom we must give account."

4:14 — "Therefore...let us hold firmly to the faith we profess."

6:4-6 — "It is impossible for those who have once been enlightened, who have tasted the heavenly gift, who have shared in the Holy Spirit, who have tasted the goodness of the word of God and the powers of the coming age, if they fall away, to be brought back to repentance, because to their loss they are crucifying the Son of God all over again and subjecting him to public disgrace."

6:11-12 — "We want each of you to show this same diligence to the very end, in order to make your hope sure. We do not want you to become lazy, but to imitate those who through faith and patience inherit what has been promised."

10:26-27 — "If we deliberately keep on sinning after we have received the knowledge of the truth, no sacrifice for sins is left, but only a fearful expectation of judgment and of raging fire that will consume the enemies of God."

10:35-38 — "So do not throw away your confidence; it will be richly rewarded. You need to persevere so that when you have done the will of God, you will receive what he has promised...And if he shrinks back, I will not be pleased with him."

12:1, 3 — "Therefore, since we are surrounded by such a great cloud of witnesses, let us throw off everything that hinders and the sin that so easily entangles, and let us run with perseverance the race marked out for us...Consider him who endured such opposition from sinful men, so that you will not grow weary and lose heart."

12:14-17 — "Make every effort to live in peace with all men and to be holy; without holiness no one will see the Lord. See to it that no one misses the grace of God and that no bitter root grows up to cause trouble and defile many. See that no one is sexually immoral, or is godless like Esau, who for a single meal sold his inheritance rights as the oldest son. Afterward, as you know, when he wanted to inherit this blessing, he was rejected. He could bring about no change of mind, though he sought the blessing with tears."

12:25, 29 — "See to it that you do not refuse him who speaks. If they did not escape when they refused him who warned them on earth, how much less will we, if we turn away from him who warns us from heaven?...for our God is a consuming fire."

JAMES

1:14-16 — "But each one is tempted when, by his own evil desire, he is dragged away and enticed. Then, after desire has conceived, it gives birth to sin; and sin, when it is full-grown, gives birth to death. Don't be deceived my dear brothers."

1:21-22 — "Therefore, get rid of all moral filth and the evil that is so prevalent, and humbly accept the word planted in you, which can save you. Do not merely listen to the word, and so deceive yourselves. Do what it says."

2:13-14 — "Because judgment without mercy will be shown to any-one who has not been merciful...What good is it, my brothers, if a man claims to have faith but has no deeds? Can such faith save him?

4:4 — "You adulterous people, don't you know that friendship with the world is hatred toward God? Anyone who chooses to be a friend of the world becomes an enemy of God."

5:9 — "Don't grumble against each other, brothers, or you will be judged. The Judge is standing at the door."

1 PETER

4:17-18 — "For it is time for judgment to begin with the family of God; and if it begins with us, what will the outcome be for those who do not obey the gospel of God? And, if it is hard for the right-eous to be saved, what will become of the ungodly and the sinner?"

5:8 — "Your enemy the devil prowls around like a roaring lion looking for someone to devour. Resist him, standing firm in the faith..."

2 PETER

1:9 — "But if anyone does not have them, he is nearsighted and blind, and has forgotten that he has been cleansed from his past sins. Therefore, my brothers, be all the more eager to make your calling and election sure. For if you do these things you will never fall."

2:20-22 — "If they have escaped the corruption of the world by knowing our Lord and Savior Jesus Christ and are again entangled in it and overcome, they are worse off at the end than they were at the beginning. It would have been better for them not to have known the way of righteousness, than to have known it and then to turn their backs on the sacred command that was passed on to them. Of them the proverbs are true: 'A dog returns to its vomit,' and, 'a sow that is washed goes back to her wallowing in the mud.'"

3:14-17 — "So then, dear friends, since you are looking forward to this, make every effort to be found spotless, blameless and at peace with him...Therefore, dear friends, since you already know this, be on your guard so that you may not be carried away by the error of lawless men and fall from your secure position."

1 JOHN

2:24-26 — "See that what you have heard from the beginning remains in you. If it does, you also will remain in the Son and in the Father. And this is what he promised us — even eternal life. I am writing these things to you about those who are trying to lead you astray."

2:28 — "And now, dear children, continue in him, so that when he appears we may be confident and unashamed before him at his coming."

2 JOHN

8 — "Watch out that you do not lose what you have worked for, but that you may be rewarded fully. Anyone who runs ahead and does

not continue in the teaching of Christ does not have God; whoever continues in the teaching has both the Father and the Son."

3 JOHN

9-11 — "I wrote to the church, but Diotrephes, who loves to be first, will have nothing to do with us. So if I come, I will call attention to what he is doing, gossiping maliciously about us. Not satisfied with that, he refuses to welcome the brothers. He also stops those who want to do so and puts them out of the church. Dear friend, do not imitate what is evil but what is good. Anyone who does what is good is from God. Anyone who does what is evil has not seen God."

JUDE

5 — "Though you already know all this, I want to remind you that the Lord delivered his people out of Egypt, but later destroyed those who did not believe."

REVELATION

2:5 — "You have forsaken your first love. Remember the height from which you have fallen! Repent and do the things you did at first. If you do not repent, I will come to you and remove your lampstand from its place."

2:10 — "Be faithful, even to the point of death, and I will give you the crown of life."

2:16 — "Repent therefore! Otherwise, I will soon come to you and will fight against them with the sword of my mouth."

2:23 — "Then all the churches will know that I am he who searches hearts and minds, and I will repay each of you according to your deeds."

2:26 — "To him who overcomes and does my will to the end, I will give authority over the nations."

3:3 — "Remember, therefore, what you have received and heard; obey it, and repent. But if you do not wake up, I will come like a thief, and you will not know at what time I will come to you."

3:11 — "I am coming soon. Hold on to what you have, so that no one will take your crown."

3:16 — "So, because you are lukewarm — neither hot nor cold — I am about to spit you out of my mouth."

3:21 — "To him who overcomes, I will give the right to sit with me on my throne..."

16:15 — "Behold, I come like a thief! Blessed is he who stays awake and keeps his clothes with him, so that he may not go naked and be shamefully exposed."

22:12 — "Behold, I am coming soon! My reward is with me, and I will give to everyone according to what he has done."

22:19 — "And if anyone takes words away from this book of prophecy, God will take away from him his share in the tree of life and in the holy city, which are described in this book."

SUMMARY POINTS

1) Some use 1 John 2:19 to support the idea that all people who fall away from the faith were never justified originally. This is not legitimate. Although the New Testament can be used to support the possibility that *some* people who fall away were never justified originally, it does not apply this to *every* case. In fact, the New Testament describes most individuals who fall away as those who truly embraced the gospel and were justified at some point in the past. New Testament writers usually confine instances in which people are said to fall away who were never justified originally to false prophets and antichrists who come into the Church to draw true believers away from the faith.

2) Hebrews 11:29's account of the Israelites falling away shows that a person or group can have the same faith that in others (for example, the "heroes of faith" recorded in the entire chapter of Hebrews 11) is true salvific faith, but later fall away from that faith and lose their salvation.

3) Romans 8:38-39 and John 10:28-29 do not support the concept of eternal security since, (a) the passages, read in context, refer only to external forces that God will prohibit from disrupting the salvation plan, not to sinful forces within the individual himself that can make him turn away from God; and (b) these passages, and others like them, speak only in general terms of the plan of predestination, and do not cite any specific individuals who belong in this category.

4) Next to the person of Christ, Scripture attends to no topic more than the warning to Christians not to fall away from the faith and lose their salvation. In fact, every book in the New Testament, with the possible exception of Philemon, in some way or other suspends the outcome of our eternal destiny based on the duration and degree of our faith and obedience. Scripture offers absolutely overwhelming evidence that a believer can fall from the salvation he once possessed.

END NOTES

[1] Other like passages are Hebrews 13:5-6, "Keep your lives free from the love of money and be content with what you have, because God has said, 'Never will I leave you; never will I forsake you.' So we say with confidence, 'The Lord is my helper; I will not be afraid. What can man do to me?'" and Jude 24, "To him who is able to keep you from falling and to present you before his glorious presence without fault and with great joy..." These verses teach only that God will faithfully help us to the end to reach salvation; they certainly leave open the possibility, as do the contexts in which they are contained, that the individual himself may refuse God's help.

HOW CAN i GET TO HEAVEN

CHAPTER 6

WHEN I'M JUSTIFIED, DOES GOD MERELY CALL ME RIGHTEOUS OR AM I TRULY RIGHTEOUS INSIDE?

Before we begin, let us once again review the terms of this debate. Imputed righteousness, as Protestant proponents usually defend it, refers to that righteousness which derives solely from the merits of Christ's active and passive obedience, which, in turn, is applied to the sinner's account. The sinner can perform absolutely no work in order to obtain that righteousness. It is a righteousness that is "alien" but which the sinner can have credited to himself by simply believing in Christ and his work. Probably the best analogy to explain the concept of imputed righteousness is that of an accountant's ledger book. Into his ledger book the accountant adds a credit entry representing a sum of money obtained as a gift which puts the total account in the black; similarly, under imputed righteousness God credits the "alien" righteousness of Christ to the sinner in order to make his standing with God positive. Since the wages of sin is death, then without a righteousness from another source to countermand the negative entries, the sinner could not be justified. Moreover, since God demands perfect righteousness, the man, being sinful and imperfect, is unable to make his own "credit entry" through his own righteous acts. Therefore, the righteousness must come from a perfect source outside of the sinner and be applied to him by a free act of God. The righteousness is "imputed" to him but it is not his own.

The Catholic concept of infused righteousness refers to that righteousness which also comes from God, but which God gives to the sinner not as a mere "credit" but as an infusion of actual righteous quality into the person. Using the analogy above, rather than say he receives a "credit entry," we could say that he becomes "credit worthy." As God infuses his divine righteousness into the individual, he instills the virtues of faith, hope and love. As the individual, through God's helping grace, maintains this personal righteousness, he becomes increasingly justified and sanctified in the eyes of God, leading to his final justification and glorification in heaven. One of the best analogies to explain the concept of infused righteousness is that of pouring a sufficient quantity of white liquid into a beaker full of black liquid so that the final solution turns from dark to light. The white liquid is analogous to the grace of God which is "infused" into the sinner, changing the whole person and sufficiently overcoming the blackness of sin. The infused righteousness restructures or renovates the sinner to the point that he becomes acceptable in the eyes of God and may enter heaven. Developing the analogy to show that the justification process is an ongoing one, we can picture God continually pouring white liquid into the dark liquid to make it whiter and whiter. At the same time, however, sin may combat this process and once again make the liquid dark or darker. It is the condition of the soul, e.g., the whiteness of the liquid, at the end of the person's life that is the criterion for final justification.

WHY DO PROTESTANTS OBJECT TO CATHOLIC JUSTIFICATION?

At this point in the discussion many Protestants recoil. If God is perfect and demands perfection, how can one expect to be "restructured" or "renovated" to the point of satisfying God's standard of perfection? Does it not seem that the only possible way to meet God's perfect standard is to have a perfect righteousness given to the individual since he cannot attain it on his own? The problem with these questions, as we have noted earlier in this study, is that they assume a premise that is not true. Granted, before the atonement of Christ, the sinner can do nothing on his own to become acceptable in God's eyes. That is why the Council of Trent insisted that neither faith nor works can merit the grace of justification.[1] No one can do anything to appease God without the atonement of Christ, let alone strive to attain a perfect righteousness to meet God's standards. But once the atonement was accomplished, the grace of God was made available to the whole world. For those who wish to avail themselves of this grace, God will no longer look at them through the eyes of the uncompromising and exacting system of law that was put in place as their judge after Adam's sin. God will now look at them as a father looks upon his children, not as a judge looks upon a criminal. As a father does not exact, without compromise and forgiveness, a perfect and faultless obedience from his children, neither does God demand such from his children. Within the system of grace, God will extend his mercy and love to those who genuinely seek him, even though they are not perfect. The perfect righteousness of Christ which satisfied God's wrath, in turn, released us from the system of law and opened the door for a gracious relationship between God and man. The change in status the sinner undergoes is one which transfers him from the system of law to the system of grace. Once in the system of grace, he must now abide by the conditions of that system. The system of grace requires that the cleansed person maintain the righteousness that was infused into him. If he does so, then God will reciprocate and grant him heaven as his eternal dwelling. He maintains this righteousness by continuing in faith, hope and love. If he falters, God can forgive and restore him, but he must seek God's forgiveness and the continual infusion of His righteousness. In short, God does not demand perfect righteousness as seen through the uncompromising edicts of the law, but perfect righteousness that is in accord with his viewing of man from his grace and mercy.

Protestants often misunderstand another aspect of infused grace, believing that the doctrine assumes the person himself is producing the righteousness, and concluding that such a system bespeaks a salvation based on human works. The typical Protestant adage, "nothing do I bring, simply to the cross I cling," which appears so God-glorifying and totally selfless, reinforces these views. Catholic theology teaches, however, that though God demands human effort, and often severe human effort as recorded in the story of

Abraham detailed earlier in this study, only the power given to us by the grace of God can provide and maintain that righteousness. Without God's gracious viewing of the work and his power to help in actually performing the work, the person would not be righteous. The good works we do are a result of the cooperation of our wills with the divine will.[2] Paul says in Philippians 2:12-13:

> Therefore, my beloved, just as you have always obeyed me, not only in my presence, but much more now in my absence, work out your own salvation with fear and trembling; for it is God who is at work in you, enabling you both to will and to work for his good pleasure.

This passage clearly shows the participation of both parties, God and man. Paul states that they have "obeyed" and then asks that they "work out their salvation with fear and trembling." This means that the fear of and reverence for God's scrutiny and ultimate judgments must always guide obedience. When Paul says they have "always" obeyed, he is indicating that they have maintained the obedience, or righteousness, that they originally received. Maintaining the obedience is the means by which they "work out" their salvation. They will continue to obey because they fear God and tremble before him, knowing that disobedience leads to damnation.[3] Yet Paul does not want them to think that they are totally on their own. That notion would plunge them into abject fear with no hope of persevering. Paul reassures them that God is there to help them in their obedience.[4] He provides sufficient grace for each act of faith, hope, and love.

THE CATHOLIC CONCEPT OF GRACE TO THE RESCUE

In order to have a complete understanding of the synergism between God's grace and man's responsive action, it is necessary to comprehend thoroughly the Catholic concept of grace, as well as the biblical evidence that supports this teaching. As noted above, when we speak of grace being infused into a person, we have to imagine it as something that can be quantified and stored. As a spirit or soul is real yet unseen and untestable, so grace has real existence. Though it comes in many forms, (e.g., sanctifying grace, actual grace, efficacious grace), it is not just a mere concept or attribute of God. Grace is a spiritual power that God gives us, not merely favor through which he observes us.[5] The more of this grace we obtain from God, the higher our spirituality can be. Although Scripture often speaks of grace as the relationship we now enjoy with God, (i.e., the state or system of grace in which God views us differently than through the system of law), Scripture also speaks of grace as coming in various measures, e.g., Acts 4:23, "*great* grace was upon them"; James 4:6, "He gives us more grace"; 1 Peter 4:10, "the *manifold* grace of God"; 2 Peter 1:2, "Grace and peace be *multiplied* to you." Scripture also speaks of grace given in proportion to the need at hand or the specific service to be performed, e.g., Romans 12:6, "We have different gifts according to the grace given to us"; Romans 15:15, "because of the grace that God gave me to be a minister to the Gentiles"; Galatians 2:9, "they recognized the grace given to me"; Ephesians 4:7, "but to each one of us grace has been given as Christ apportioned it"; Hebrews 4:16, "Let us then approach the throne of grace with confidence so that we may find mercy and find grace to help us in the time of need." Paul says in 1 Corinthians 15:10: "But by the grace of God I am what I am, and his grace to me was not without effect. No, I worked harder than all of them — yet not I, but the *grace of God* that was with me." In Hebrews 13:9 it states: "It is good for our hearts to be *strengthened by grace*, not by ceremonial foods, which are of no value to those who eat them." And in 2 Corinthians 1:12: "We have conducted ourselves...in holiness...according to God's grace." And in 2 Corinthians 9:8: "And God is able to make *all grace abound* to you, so that in all things at all times, having all that you need you will abound in every good work."

These passages represent grace not merely as an attribute of God but as a spiritual power that God gives to the individual. When God gives his grace, a *strengthening* occurs. When Paul says in 1 Corinthians 15:10, "by the grace of God that was with me," the impression we receive is that of a power resident in Paul which allows him to do his work. Paul repeats this theme again in Philippians 4:13, "I can do all things through Christ who strengthens me."[6]

From these passages we learn two lessons: (1) Grace is not merely a way God views us but it is also a power emanating from God given to help the individual lead a Christian life; (2) The individual's works incorporate both his free will to do the work and the grace of God that prompts him and provides the power to do the work. The Christian cannot take strict credit for his work since it was God who enabled him to do the work. God does, however, graciously reward him for cooperating with him, for example, in Hebrews 6:10 it says, "God is not unjust; he will not forget the work and the love you have shown him..."

REVELATION 21:27
"NOTHING IMPURE WILL ENTER"

One of the passages often cited to support the Catholic view of infused righteousness, (i.e., righteousness which is sufficient to enter heaven) is Revelation 21:27: "Nothing impure will ever enter it, nor will anyone who does what is shameful or deceitful, but only those whose names are written in the Lamb's book of life." Catholic theology argues that if we are only legally righteous (as in the Protestant view), not intrinsically righteous, then we will not fulfill the requirement of Revelation 21:27 to be "pure" as we enter heaven. Protestants invariably interpret such a verse to mean that only Christ's righteousness imputed to the individual can make him pure in God's sight and able to enter heaven. Although in the Protestant view the Christian may attain a certain degree of sanctification and holiness as he leads his life, this is not what gets him into heaven. In the Protestant scenario, when the individual stands before God to be judged for his sins, he is said to "plead the blood of Christ," and God responds not by looking at the individual's sinful life but upon the perfect righteousness of Christ. Since Christ was his substitute at his initial justification, he will also be his substitute when he stands before God at the final judgment seat. The Christian's works will determine not whether he enters heaven, but rather what kind of reward, if any, he will receive in heaven. We will cover the aspect of reward for works more fully in chapter 9. For now, we must analyze the Protestant concept of imputed righteousness more thoroughly.

To many, the Protestant concept of imputation seems to be the most appropriate theory. After all, looking at ourselves in a moment of sin we wonder if we will ever be worthy enough in God's eyes to enter heaven. If Catholics claim to be infused with righteousness in justification yet also know that God examines and judges every motive and action, then how, one may ask, can we ever expect to please God sufficiently to enter heaven? Does not the Protestant view sound so much easier and simpler? Doesn't it give us more certitude to claim that Christ is our righteousness and then let God figure out what kind of personal reward we will receive once we enter heaven? Certainly one could create many plausible scenarios of salvation. Protestant denominations have given us many of them, e.g., Lutheranism, Calvinism, Arminianism, Methodism, Dispensationalism, etc. All of these seem to be plausible, reasonable systems, at least to some degree. However, one obvious problem with such a variety of plausible systems is precisely the disagreements among them. At best, only one could possibly have the truth. Moreover, each claims to use Scripture alone to arrive at its particular soteriological system. In reality, each denomination tends to stress a particular set of Scriptures while downplaying others. The set of Scriptures stressed by one denomination inadvertently overrules another set that provides a rival denomination with a differing view of a particular doctrine. We have seen many examples of this tendency thus far. Apparently, something is missing in each of these "plausible" salvation scenarios.

Although the Protestant explanation of Revelation 21:27 is plausible, one immediate problem with such a view is that it does not do justice to the literal or "face value" language John chooses. John does not speak in terms of "imputed righteousness" in Revelation 21:27. He speaks only of what is observable as the person attempts to gain entrance into heaven. Those who are "impure" are also those who do what is "shameful" or "deceitful." It is not a matter of whether they have accepted the alien righteousness of Christ; it is a matter of whether they have been obedient. The remaining context provides corroboration that the internal righteousness which qualifies them for heaven is John's intended meaning. He points to the obedience or disobedience of each individual as the distinguishing mark between them. In Revelation 22:11 he writes, "Let him who does wrong continue to do wrong; let him who is vile continue to be vile; let him who does right continue to do right; and let him who is holy continue to be holy." Again, in Revelation 22:15 he writes, "Outside are the dogs, those who practice magic arts, the sexually immoral, the murderers, the idolaters, and everyone who loves and practices falsehood." The focus is on the good or evil actions of the individual, not the reception of an imputed righteousness.

We see, then, that while the Protestant system may seem plausible, it often misses the simple language of Scripture. Rather than taking each verse as it stands and allowing the differing "face-value" facts of Scripture to create as many theological categories as necessary to explain its complete message, the Protestant hermeneutic invariably elevates "faith alone," and its counterpart "imputed righteousness," as all-encompassing theological categories into which the rest of the Scripture's language must fit. The theological category of *faith alone* becomes the overriding criterion — the *sine qua non* of biblical hermeneutics — by which to judge or interpret any other Scripture. Passages like Revelation 21:27; 22:11, 15, and many others, instead of simply being taken at their own face-value, become the victim of a theological system.

WHAT ELSE DOES THE NEW TESTAMENT SAY ABOUT JUSTIFICATION?

In New Testament language, if a person has been "justified," he is "righteous" or possesses "righteousness." These terms refer both to how God views us and to what God gives us. Simply put, if a person is "justified" or "righteous" this means that from God's perspective he is worthy to enter heaven. The main difference between the Catholic and Protestant interpretations of these terms, as stated earlier in the chapter, is that the Catholic view holds that the individual is worthy for heaven only after God has sufficiently prepared him. It is the Holy Spirit who prepares him by "restructuring" or "renovating" his once sinful soul. All the trials, suffering, prayers, and good works a Christian experiences on earth serve for the express purpose of preparing his person to be worthy of heavenly citizenship. As Hebrews 11:6 requires faith that "pleases" God, this faith must (1) believe that God exists, and (2) believe that "God is the rewarder of those who diligently seek him." As the Christian increases in holiness by the infusion of God's grace, he is showing that he is "diligently seeking" the God who will reward him.

In using the words "just" or "righteous," the Scripture often refers to specific men as being such. Joseph is a "righteous man" (Matt. 1:19). John the Baptist is a "righteous and holy man" (Mark 6:20). Simeon is "righteous and devout" (Luke 2:22). Lot is "righteous Lot" (2 Peter 2:7-8). A passage of this kind that especially stands out is Luke 1:5-6: "...there was a priest named Zechariah...his wife Elizabeth was also a descendant of Aaron. They were both *righteous* before God, walking in all the commandments and ordinances of the Lord, blamelessly." The key facet of this passage is that *God* is the reference point in determining the righteousness of Zechariah and Elizabeth. It is not men, who see only the outside, doing the evaluating. God, who peers into the hearts of this couple, sees them as righteous. This would certainly lead us to reevaluate the meaning and extent of the statement by Paul in Romans 3:10 that there are "none righteous, no not one." How can God view the whole human race as unrighteous sinners in Romans 3:10 and yet speak of Zechariah and Elizabeth as "righteous before God"? The answer, as we have been arguing thus far, is to take Luke 1:6 at "face-value" and conclude that they were seen as righteous because they actually "walked in all the commandments and ordinances of the Lord blamelessly." The second and more general answer, as noted throughout this study, is that prior to God's grace and the repentance that grace prompts from man, Paul is absolutely correct that all men are sinners and unrighteous. Moreover, there is nothing they can do in themselves to rectify that situation. God must make the first move. God provides the grace, through the atonement of Christ, which allows him to forgive men's sins and look upon them much differently than he was required to do through the uncompromising system of law. Thus, within the system of grace, Zechariah and Elizabeth pleased God sufficiently that God could look upon them as "righteous." They fit the category of Paul who said that faith which "pleases" God is that which acknowledges his existence and believes that he rewards those who diligently [by obedience] seek him" (Hebrews 11:6). This means not that they were sinless but that they understood their sinful nature and used God's grace to subdue it. The subduing of sin allowed them to "walk in the commandments and ordinances of the Lord, blamelessly." This is the same language used of Noah, for example, who is said to be "a righteous man, *blameless* among the people" (Genesis 6:9); of Job who is said to be "*blameless and righteous*; he feared God and shunned evil" (Job 1:1), or of Abel who is called "*righteous* Abel" (Matt. 23:35). Scripture also speaks of individuals or groups of men as righteous without specifying a name, e.g., "the righteous and the unrighteous" (Matt. 5:45), "he that receives a righteous man" (Matt. 10:41), "prophets and righteous men" (Matt. 13:17), "you garnish the tombs of the righteous" (Matt. 23:29), "the resurrection of the righteous" (Luke 14:14; Acts 24:15), "the eyes of the Lord are over the righteous" (1 Peter 3:12), "the prayer of a righteous man" (James 5:16); "her parents were righteous" (Susanna 1:3).

An interesting parallel between Christ and righteous men, and one that Scripture is not in the least ashamed of making, regards the righteousness of Christ and the righteousness of godly men. To set up this parallel, Scripture first refers to Christ as a "righteous man" (Acts 3:14; 7:52; 22:14; 1 John 2:1); then 1 John 3:7 makes the parallel: "He who does what is right is righteous, just as he is righteous." In very simple language that does not mince words, John tells us that one acquires the state of being righteous by doing righteousness. In fact, the measure of the righteous state is such that it is equal to the righteous state of Christ. This is quite a statement. God says we are righteous not merely to placate our sensibilities and make us feel good, but because, as God views us within the system of grace, we are as righteous as Christ. The degree of our sins and faults is not in view here. It is understood from John's earlier writing that if one sins he can confess that sin and God will forgive him (1 John 1:8-10). The sins being set aside, John then goes on to tell us that we are as righteous as Christ is righteous.

The New Testament word "righteousness" similarly conveys recognition of individual righteousness. For example, Jesus requires that our righteousness "must exceed the righteousness of the scribes and Pharisees" or we shall "not enter into the kingdom of heaven" (Matt. 5:20). There is no thought here of entering heaven merely because we have obtained an "alien righteousness." The responsibility is on the individual to make sure his righteousness is true righteousness. Jesus goes on to explain exactly how one can measure his own righteousness. In the remaining context of Matthew 5, Jesus refers to the "sayings" or code of ethics that the Old Testament formerly required but that he is now going to enhance in the New Testament. Thus, in Matthew 5:21, it is no longer sufficient to refrain only from physically killing someone; rather, Jesus says that even being angry with one's brother puts one in danger of judgment, i.e., judgment that results in not being able to "enter the kingdom of heaven" as he has just stated in Matthew 5:20. Hence, the way our righteousness "exceeds" the righteousness of the Pharisees is by refraining from anger, whereas the Pharisees, though they did not murder their brother, hated him and reviled him in their heart. Again, by interpreting the biblical language for its "face value" meaning within its own context rather than superimposing a theological system upon it, we learn that we do not exceed such Pharisaical righteousness by laying claim to someone else's righteousness [i.e., Christ's], but by exercising our righteousness by the power of God's grace unto the God who views us under his grace. In the remaining context, Jesus tells us many ways that our righteousness must exceed that of the Pharisees, e.g., not looking with lust on a woman (verse 28), not divorcing illegitimately (verse 32), not swearing (verse 34), not seeking vengeance (verse 39), loving one's enemy (verse 44). We must do these things, according to verse 45, "that you may be the children of your Father which is in heaven," not merely because we "are" his children.

The word "righteousness" is also used in Luke 1:75 where Zachariah, the same person who is said to be "righteous before God" in Luke 1:6, upon the birth of Christ, says, "that we might serve him without fear, in holiness and righteousness before him." This again shows the reason why Zachariah was recognized as "righteous before God" — he was one who sought to live that way.

HOW DO I ATTAIN "THE RIGHTEOUSNESS OF GOD"?

Scattered throughout the New Testament are references to "the righteousness of God." A total of ten passages use this phrase.[7] The phrase "the righteousness of God" is important to study because Martin Luther claimed that it was the watershed that gave him clear insight into the nature of justification. Before his new understanding, Luther was under the impression that the phrase referred to the vindictive nature of God who, if the individual did not measure up to the highest form of spirituality, would come down with his righteous vengeance. Luther's notion of such a God fits in well with his extremely scrupulous nature. It is said that Luther whipped himself with chains as a self-imposed chastisement in order to show God sorrow for sin and receive his favor. According to Luther's own account, one day he awoke from his dogmatic slumber and saw the "righteousness of God" in a whole new light. In reading Romans 1:17, Luther reasoned that the clause "For in the gospel a righteousness from God is revealed..." was referring to the status of righteousness into which God's judicial verdict places the believer. Having attained the "status" of righteousness, one could be considered righteous by God without actually being righteous. One acquired the status of righteousness by faith — faith alone. This "discovery" became the hallmark of Luther's theology. Indeed, if it is possible to point to one verse that spawned a reformation, Romans 1:17 may be the most likely candidate.

From Luther's interpretation of Romans 1:17 came the beginnings of the Protestant concept of *imputation*. A righteousness which God's verdict establishes, the argument goes, is a righteousness beyond dispute and one that will hold up even in God's strict court of justice. Though a man may bring many versions of his own righteousness to God, no man could claim his own righteousness in God's court. The righteousness must be credited to the man's account, even though the man was not righteous in himself. Indeed, Luther believed that the person, even at the moment of imputation, was, figuratively speaking, simply a pile of dung. The righteousness of God that was given to him was analogous to a covering of snow over the dung in such a way that when viewed from the surface only the white snow would be observable. Luther obtained this imagery from his own culture and economy. The farmers in his area used to show off their economic status by mounting a pile of dung in their front yards, which they eventually used as fertilizer for their crops. When winter came, snow would fall on the dung and thus change its appearance and mask its odor. To Luther, this served as a perfect example of his new interpretation of Romans 1:17.

The problems with Luther's interpretation of Romans 1:17 are manifold. First, no theologian prior to him had understood the "righteousness of God" as an imputation. Naturally, then, the burden of proof lay upon Luther, and what a great burden it was. The same men of previous centuries who had defined such esoteric and enigmatic doctrines such as the Trinity, the Deity of Christ, the Inspiration and Canonicity of Scripture, Heaven and Hell, and many other doctrines, had, Luther said, missed the boat, as it were, when it came to the very nature of salvation. Second, Luther's proof texts for the concept of imputation simply begged the question. Since the very verses he offered as proof could logically and consistently be understood in a totally different way than he was presenting, extracting a theory of imputation out of such passages really had no substantive and irrefutable proof. Imputation became simply a plausible theory without historic precedent and without unambiguous Scriptural proof. The many and varied interpretations of "the righteousness of God" that followed in Protestantism after Luther bear this out.

The early fathers and medieval theologians before Luther had, to be sure, understood "the righteousness of God" as a quality of God. But they had gone a step further. They taught that God could give this righteous quality to men, not through an imputation, but as a qualitative sharing of God's righteousness. In other words, God put his righteous qualities into man — in a word, he *infused* it into them. This made them righteous internally, not merely externally. When God looked at them he saw a righteous individual, not someone who just appeared to be righteous on the outside because God gave him a label of "righteous." We have already noted the use of "righteous" in Scripture which referred to several men and women as "righteous before God," e.g., Noah, Job, Zachariah, Elizabeth, et al. These texts make it clear that it was for their particular faith and obedience that the term "righteous" was attributed to them, not because God had merely labeled them with his righteousness. Granted, the only way God could recognize their internal righteousness was through the grace provided by Christ's atonement to forgive their sins. Nevertheless, the resulting righteousness that men actually possess through faith is what Paul and the other New Testament writers are speaking of when they refer to the righteousness which justifies.

How can we better understand the "righteousness of God" as used in Scripture? If the phrase is subjective, then the righteousness would be a quality of God, i.e., his righteous character. If the phrase is objective it would refer to the righteousness that God expects to view in others or gives to others. Scripture uses both senses. In Romans 3:5, for example, the subjective sense is evident: "But if our unrighteousness brings out the *righteousness of God* what shall we say? That God is unrighteous for bringing his wrath on us?" This passage establishes God's righteousness by contrasting it with the unrighteousness of men. Both by verse 3, which refers to the "faith of God" or "God's faithfulness" in contrast to the unbelief of the Jews, and verse 7, which refers to the "truth of God" in contrast to the "lies" of men," each clearly refers to the righteous quality of God. Since these phrases are subjective, the "righteousness of God" is also subjective.

On the other hand, a passage in which "the righteousness of God" is used objectively in reference to the kind of righteousness God instills into and expects from man is James 1:19-20: "...Let every man be quick to hear, slow to speak, slow to anger. For the anger of man does not produce the righteousness of God." Here it is clear that the "righteousness of God" is a quality that God desires to see in man. Being slow to anger is how one produces the righteousness that is pleasing to God. Since God infuses his own righteousness into the individual, then it is only logical to understand that as God "reveals" his righteousness to man, as taught in Romans 1:17, he disseminates it not by mere gospel proclamation but by the actual implantation of that righteousness into the hearers and believers of that gospel. In essence, God "reveals" himself *to man* (in the gospel) and *in man* (infusing his righteousness).[8]

In Romans 1:17 and subsequent passages in the epistle, Paul faults the Jews for trying to manufacture their own righteousness rather than seeking the righteousness that appeals to God. Paul notes this contrast clearly in Romans 10:3: "For not knowing the righteousness of God, and seeking to establish their own, they did not submit to the righteousness of God." Here Paul describes the "righteousness of God" as a quality of God to which they did not submit. Similarly, Romans 1:17, says in two ways that the righteous quality of God is "revealed," and it is up to man to access it and live by it. First, the phrase "from faith to faith" implies a continuity of faith in the life of the individual. Second, the quote taken from the book of Habakkuk, "the just by faith shall live," also implies such a continuity by specifying that one "lives" by faith. The section immediately following, Romans 1:18, speaks of the "unrighteousness of men," thus contrasting the righteousness that comes from faith with a merely human quality of righteousness which in God's eyes is so unsatisfactory as to be unrighteous.

The Habakkuk passage has several additional facets: (1) Nowhere does the Old Testament book of Habakkuk suggest that faith has anything to do with imputed righteousness. Chapter 1 of this book points out Habakkuk's complaint that God was ignoring the plight of the righteous by not bringing swift judgment upon the evildoers of Israel. In answering, God tells Habakkuk that he will bring the Babylonians to punish Israel at the appointed time. Habakkuk then complains that God would be punishing Israel by using an unrighteous heathen nation, that itself is worthy of punishment. God retorts that in due course he will also bring judgment upon the Babylonians. Habakkuk must wait patiently for God's complete vengeance, and not lose heart. He must believe that God will do what he says he will do even when it seems he is never going to do it. In the midst of this trial, Habakkuk wrote those famous words concerning the Lord's judgment on Israel and Babylon: "For the revelation awaits an appointed time; it speaks of the end and will not prove false. Though it linger, wait for it; it will certainly come and will not delay" (Habakkuk 2:3). He then describes the wicked disposition of the Babylonians: "he is puffed up, his desires are not upright." He contrasts this with the disposition of the righteous person, namely Habakkuk himself: "but the righteous will live by his faith." Habakkuk, already a righteous man, must now continue to live out his faith by believing that God is doing everything in the best and swiftest way possible, even though it doesn't seem that way. Later, Habakkuk reassures himself of God's integrity by reminiscing about God's ancient fame and wonderful deeds (Habakkuk 3). Hence, nowhere do we find in the book of Habakkuk Luther's concept of the "righteousness of God" as a judicial verdict of righteousness. Habakkuk is merely demonstrating that a righteous man will continue to live by faith in the face of circumstantial evidence that tempts him not to believe in God. The issue is continuity of faith. That is the kind of faith God desires to see in man. That is the faith that pleases God; the faith he will credit as righteousness, and which will allow man to enter heaven.

The last usage of the Habakkuk quote in the New Testament also opposes Luther's concept of a judicial imputation of righteousness. Hebrews 10:36-38 states: "You need to persevere...He who is coming will come and not delay. But my righteous one will live by faith. And if he shrinks back I will not be pleased with him." Paul displays the same theme that was evident in Habakkuk, that is, persevering in faith while one waits on the Lord to act. The object of the waiting is the "eternal promise" and thus the faith must continue for their entire lives. The continuity of the faith is crucial since those who "shrink back" from it will not "please" God. Just a few verses later, we see Paul describing the kind of faith that does "please" God. It is faith that believes both that God exists and that he is the rewarder of those who diligently seek him (Hebrews 11:6). This demonstrates again why justification cannot be by a one-time juridical act sparked by faith alone. Since one's faith must be measured in order to have value, and since the measurement of that faith cannot be determined until the end of one's life, therefore one cannot be justified "once-for-all" in a legalistic framework.

We see another facet of the principle that the righteous will live by faith when we understand that, as Paul speaks in Romans 1:17 of the righteousness of God being revealed in the "gospel," the gospel about which he speaks is not confined to the New Testament. In fact, Paul's quote from the Old Testament book of Habakkuk already contains the very gospel message Paul is preaching![9] In turn, the reference in Romans 1:18 to those who "suppress the truth by their wickedness" must refer to those who suppress the gospel — a gospel that requires men to live by faith. It does not merely refer to the world of pre-New Testament Gentiles who did not have the written word. In fact, the Jews committed many of the sins that Paul enumerates in Romans 1:21-32 just as much, if not more, than the Gentiles. We see, then, that not only disbelieving the gospel, but also "wickedness," suppresses the truth of the gospel. Those who act wickedly show that they are not living by faith in God. This is why Paul stresses *obedience* in relation to the kind of faith he seeks when he says in Romans 1:5: "...we received grace and apostleship to call people from among the Gentiles to the *obedience that comes from faith.*" Paul is not calling them to a *faith alone* but to *obedience*. Paul says the same in Romans 16:26: "the gospel...which was made known to all the nations for the *obedience of faith.*" Here again Paul equates the gospel of salvation not with *faith alone* but with the obedience God requires of those who claim faith. Not only is obedience coupled with faith but the mere act of faith in response to the command of God is itself an act of obedience.

The next instance of "righteousness of God" appears in Romans 3:21-22: "But now a righteousness of God, apart from law, has been made known...this righteousness of God comes through faith in Jesus Christ to all who believe." As stated above, the use of "righteousness of God" refers both to God's personal righteousness and the righteousness God instills in man for justification. The phrase "but now" develops a contrast with the previous verses, i.e., verses 19- 20, which speak about the system of law under which the whole world is held accountable in sin. These verses further state that no one can be justified by law, rather, the law makes us aware of how sinful we are. Paul further develops the contrast in verse 24 in speaking of being "justified freely by his grace through the redemption that came by Jesus Christ." In other words, the opponents are the law on the one hand and grace on the other — two competing systems, one of which cannot save, while the other can. We understand the system of grace which does save as "the righteousness of God." The passage describes the kind of righteousness that God has revealed and requires. It is not a legal righteousness but a godly righteousness. As Paul proceeds to explain further in Romans 4:3-4, we see that the righteousness that God accepts from man is not a righteousness whereby man seeks strict payment from God for his righteous acts. Under the system of law, nothing man does can be viewed as righteous since the law will always expose the sinful side of man. Rather, the righteousness of God that he imparts and wants reciprocated comes first when the individual admits his sinful condition by acknowledging the law's case against him. He then seeks to be included in the system of God's grace, apart from law, so that God can now view his faith and works as righteousness. It is the atonement of Christ that makes all this possible. All men need do at this point is to obey the command of God to believe it and act upon it.

Another important usage of "the righteousness of God" appears in 2 Corinthians 5:21: "He made the one not knowing sin to be sin on our behalf in order that we might become the righteousness of God in him." Taking this verse in isolation from its context, many Protestants have concluded that 2 Cor. 5:21 teaches an imputed righteousness since Paul speaks of righteousness that resides "in him," i.e., in Christ. Thus they say that the Christian, being "in him," is one and the same with Christ. They then stipulate that God is not looking at the righteousness in the Christian but at the righteousness of Christ. Hence, the righteousness of Christ is imputed to the Christian and thus we, in Christ, become the righteousness of God. The problem with this interpretation, as with most Protestant interpretations of the atonement and justification, is that although there is some truth to their view, it is at best a half-truth and as a result distorts the full meaning and intent of the passage. We can see this in two ways. First, the grammatical construction of 2 Cor. 5:21 does not necessarily treat the subordinate clause ("in order that we might become the righteousness of God in him") as an actual or definite result of the main clause ("He made the one not knowing sins to be sin on our behalf"). The English correctly translates the main verb in the subordinate clause as "might become" showing a *potential* result in process rather than a punctiliar event. Second, the context of 2 Corinthians 5-6 specifies the *impediments* to the realization of the subordinate clause of 2 Corinthians 5:21. We first note this in verses 19-20 in which Paul states that he is an ambassador for Christ with the message of reconciliation. He then says in verse 20: "We implore you on Christ's behalf: Be reconciled to God." The command to "be reconciled" is a present imperative. Hence, if becoming the righteousness of God was a punctiliar event in the past no longer to be questioned, we must ask why Paul is appealing ("begging" in Greek) for them to be reconciled? The audience to whom he is speaking consists of recognized Christians. This is the second letter he has written to them and thus their Christian faith has long been established. What, then, is the problem? It is the same problem the Corinthian church has had from the beginning. The faith of many in the church is becoming lax and on the verge of disappearing. Paul had consistently warned them of this fact in his first letter. In almost every chapter of 1 Corinthians he brings an indictment against them for their sin and lack of faith. He carries this over into his second letter which concludes in 2 Corinthians 13:5 with, "Examine yourselves to see if you are in the faith; test yourselves. Do you not realize that Christ Jesus is in you — unless of course you fail the test."

We see other indications of their slipping away from the faith in the context under discussion. In 2 Corinthians 6:1-2 Paul says: "As God's fellow workers we urge you not to receive the grace of God in vain. For he says, 'In the time of my favor I heard you, and in the day of salvation I helped you.' I tell you, now is the time of God's grace, now is the day of salvation." This is quite a stinging indictment and warning to the wretched Corinthians. Paul is so worried about whether they will remain in the faith that he warns them not to receive God's grace "in vain." He further reinforces what he means by pleading for them to recognize "the day of salvation." In other words, if they receive the grace of God in vain they will lose their chance for salvation. Paul is not playing around with them. If they continue on the path they are on, they will not "become the righteousness of God." We also note that Paul sandwiches 2 Corinthians 5:21, which speaks of Christ becoming sin for them so that they might become the righteousness of God, between verse 20 in which Paul pleads for them to be "reconciled" to God, and verse 6:1 which warns them not to receive the grace of God in vain. Verse 21, then, is a reminder to them of the potential result of Christ becoming sin for them, a potential result that in many of the Corinthians has thus far not been thoroughly realized. Though they started out with the "righteousness of God," the remaining question for the Corinthians is whether they will continue to possess and cultivate that righteousness to the end.

WHAT DOES PAUL MEAN WHEN HE SAYS: "AND IT WAS CREDITED UNTO HIM AS RIGHTEOUSNESS"

We must now investigate one of the most popular Protestant arguments for the concept of imputed righteousness. This matter concerns the use of the word "credited."[10] This word can refer to reckon, calculate, take into account, put on someone's account, estimate, evaluate, look upon as, consider, think, dwell on, believe, be of the opinion of. Protestant exegesis, especially that of Romans 4 where the Greek word appears twelve times, has consistently understood the word in the sense of "credited." As noted earlier, the analogy drawn to describe the righteousness credited to Abraham in Romans 4 is that of an accountant giving a "credit" to Abraham's ledger book, a credit that was secured completely by the work of Christ in the atonement. Abraham is understood as one who has "something to his credit" so that when God looks at his ledger book, as it were, he sees that, in accounting terms, Abraham is in the black. One Evangelical Protestant comments:

> This verb most often indicates "what a person, considered by himself, is not, or does not have, but is reckoned, held or regarded to be, or to have. It is clear then that when Abraham was justified by his faith, the righteousness which was reckoned or "charged to his account" was a righteousness not his own but that of another, namely, the righteousness of Christ.[11]

Unfortunately, this analysis presents a false premise which leads to a false conclusion. First, the Greek verb for "credited" does not "most often indicate" what someone or something is merely "considered" to be but is not so in reality. The New Testament uses the Greek word 41 times. But most of these refer to what someone is thinking as a mental representation of the *reality* they are witnessing.[12] In only a few instances is the word used as a mental representation of something that does *not exist* in reality.[13] Hence, the preponderant evidence shows that the word "credited" denotes more of what is *recognized* or *understood* intrinsically of a person or thing than a mere crediting to the person or thing something that is not intrinsic to it. In the case of Abraham, for example, we can understand the phrase "his faith is credited as righteousness" in Romans 4:5 such that God is recognizing or viewing Abraham's faith as righteousness, or that God interpreted the faith Abraham demonstrated as righteousness, or both. This is very different from saying that God merely "credited" Abraham with righteousness as if to say that Abraham was not really showing any righteous qualities when he demonstrated his faith but that God, because of the alien righteousness of Christ, merely gave him the label of righteousness.

Let's look at other evidence Scripture gives us for the concept of infusion. In Psalm 32:1. David declares: "Blessed is he whose transgressions are forgiven, whose sins are covered. Blessed is the man whose sin the Lord does not count against him and in whose spirit is no deceit." Notice that in connection with being "forgiven," "covered," and "sin...not counted against him," David speaks of one "in whose spirit is no deceit." This statement is speaking of the inner quality — the spiritual essence — of the person as he is being forgiven. His spirit has no deceit. It is not merely a legal covering given to David but a restoration or recognition of his inner nature. Lest we be confused about this additional dimension to David's justification, he reiterates these same terms even more vividly in the companion passage of Psalm 51, a passage which is concerned with the same sin of David. In Psalm 51:9-12, David writes of himself:

> Hide your face from my sins and blot out all my iniquity. Create in me a pure heart, O God, and renew a steadfast spirit within me. Do not cast me from your presence or take your Holy Spirit from me. Restore to me the joy of your salvation and grant me a willing spirit to sustain me.

As we learned in chapter 4, Paul is using David's experience in Psalm 32 and its companion passage of Psalm 51 as the reference point and definition for justification. In other words, what happened to David in Psalms 32 and 51 is what happens when one is justified. His sins are blotted out, but in addition, David speaks of his inner nature being changed. He wants God to create a "pure heart" and "renew a steadfast spirit" within him. He asks that God not take his "Holy Spirit" from him and desires that God will grant a "willing spirit" to sustain him. What clearer language could there be to describe the subjective change of the one whose sins are blotted out and covered? Similarly, statements such as "Wash away all my iniquity and cleanse me from my sin" in 51:2 and "Surely you desire truth in the inward parts; you teach me wisdom in the innermost place" in 51:6 show the convergence of God's mindful forgiving of sin at the same time that he changes the inner essence of the person he forgives. The two events are simultaneous and it is Paul who is combining the simultaneity under the exclusive term *justification* in Romans 4:5- 8, not the Protestant notion of sanctification.

As we learned in chapter 4, justification is a process. The process comprises both the infusion of righteousness into the individual and God's recognition of that righteousness. These two facets of justification are like two strands of a rope, intertwining and interweaving with each other. It is the action of God's grace that initiates and accomplishes the process. God makes the first move in the life of the individual through "prevenient" grace, i.e., "that which comes before."[14] As the individual responds to this grace both by faith and works, he attains a specific righteous quality in the eyes of God by merely responding to God's call and continuing to respond in faith, hope, and love. As we learned in previous chapters, God can look upon man's faith and works as meritorious and with the potential to gain righteousness because God is not viewing them from the system of uncompromising law but through the eyes of grace. It is the atonement of Christ that has made this new view of man possible. Thus, grace is both the lens through which God views us and the infused quality we receive from God to help us maintain his gracious view. At each point that God gives the individual his grace and he responds to that grace, one can say that he is "justified" in God's eyes. God gives both a justifying quality (infused grace) and continually recognizes and pronounces the individual "just" because he has the quality of righteousness within him. Hence, "to justify" refers both to the making righteous of the individual and the recognition of that same righteousness in God's eyes.

WHAT DOES PAUL TEACH IN ROMANS 8:33?

Romans 8:33 is one of the more popular verses of Scripture for theorists of imputed righteousness. Analyzing this verse in its context, however, shows that it not only denies the theory of imputation, but it resolutely confirms justification by infusion.

We can start with the stipulation that the opposite of "condemnation" is "justification." But a person is not condemned who does not have qualities about him that can be condemned — qualities that by his conduct he has exhibited to the world. He does not receive a sentence of condemnation for something he is not or that he has not done or with which he has not been identified. That would be a "legal fiction." Similarly, in a court of law, the judge does not justify a person he knows is guilty of the crime in question. He cannot pronounce him just if he is unjust. Moreover, if he is condemned for what he *is* or *has done*, by the same token, it is only equitable that he is justified for what he *is not* or the crime he *has not done*.

These elementary principles of equity hold as regards the *justification* and *condemnation* in Romans 8:33. For example, in Romans 8:30, Paul lays out the *ordo salutis* (order of salvation), "And those he predestined, he also called; those he called, he also justified; those he justified, he also glorified." This *ordo salutis* is connected to the previous verse which adds "foreknowledge" to the order: "For those God foreknew he also predestined to be conformed to the likeness of his Son, that he might be the firstborn among many brothers." Here we see that the purpose of predestination is to conform one to the likeness of Christ. This verse uses two concepts: "conformed to the likeness" and "firstborn among many brothers," which have their end result in the final resurrection of the body, or what Romans 8:33 terms "glorification." The same usage of these phrases in other parts of the New Testament supports this interpretation.

Immediately noticeable by its absence from the order of salvation of Romans 8:33, however, is the aspect of *sanctification*. This is no accident. It shows us that Paul is subsuming sanctification within the realm of justification. In Paul's view, justification occurs after the "call" and continues until the "glorification." Protestant theology holds that sanctification occurs between justification and glorification and is distinct from both. As we have noted previously, this is not the way Paul or other New Testament writers portray justification. Although justification is used in reference to the past, it is also used in reference to the present and future.[15]

To demonstrate the transformational aspect of justification, even though the primary reference to being *conformed to the image of the Son* is to the future glorification, the New Testament uses such terminology in reference to the process of justification/sanctification. We note this in the verbal cognate of the word "conformed" used in Philippians 3:10-12:

> That I may know him and the power of his resurrection and the fellowship of his sufferings, *being conformed* to his death, if somehow I may attain to the resurrection from the dead. Not as though I had already received it or been made perfect, but I follow after if indeed I may lay hold of that for which I was laid hold of by Christ Jesus.

Here Paul speaks of presently "being conformed to his death" in expectation of attaining to the resurrection, hence, the *conforming* that is taking place here is prior to the resurrection. Within the present *conforming*, Paul includes "the fellowship of his sufferings" and that he has "not already...been made perfect." His final goal is to be totally conformed to the image of Christ in the resurrection, but prior to that he is "being conformed to his death" through his suffering and his striving for perfection on earth. In other words, he must be conformed to his death before he can be conformed to his resurrection. Because Christ's death entailed suffering, Paul must also go through similar suffering so that he may finally attain to the resurrection. As Paul goes through this suffering, he is justified and sanctified more and more.

Paul speaks similarly of the justification/sanctification process in other passages. For example, in 2 Corinthians 3:18 he writes: "And we, who with unveiled faces all reflect the Lord's glory, *are being transformed into his likeness*, with ever-increasing glory..." Here Paul speaks of the ongoing "transforming into the likeness" of Christ. This is occurring presently in the life of each Christian as his will is conformed to Christ's. As Paul said above in Philippians 3:10, this transformation into Christ's likeness occurs through the sufferings he sustains and his striving for perfection. According to Colossians 3:10, it is also accomplished through knowledge: "And having put on the new self which is being renewed in *knowledge* in the image [likeness] of his Creator." Paul also speaks of the "trans-formation" and "renewal" in Romans 12:2: "Do not conform any longer to the pattern of this world, but be *transformed* by the *renewing* of your mind."

We can see from all these interconnecting passages that Romans 8:29's teaching that we are conformed into the image of Christ involves both our present life and our future life at the resurrection. Under the terms of Paul's *ordo salutis* in Romans 8:30, the present "conforming," "transforming," and "renewing" into the likeness of Christ falls under the rubric of "justification." It is in this justification that we are conformed to the image of Christ presently, awaiting our final conforming at the glorification as we receive our resurrection bodies.

Paul also makes clear that our conforming to the likeness of Christ involves our justification by the way he uses the word "justified" in connection with sanctification. We note this in 1 Corinthians 6:11 where Paul writes:

> ...nor thieves nor the greedy nor drunkards nor slander-ers nor swindlers will inherit the kingdom of God. And that is what some of you were. But you were washed, you were sanctified, you were justified in the name of the Lord Jesus Christ and by the Spirit of our God.

The context of this passage concerns the present life of the Corinthians. The reference to "washed" probably refers to their baptism (cf., 1 Cor. 1:14-17; 12:13; Acts 22:16). It is at this "washing" that they are "sanctified" and "justified." Clearly, by the context in which these words are placed in 1 Corinthians 6:10-11, this tripartite event in the past refers exclusively to the time they were *intrinsically* made righteous. They were once despicable sinners engaging in many and varied sins but at their washing, sanctification, and justification, these sins were removed and they became righteous — new creations (cf. 2 Cor. 5:17; Gal 6:16). Thus, 1 Corinthians 6:11 associates the term "justification" with the trans-formational change in the individual that we have seen above in Romans 12:2; 2 Corinthians 3:18; Philippians 3:10; and Colossians 3:10.[16] Paul reinforces this concept in 1 Corinthians 6:11 by referring to the action of "the Spirit of our God" which is normally associated with the transformational aspects of the Christian life, especially in the extended context of the verses in question, i.e., Romans 8:1-27. That Paul is subsuming sanctification under justification (or vice-versa) is also evident by his listing sanctification *before* justification in 1 Corinthians 6:11 as if to break down any notion that the two are separate, distinct or follow any particular order. This agrees with the evidence in Romans 8:30, which leaves sanctification out and subsumes it under the title of "justified."

We see the Spirit's action in justification as well in Titus 3:5-7:

> ...he saved us not because of righteous things we had done but because of his mercy. He saved us through the *washing of rebirth and renewal by the Holy Spirit* whom he poured out on us generously through Jesus Christ our Savior, so that, *being justified by his grace...*

Here we notice that in the same breath that Paul speaks of "being saved through the washing of *regeneration and renewal* by the Holy Spirit," he pinpoints the time this was done for us as "being justified by his grace." Justification occurs when we were "saved," "rebirthed," and "renewed." The New Testament uses the word "renewed" in only one other passage, Romans 12:2, cited above. In that verse Paul refers to the "renewing of your mind" in the context of the holiness expected in Christian life. The word "rebirth" is used only one other place in the New Testament, Matthew 19:28, in which Jesus speaks of the final glorification as the "regeneration" As we have seen, other New Testament passages use similar terms for justification, sanctification and glorification. The terminology is fluid such that one aspect can stand for another or overlap into another's territory. Justification is a "rebirth" and "renewal" as much as sanctification and glorification. Hence, one cannot escape observing that justification is spoken of as an inner *transformation* by Paul.

In the description of justification in Titus 3:5-7, the phrase in verse 6 accentuates the Holy Spirit's life-changing action: "by the Holy Spirit whom he ["God our Savior," from verse 4] poured out on us...so that being justified..." Here we see that Paul uses the term "pouring out" of the Holy Spirit to describe the "justification," "rebirth" and "renewal."

Paul uses the words "pouring out" in another passage that speaks of justification — Romans 5:1-5. He begins in verse 1 by declaring, "Therefore, since we are justified through faith..." This statement treats the justification as a past event. Paul uses another past tense verb in verse 5 as he says, "God has *poured out* his love into our hearts by the Holy Spirit." The past reception of faith and love is coupled with "hope" as Paul says in verse 3, "we rejoice in the hope," and in verse 5, "hope does not disappoint us." Hence, we understand that at the justification introduced in Romans 5:1, the individual received an infusion of faith, hope and love.[17]

Romans 6:6-7 also uses the term justification in reference to sanctification: "For we know that our old self was crucified with him so that the body of sin might be done away with, that we should no longer be slaves to sin — because anyone who has died has been *justified* from sin." As in 1 Corinthians 6:11 cited above, the context of Romans 6 concerns the Christian life. In fact, Paul, just as he reminded the Corinthians, reminds the Romans of their baptism. Paul mentions baptism specifically in verses 1-4:

> What shall we say, then? Shall we go on sinning so that grace may increase? By no means! We died to sin; how can we live in it any longer? Or don't you know that all of us who were baptized into Christ Jesus were baptized into his death. We were therefore buried with him through baptism into death in order that, just as Christ was raised from the dead through the glory of the Father, we too may live a new life.

As Paul pointed to the "washing" in 1 Corinthians 6:11 and Titus 3:5, so he points to "baptism" in Romans 6:1-4. As it was for the Corinthians, baptism is the beginning of justification and sanctification for the Romans. In being baptized, they become partakers in Christ's death and thus become "dead" to sin. Paul tells them that they must live a new life — a life free from sin. Paul concludes in Romans 6:7 that one who has "died" [died with Christ in baptism] has been *justified* from sin. One of the more curious aspects of this verse is that Paul could have used two other words in place of *justified* that would have given the same meaning he intended. He uses them elsewhere in this context. One appears in Romans 6:18, where Paul says, "you have been set *free* from sin and become slaves to God." Romans 6:20, 22 uses the same phrasing. In all three cases Paul is using the "free/slave" metaphors for illustration. The other word Paul could have used is "sanctified" (e.g., "anyone who has died has been sanctified from sin"). Since "sanctified" carries the meaning of "set apart from" or "separated from" it would have been an appropriate term to show the Christian's separation from sin. In fact, "sanctified" may have been a better word to use since it specifically denotes cleansing and holiness. Its noun cognate is used in Romans 6:19 ("leading to holiness") and 6:22 ("leads to holiness").[18] Yet Paul chose to use the word "justified" in Romans 6:7, the same word he used singularly in reference to God "justifying the ungodly" in Romans 4:5, for example. In other words, in Romans 6:7 Paul understands and is using the term "justification" as a synonym for sanctification. Now we can understand even more why Paul's usage does not refer to a forensic justification but can and must refer to a transformational justification. The justification involves a separation or cleansing from sin. The ungodly become justified because sin has been washed from their soul and they have become renewed.

Further evidence regarding the transformational aspect of justification in Romans 6:7 is the emphasis beginning in 6:5-6 in which Paul states: "If we have been united with him in the likeness of his death, we will certainly also be united with him in his resurrection. For we know that our old self was crucified with him so that the body of sin might be done away with..." We will recall that Paul spoke of the same occurrence in Philippians 3:10: "I want to know the power of his resurrection and the fellowship of sharing in his sufferings, becoming like [conformed to] him in his death..." In the former verse, Romans 6:5, Paul is connecting "being united with Christ in his death through baptism" with the death of the old self and renunciation of the sinful life. In the latter verse, Paul speaks of becoming like Christ in his death by going through the "fellowship of his sufferings." Both are speaking about the sanctified Christian life and both anticipate its completion in the resurrection of the body.

We will also recall that Paul used a particular word in Philippians 3:10 that was used in Romans 8:29 — the word *conformed*. In Philippians 3:10, Paul indicates that he is "conformed to the death of Christ" in anticipation of the resurrection, whereas in Romans 8:29 he is "being conformed to the image of the Son" in anticipation of his glorification, i.e., the resurrection. In Romans 6:1-6 it is baptism that initiates the conforming to the Son in his death. According to 1 Corinthians 6:11, it is the "washing," i.e., baptism, that initiates the justification and sanctification to make one righteous and pure, conformed to the image of Christ. What all of this points to is that when Paul says in Romans 8:33, "It is God who justifies, who is he that condemns," the justification to which he is referring encompasses the entire life of the Christian. The sanctification of the Christian is subsumed under the term justification in Romans 8:33 just as it is in Romans 8:30. It is the process by which sin is eradicated from the life of the individual so that he may be conformed to the image of Christ presently in his soul and finally in his body at the physical resurrection of the last day.

BACK TO ABRAHAM

The difference between God viewing Abraham's faith as a measure of righteousness (the Catholic view) and God merely crediting Abraham with an alien righteousness (the Protestant view), hearkens back to the distinction made earlier in chapters 1-2 concerning the kind of faith that Abraham was required to give to God. Abraham's faith was not merely believing that God was his Savior. He did not merely accept God into his heart and then go on his way never having to be concerned about his salvation again. Rather, from the beginning to the very end in Abraham's life, God required great faith and love from Abraham. God placed Abraham in situations that seemed to question the very integrity of God, e.g., calling him from his home to go to a promised land that he never received (Gen. 12; Heb. 11); promising a child to parents who were a century old (Gen. 15; Rom. 4:16f); telling him to slay his own son (Gen. 22). In putting Abraham through these tests, God was attempting to draw out something deep within the heart of Abraham. In other words, God was looking for something intrinsic to Abraham

— an uncompromising, undaunted faith and love in God that accepted Him regardless of the circumstantial evidence. When God determines, from the capacity given, that a person such as Abraham has developed this kind of deep and seasoned character, he in turn views that faith and love as *righteousness*. In short, it is faith, hope and love, that *is* the righteousness of Christ, not faith that forensically apprehends the righteousness of Christ.

The object of Abraham's faith in Genesis 12-22 is God Himself, in *all* his plans, works, and majesty. The preponderant message in Genesis is that Abraham must believe not only that God is his Savior, but also that *God is all that he says he is*, despite the circumstantial evidence suggesting otherwise. The descriptions of faith in the Genesis accounts, and in Hebrews 11, state clearly that it is not merely that Abraham acknowledge the promised seed, but that he fully make God his Lord — that he believe and obey without question everything that God tells him no matter how difficult it may be to accept. Paul, likewise, makes this very clear in Romans 4:17-21 where he takes great pains to describe the tremendous inner quality of Abraham's faith by such phrases as "against all hope," "without weakening," "not wavering," and finally "was fully persuaded that God had power to do what he promised." These words would be superfluous if all Abraham had to do was accept God as his Savior.

Romans 4:18 explains that precisely because of Abraham's undying faith in God, it *then* becomes possible for him to become the father of many nations and produce the promised seed of Galatians 3:16. Paul writes in Romans 4:18, "Against all hope, Abraham in hope believed and so became the father of many nations, just as it had been said to him, 'So shall your offspring [seed] be.'" The very salvation of Abraham, and the salvation of the nations coming from him, rides on the deep and sustained faith of Abraham. Paul insists that it was *this* faith — the faith that believed God had power to do what he said despite the circumstances — that was "credited to him as righteousness," as Paul says in Romans 4:22: *"This is why"* it was credited to him as righteousness."

Paul reinforces this meaning by the next two verses which speak of the faith that those coming after Abraham must also have to be credited with righteousness: "The words, 'it was credited to him,' were written not for him alone, but also for us, to whom God will credit righteousness — for us who believe *in him* who raised Jesus our Lord from the dead." Here we see that it is not merely believing in the atonement, but believing *in him* [God] — the God who calls things that are not as if they were — behind the atonement. Just as Abraham believed that God had the power to raise Isaac from the dead, so we who believe God had the power to raise Jesus from the dead will be credited with righteousness for that belief. This faith, combined with a continuing life of love and hope, even as Abraham exhibited, will procure our salvation. God can graciously accept our faith, hope, and love because Christ provided such gracious acceptance of us in the atonement and resurrection. Through grace, God infuses these qualities into the individual, making him righteous in God's eyes and worthy of salvation.

As Protestant theologians attempt to confine the object of faith to "faith in the alien righteousness of Christ," in effect, faith becomes merely a "code word" for "Christ's righteousness" so as to confine faith to the soteriological area of legal imputation. *It is a fact, however, that the New Testament never uses such language.* Although no one would dispute that faith certainly includes the righteousness of Christ as its object, it is never limited to that dimension. The New Testament uses the phrase "faith in Jesus Christ" several times but never in a one-to-one correspondence with the atonement; rather, it refers to faith in the whole person of Christ as creator, sustainer, provider, redeemer, helper, healer, etc. In other words, it is belief in *Him,* as a personal being, that is the substance and object of faith. As noted in chapter 1, Romans 4:24 specifies belief "in *Him* (God) who raised Jesus our Lord from the dead," not just a belief that Jesus was raised. Hence, we are not "appropriating" Christ's righteousness, we are believing in God, the Trinity, in all his splendor and magnificence, though we cannot see Him physically. It is the belief in Him, personally, and in all that he stands for and has done that is recognized as righteousness in the eyes of God precisely because we cannot see him.

One might ask that if God is viewing Abraham's faith as the righteousness itself, then what part does the righteousness of God or the atonement of Christ have in the righteousness of Abraham? The answer is very simple. God and Abraham are working together. God has provided the means by which he can place Abraham in the way of grace. The means is the atonement of Christ. As we learned from Romans 3:25, "God presented him as a sacrifice of atonement...and in his forbearance he had left the sins committed beforehand unpunished..." Abraham's sins, like those of everyone else who receives the grace of God, are atoned for and forgiven in anticipation and on the basis of the death and resurrection of Christ. Through the power of the atonement, God puts Abraham in a gratuitous relationship. Within this relationship, Abraham is expected to continue in faith, love, and obedience in order to please God and develop an intimate relationship. To do this, God tests him, at times very severely, to cultivate and draw out faith, hope, and love. Through the grace that God has infused into Abraham, Abraham is able to act in faith. It is not just Abraham who is involved in the act of faith. God also is intimately at work in Abraham's heart. Although God is at work in Abraham, Abraham must respond and cooperate with the grace of God to procure the faith that God requires. God will not test Abraham above what he can bear but Abraham must act on the measure of grace that God gives him (cf., 1 Cor. 10:13; 1 Peter 1:6-7; 2 Peter 2:9).

We are not any different from Abraham. Paul states that we must also "walk in the footsteps of faith that our father Abraham had..." (Romans 4:12). As Abraham did, we must believe in a God who "calls things that are not as though they were" (Romans 4:18); we must "not weaken in faith" or "waver in unbelief regarding the promise of God" (Romans 4:19-20); we must be "strengthened in faith" and "give glory to God" being "fully persuaded that he has the power to do what he promised" (Romans 4:20-21). In short, God will view us as righteous if we "believe *in him* who raised Jesus our Lord from the dead." It is not just a belief in the resurrection, per se, but a belief in "him" (that is, God) who we believe has the power to raise Jesus even though it seems impossible. We must believe he has done what he promised and will do what he promises, even though we face many temptations to believe otherwise (cf. 1 Cor 15:1-18; Hebrews 3:12-14; 2 Peter 3:3-9). As God tested Abraham's faith, so he will test our faith, over and over for our entire lifetime. At each point God will attempt to draw out of us the faith that "pleases" him — a faith, as Paul says, "believes that he exists <u>and</u> is the rewarder of those who diligently seek him" (Hebrews 11:6). We work out our salvation in faith and obedience and we have the confidence that God, through his grace infused in us, is enabling us to please him.

SUMMARY POINTS

1) The general Protestant concept of justification teaches that by an act of faith man is credited or imputed with the alien righteousness of Christ. Although there are many views of justification among them, generally speaking, Protestants understand justification as an single, extrinsic, legal act of God which does not involve any transformation of the individual's inner nature. They reserve the inner change of the individual for the area of sanctification. The Catholic concept of justification teaches that God infuses man with sanctifying grace which justifies the individual before God by transforming his inner nature. The individual increases in sanctifying grace and thus his justification increases and progresses throughout his life.

2) Catholic theology teaches that God prompts the individual to seek for justification through the action of *actual* grace. God requires that man respond to and cooperate with his grace in order to receive salvation. Once justified, man continues to cooperate with God within the realm of grace.

3) Scripture consistently uses the words "righteousness" and "justified" to refer to the righteousness and justified state of the individual, thus affirming the Catholic view.

4) The phrase "righteousness of God" refers to the righteous quality of God but also to the righteousness that God infuses into the individual.

5) Habakkuk 2:4 ("the just shall live by faith"), which Paul quotes in Romans 1:17, does not teach righteousness by imputation; rather, it refers to the intrinsic faith God expects of Habakkuk while he waits for God's providence.

6) The Protestant claim that the word "credited" or "reckoned" refers not to what actually exists within the person, but only what God designates or classifies him to be, is incorrect. The preponderant usage of these words in Scripture refers to what actually exists within the individual, thus affirming the concept of infusion.

7) The New Testament is replete with evidence connecting the inner renewal or transformation of the individual with justification.

8) Attempts to alter the language of Romans 4:3, 4:22 and Galatians 3:6 to say that Abraham's belief is *not* what God counts for righteousness, are incorrect. God recognizes Abraham as righteous precisely for his faith.

9) The Catholic view understands that what God declares is in accord with what he views in the object he is addressing. In other words, God declares man righteous in justification because he has made him intrinsically righteous.

10) The Protestant theory of legal imputation neither offers no adequate answer as to why God requires faith from the individual in order to attain justification, nor does it adequately explain why God requires a certain quality of faith. Some Protestants understand faith as a condition for justification, others do not.

11) Some separate faith from repentance in order to maintain the stance that no works are required for justification. This dichotomy is not supported by Scripture.

END NOTES

[1] Council of Trent, Session 6, Chapter 8: "...because faith is the beginning of human salvation, the foundation and root of all justification, without which it is impossible to please God and to come to the fellowship of his sons; and are, therefore, said to be justified gratuitously, because none of those things which pre-

cede justification, whether faith or works merit the grace itself of justification; for if it is a grace, it is not now by reason of works; otherwise (as the Apostle says) grace is no more grace."

2 Council of Trent, Session 6, Chapter 5: "...freely assenting to and cooperating with the same grace...nor on the other hand can he of his own free will without the grace of God move himself to justice before Him."

3 Council of Trent, Session 6, Chapter 13: "For God, unless men be wanting in his grace, as He has begun a good work, so will He perfect it, working to will and to accomplish [Phil. 2:13]. Nevertheless, let those who think themselves to stand, take heed lest they fall [1 Cor. 10:12], and with fear and trembling work out their salvation [Phil. 2:12] in labors, in watchings, in almsdeeds, in prayers and oblations, in fastings and charity [2 Cor. 6:3]. For they ought to fear, knowing that they are born again unto the hope of glory, and not as yet unto glory in the combat that yet remains with the flesh, with the world, with the devil, in which they cannot be victors, unless with God's grace they obey the Apostle saying, 'We are debtors, not to the flesh, to live according to the flesh. For if you live according to the flesh, you shall die. But if by the spirit you mortify the deeds of the flesh, you shall live [Rom. 8:12].' " Session 6, Chapter 16: "And whereas in many things we all offend, each one should have before his eyes the severity and judgment as well as mercy and goodness; neither ought anyone to judge himself, even though he be not conscious to himself of anything, since the whole life of man must be judged and examined not by the judgment of men, but of God, who will bring to light the hidden things of darkness, and will make manifest the counsels of the heart, and then shall every man have praise from God, who, as it is written, 'will render to every man according to his works.' "

4 Council of Trent, Session 6, Chapter 16: "For since Jesus Christ Himself...continually infuses His virtue into the said justified, a virtue which always precedes their good works, and which accompanies and follows them, and without which they could in no wise be pleasing and meritorious before God...Thus neither is our own justice established as our own from ourselves, nor is the justice of God ignored or repudiated; for that justice which is

called ours, because we are justified through its inherence in us, that same is (the justice) of God, because it is infused into us by God through the merit of Christ." The grace given to the faithful for the purpose of performing some special task or overcoming a certain obstacle is called "actual" grace (*Catholic Catechism*, Sections 1084, 1127-31, 1392- 1395, et al.). One obtains it through the sacraments and prayer (CC, Section 1966, 2003, 2558-2865).

5   Council of Trent, Session 6, Chapter 7: "...but we are truly called and are just, receiving justice within us, each one according to his own measure, which the Holy Spirit distributes to everyone as he wills [1 Cor. 12:11], and according to each one's own disposition and cooperation."

6   The Old Testament also speaks of such action of God, cf., Exodus 31:2-3; Psalm 84:11; Numbers 6:25.

7   Matt. 6:33; Rom. 1:17; 3:5,21,22; 10:3; 2 Cor. 5:21; Phil. 3:9; James 1:20; 2 Pet. 1:20.

8   Council of Trent, Session 6, Chapter 16: "Thus neither is our own justice established as our own from ourselves, nor is the justice of God ignored or repudiated; for that justice which is called ours, because we are justified through its inherence in us, that same is (the justice) of God, because it is infused into us by God through the merit of Christ."

9   Compare the following: Romans 1:2, "the gospel of God — the gospel he promised beforehand through his prophets in the Holy Scriptures regarding his Son..."; Romans 3:2, "But now a righteousness from God, apart from the law, has been made known, to which the Law and the Prophets testify"; Hebrews 4:2, "For we also have had the gospel preached to us, just as they did..."; Hebrews 4:6, "...and those who formerly had the gospel preached to them did not go in, because of their disobedience."

10   From the Greek "logizomai."

11   Joel Beeke in *Justification by Faith Alone*, ed., Don Kistler, (Morgan, PA: Soli Deo Gloria Publications, 1995), p. 56.

12   cf., Luke 22:37; Rom. 3:28; 6:11; 9:8; 1 Cor. 4:1; 13:5,11; Phil, 3:13; 4:8; Heb. 11:19, et al.

13   cf., Rom. 2:26; 2 Cor. 12:6

14   Council of Trent: "It furthermore declares that in adults the beginning of that justification must be derived from the predispos-

ing grace of God through Jesus Christ, that is, from his vocation, whereby without any existing merits on their part they are called, so that they who by sin were turned away from God, through His stimulating and assisting grace are disposed to convert themselves to their own justification, by freely assenting to and cooperating with the same grace..." Session 6, Chapter 5, (cf., Lamentations 5:21; Jeremiah 3:22; Zechariah 1:3).

[15] *Past*: Romans 5:1; 1 Cor. 6:11; Titus 3:7. *Present*: Romans 8:33; Acts 13:39; Gal. 2:17; James 2:24. *Future*: 1 Cor. 4:4-5; Matt. 12:37; Romans 2:13.

[16] To this we can add Scripture's numerous metaphors which illustrate the soul's transformation by the removal of sin. Sin is said to be: (1) washed or cleansed away: Psalm 51:2,7; Isaiah 1:16; Ezek. 36:25; Acts 22:16; Hebrews 1:3; 1 John 1:7; (2) blotted out: Isaiah 43:25; (3) swept away: Isaiah 44:23; (4) wiped out: Acts 3:19; (5) taken away: 2 Sam. 12:13; 1 Chr. 21:8; John 1:29; (6) removed: Psalm 103:12; (7) leaving no deceit: Psalm 32:2.

[17] The Catholic Council of Trent held that "...he is ingrafted, receives in the said justification together with the remission of sins all these [gifts] are infused at the same time: faith, hope, and charity" (Session 6, Chapter 7, DS 800).

[18] The noun cognates are usually translated as *sanctification* (e.g., 1 Cor. 1:30; 1 Thess. 4:3,4,7; 2 Thess. 2:13; 1 Pet. 1:2).

HOW CAN I GET TO HEAVEN

CHAPTER 7

IS JUSTIFICATION LIKE A COURTROOM PROCEEDING OR A FAMILY RESTORATION?

The Protestant view of justification begins with the idea that God is a Judge who must bring the accused sinner before the bar of justice to be condemned for his crimes. In God's courtroom, the law stands as the prosecuting attorney exposing the utter imperfection and multitude of sins of the defendant. Having no defense against these charges, the sinner is convicted as a criminal and sentenced to condemnation. But there is a way of escape. God has provided a substitute who will stand in place of the accused criminal. The substitute is Christ. Christ stands before the bar of God's justice in place of the sinner and takes the full wrath of God for the latter's crimes. Prior to taking the punishment for the sinner, Christ shows the judge by his perfect obedience to the law that he himself is not a criminal. Thus, Christ's active obedience (living a sinless life) and his passive obedience (suffering condemnation) constitute the "righteousness of Christ." In turn, this righteousness of Christ is "imputed" to the sinner, that is, the righteousness is transferred or credited to the sinner so that God's scrutiny as judge is directed towards the transferred righteousness, not the sinner himself. Having the perfect righteousness of Christ given to him, the accused criminal, though still a sinner within his nature, can be set free from the court of law. Once freed, the justification process is over. He is granted all the rights and privileges of the pardon that stems from his release. In his freedom, he must now imitate Christ and be obedient to his new Father, God Almighty. There is one requirement in this gracious provision, however. In order for it to be appropriated by him, the convicted sinner must *believe* all this is possible. Even though he does not have to show that he himself is perfectly righteous to the Judge, he must exercise the proper faith in order for the Judge to allow Christ to serve as his perfect substitute. If he does not believe, then he must stand before the Judge on his own and with the certainty that he will be convicted and sentenced.

Catholicism's view of justification, although it may have its legal facets, is not defined nor dependent on western society's notion of courtroom legality. The first fact we must recognize is that Scripture does not use courtroom imagery to describe our initial justification. Paul does not appeal to the Roman court system when describing justification, rather, he appeals to the covenant fathers such as Abraham, Moses and David. If the courtroom model were being portrayed, we would expect Scripture to create vivid scenes of a criminal standing before a judge, perhaps with an attorney present to defend his case. We would expect, in reference to justification, to see terminology associated with a courtroom scene, e.g., court, judge, jury, verdict, books, defendant, witness, attorney, acquitted, etc. Although Scripture employs scenes and descriptions of this nature, it does so only in reference to the Final Judgment.[1] Instead, we invariably see Scripture using *familial* imagery to describe our initial justification. For example, Romans 8:15- 33; Galatians 3:24-4:5 and Ephesians 1:5 describe justification in terms of filial *adoption*.[2] To illustrate related topics, Paul uses the imagery of the marriage and its dissolution through death in Romans 7:1-4 as a prelude to his discussion on the relationship between law and grace in Romans 7:5-25. Similarly, he uses the allegorical account of the two wives of Abraham, Sarah and Hagar, in Galatians 4:21-31 to illustrate the difference between the promise and law. These, and other passages, suggest that there is much more to the understanding of justification which is beyond the courtroom. As we have learned from chapters 4–6, justification is a process whereby God continually infuses his grace into the individual, substantially changing him to be pleasing to God and acceptable for citizenship in his kingdom. The present chapter will show us that it is the familial model, not the courtroom model, that effectively incorporates these two elements into justification.[3]

The following is a brief sketch of how this takes place. God calls the sinner, who is estranged from his heavenly Father because of the sin of Adam, back to join the heavenly family. A judge does not acquit him; rather, his father forgives him (as in the parable of Luke 15 when the Prodigal son came home to his father and received forgiveness). In reuniting with his spiritual family, he must resume the qualities of a son, and in order to be a divine son, he must be divine-like. Through his grace, God infuses these divine-like qualities into him, and he is now ready to become the *adopted* son of God, for God can only adopt that which is like Himself. It is because of the infusion of grace that the individual is given the legal title of "son," not vice-versa. The adopted son now in line for the inheritance, must show himself faithful and obedient to his Father, after which he, in turn, will receive a reign in the heavenly kingdom and live with the family of God forever. The process whereby he, under the tutelage of his Father, shows himself faithful and obedient, is justification. He continually pleases the Father and in turn shows himself to be a worthy son, justly deserving of the Father's blessing and inheritance.

To understand the familial model better one can simply look to the basic structure of family relationships. The relationships between the members of the family are primarily based on the mutual love and concern generated from emotional attachment. Within this framework, the family members show spontaneous and continual care and affection for each other. The parents love, protect, teach, and discipline their children, giving top priority to their spiritual, physical, emotional, and social well-being. The parents themselves show mutual love and respect to one another. When friction occurs among the family members, the offender is expected to seek forgiveness from the one harmed, and, of course, the one harmed is expected to forgive. Then, except in very serious confrontations, the concerns evaporate without thought of revenge. A family member does not, for example, seek "compensatory damages" from a court of law if one family member happens to get into a minor altercation with another. The emotional bond usually supersedes any recourse to legal action outside the family. Families usually settle altercations "in-house," as it were, as each family member, stimulated by the bonds of love, strives to work out any differences by mutual respect and forgiveness. If spouses are at odds with one another we expect them to reconcile in due time and make up for any harm by resuming acts of love and affection. If children disobey certain household rules, we expect the parent to deal with the infraction, discipline the child, and put things back to normal so that the household runs smoothly.

Yet while the familial model is for the most part based on the personal and emotional relationship between the members that supersedes recourse to law, there is a degree of overlap between the familial and legal dimensions of life. For example, before they are married, the bride and the groom must secure legal documentation stating that each partner is legally free to marry, e.g., that he or she has not previously created another family with someone else. Once married, the husband and wife, are expected to treat each other with mutual respect and love. Even in these emotional family bonds, each spouse is expected to obey certain household "rules" for the benefit of the entire family. If, for example, the husband abuses the wife, it may become so serious (e.g., her life is threatened) as to force the wife to avail herself of the legal authorities outside the home to put a restraining order on her husband. If one of the spouses engages in sexual intimacy with another person, the other spouse may eventually see no option except a legal divorce to terminate the spousal relationship. Similarly, parent and child are expected to have a reciprocal relationship. The parent is expected to love, protect, and provide for the child, and, the child, in turn, is expected to honor and obey the parent. If, however, the parent begins abusing the child, the legal authorities are brought in to separate the family member, punish the abuser, or both. Likewise, if the child shows himself to be unduly insubordinate (e.g., threatening the family with bodily harm or destruction), the civil authorities can become involved and put the child in juvenile detention. Hence, though the family is based on the mutual love and concern of each member for the other, a breakdown of that love and concern leaves only the law to deal with the deteriorated relationship. Relationships within the family can only supersede recourse to law if the family members maintain the dimensions of relationship that law does not have, i.e., love and forgiveness.

In contrast to family relationships, the relationship between a member of western society and his government, or other legal entity, is quite different. Each sector of society has a specific code of law by which it regulates and judges the conduct of its citizens. The government expects each member of society to obey all the rules and regulations stipulated. Whereas the family's laws are usually unwritten, the society's laws are written in fine detail. Specific laws prohibit every offense from jaywalking to murder. For example, if the speed limit is 55 mph and one travels 56 mph, technically, he has broken the law. In that sense, the law is exacting and uncompromising, showing no mercy to the offender and exacting a specific punishment or fine for every infraction.

Yet strict though the law may be, it often overlaps with elements of personality and emotion seen in family relations. In other words, it contains aspects of forgiveness and leniency. For example, a police officer does not always issue a ticket for a person who goes over the 55 mph speed limit. He may show mercy to someone who travels 56 mph. The police officer also has certain limitations in enforcing the law. He cannot physically stop everyone at the same time. Thus, there is a certain amount of involuntary forgiveness associated with law, as well as a certain amount of voluntary forgiveness depending on the disposition of the judge who is evaluating a particular infraction against the law. The judge may decide to give someone the "full extent of the law" for a particularly heinous crime or because of a defendant's belligerent attitude. Within the bounds set by the law, he may be more lenient to one person or another depending on the circumstances. Whereas the law itself is a rigid and uncompromising code that requires unconditional compliance, the judge is a thinking personality who can evaluate one contingency against another and make a final balanced decision that will serve the best interests of the law, the individual and the society as a whole. Because life and the situations it presents are frequently complex, judgments cannot always be made simply on the strict basis of law in computer-like fashion. Nevertheless, there is one thing about the law to which even the judge must submit. Once a person is brought before the law for an alleged crime, the law requires that the accused person receive a verdict of guilty or not guilty. The judge may determine the degree of punishment for a convicted criminal, or he may even decide that the case has no merit and thus throw it out of court. In any case, however, he must decide whether the accused has broken the law or not. He must convict him with a certain degree of punishment or he must set him free. Moreover, he cannot do this arbitrarily. If the accused is guilty of the crime, the judge, in his striving to be just, must punish the criminal; otherwise, law and justice have no meaning. As we move on in this study we will see more clearly the relationship between love and law, or mercy and justice.[4]

THE TRINITY: THE FIRST FAMILY

From all eternity God has existed. He had no beginning and will have no end. As He said to Moses when the latter inquired who God is, He simply yet profoundly replied, "I am who I am" (Exodus 3:14). In relation to our discussion comparing and contrasting family and law, God's identity is defined within himself, specifically in his Trinity. The Church has best defined the Trinity as "three persons in one God" or "three persons in one nature," that "nature" being Divinity. Within the Trinity, the position of each person defines his role; thus there is a Father, a Son, and a Holy Spirit. These are three distinct persons yet all are one God — a mystery indeed. For our purposes, however, as God identifies himself as Father, this forms the basis of our understanding of his relationship with the other members of the Godhead and with his creation. From all eternity God is a Father. He is not *like* a father nor does he merely have fatherly qualities. He is a real Father and he has a real Son, who one day became flesh. There was love and communication within the Trinity before the creation, during the creation, and there will be forevermore.

Being a Father to his eternal Son, God was also a father to his newly created son, Adam. This is where the Catholic understanding of God's filial relationship to man begins. Although not identical to Christ who is the natural Son of God, Adam was the "adopted" son of God. In Luke 3:23-38, Scripture even provides the genealogical record showing that the relationship between God and Adam is as father and son: "He was the son...of Enosh, the son of Seth, the son of Adam, the son of God."

For Adam, God the Father provided everything necessary to sustain life, both spiritually and physically. God gave Adam a garden that could produce various kinds of nourishment, and he protected Adam and Eve from all harm. In turn, God established certain "family" rules. He gave Adam and his wife, Eve, a "household rule" that they were to take care of the garden God created, to be its protector and cultivator. One specific rule God gave to Adam and Eve was not to eat of the tree of the knowledge of good and evil. This was to test their faithfulness and obedience. If Adam passed the test, he and all his sons would enjoy the position of remaining the sons of God forever.

Failing the test, Adam plunged himself and the whole human race into sin and death. In place of the intimate relationship of sonship, the Father convicted him and all his future sons of sin and they became outcasts in the eyes of God under sentence of death. Adam became a rebellious son, who was disinherited by his Father. Fortunately for Adam and the rest of the human race, God, in his mercy as Father, did not carry out the punishment of death immediately. God threw Adam out of his "house" and made him struggle for his sustenance in pain and sweat. Eventually, it would be necessary for something to be done concerning the impending sentence of death. If not, it would be carried out and condemn Adam and the human race to eternal banishment from sonship with God.

God, as Father, is gracious, merciful, and ready to forgive. He seeks to restore the familial relation that was severed with his adopted son. Fathers do not want to see their sons become victims of the unmerciful law which will utterly condemn them. God the Father is merciful with the human race. He is not willing that any should perish but that all should come to repentance (2 Peter 3:9). Or, as in the parable of the Prodigal son, the father wishes for the son to come to his senses and make his way back home to the family in repentance. As Peter says, "we call on a Father who judges each man's work impartially (1 Peter 1:17). After Adam's sin, God's first sign of fatherly mercy was Genesis 3:15's promise of a redeemer. In anticipation of this redeemer, God offered Adam and his progeny a way back. Although God had put Adam under the curse of sin and death, through his grace as Father, he did not totally forsake Adam nor leave him totally incapable of responding to God's invitation to be restored to the full rights of the family. Rather than execute him immediately for his crime as a Judge and Jury would do, God allowed Adam to exist, produce children, and subdue the earth, yet all the while facing the residual punishment for his disobedience if he did not make his way back to a full-fledged membership in the family. If God did not make provisions for him to rise from the dead, he would remain in a condemned state for eternity — unable to rise to eternal fellowship with his Father, forever abandoned to the abyss of the second death, eternal disinheritance.

GOD AND US: A FAMILY COVENANT

Scripture also speaks of the agreement between God and Adam as a covenant — a covenant that was broken. Hosea 6:7 states: "Like Adam, they have broken the covenant — they were unfaithful to me there." Here Hosea compares Israel's breaking of the covenant God established with them to the covenant Adam broke with God. Through his grace, God made the covenant with Adam which stated that he and all his progeny would be blessed if he would be faithful to the commands that God gave him. On the other hand, the covenant required that if Adam did not abide by its stipulations then he would have to suffer its penal sanctions. The penal sanctions of the covenant between God and Adam required that Adam, the one who sinned against the covenant, be put to death for his violation. Similarly, in Israel, those who broke the covenant, either of the nuclear family, the extended family or the remainder of society, were punished. Those of a serious nature were punished with death.

Pre-western cultures, like that of Israel (and upon which the Old Testament is based), exhibit a higher degree of convergence between the family and the society. The family was the basis of society; and kinship among its members was very strong. The Old Testament describes families and extended families in very intimate language, e.g., one member was the "flesh and bone" of another.[5] It would not be an exaggeration to say that Israel was originally one big family, which then filtered down into and made up the society on all levels. It was through the family unit that one understood reality and comprehended his standing with God and his place in the world. Within the family, each member learned the rules of life and was expected to carry this knowledge and commitment to the relationships within his extended family of grandparents, uncles, aunts, cousins, and other generic groups such as tribes and clans (e.g., Joshua 7:16-18).The father was the head of his family, yet he was only one of a long line of fathers that could be traced back to the beginning of Israel's history. To be a true Israelite, one had to know his "line of fathers" or genealogy. This is one reason why the Chronicler, after the Jews returned from 70 years in captivity in Babylon, records the history of Israel by first listing the genealogy of Israel in minute detail (1 Chronicles 1-10). The time after the Babylonian captivity began a new era and in doing so each family had to know whence it came and all the families preceding it. Israelite society knew and defined families by the father's family name and reputation. These fathers were kings, priests, elders, prophets, soldiers, etc. The father of one family had intimate ties with the father of another family. Even in death, one was said to "go to his fathers" (Gen. 15:15). In the father and son relationship, the son inherited everything that the father was, e.g., his character, his aspirations, his accomplishments, his possessions, his learning, his trade. The son was so identified with the father that he was known as "the son of" his father's name.[6] If a son became disobedient, he disgraced his father, and, particularly, his father's name. Honor then had to be restored to the father. Sometimes the father publicly repudiated and punished his son for his sins. This restored the honor of the father in the eyes of his fellow fathers.

The glue that held the nuclear family together, and connected it with all the extended families of Israel, was the concept of "covenant." Basically, covenant was an agreement between two or more consenting parties to show mutual love and concern and to abide by certain rules agreed upon by both parties for the benefit of each. The covenant's purpose was to perpetuate the relationship between the parties and thus avoid its disintegration and destruction. Hence, while personal interest motivated those within a covenant, rules of legality also prohibited one party from taking advantage of the other. Such covenantal relationships permeated Israelite society. If one of the parties broke the covenant, the guilty party incurred specific penalties.

As an agreement between two parties that involves penal sanctions for violations, the concept of covenant incorporates a certain degree of legality into the various relationships it encompasses. In effect, no matter how personal and emotional the relationship between two parties, a legal dimension is always present. In other words, as we have noted earlier in this chapter, to one degree or another, personal relationships and legal relationships overlap and converge. This is especially true in a sinful world in which there is a high likelihood that one party will violate the established personal relationship and thereby force the other party to take legal action to rectify the damage caused by the breach of trust and receive punitive compensation. This relationship between the personal and the legal is also true of God's relationship to man. In fact, the personal and the legal meet in the concept of *covenant*. As understood in the Old Testament, a covenant implied a very personal relationship between two parties, yet a relationship which also bound both by law to be faithful to the covenant. When Adam sinned against God, for example, Adam broke trust with the personal relationship God had established with him. As a result, Adam had to suffer the legal consequences of his breach with God, as did his progeny. They are all covenant breakers, having spurned the personal relationship God desired with them, and thus they suffer the penal sanctions of the covenant, e.g., the curse of sin and death.

The same relationship between the personal and the legal exists in the human family. The members of the family have a very personal relationship with one another, but a severe violation of the personal relationship may require the guilty party to incur legal sanctions. Israelite society furnishes a dramatic example of this in the civil actions taken against a rebellious son. Deuteronomy 21:18-21 records:

> If a man has a stubborn and rebellious son who does not obey his father and mother and will not listen to them when they discipline him, his father and mother shall take hold of him and bring him to the elders at the gate of his town. They shall say to the elders, 'This son of ours is stubborn and rebellious. He will not obey us. He is a profligate and a drunkard.' Then all the men of his town shall stone him to death. You must purge the evil from among you. All Israel will hear of it and be afraid.

Here we see that if the son does not obey the rules of the family, his parents hand him over to the legal authorities to be put to death. Prior to this, parents could tolerate their son's minor infractions. Through their grace, love and mercy, their child was not expected to be absolutely perfect. Yet when the son crosses the line of propriety and continually engages in insubordinate behavior, they disown and condemn him.

Because God, is a Father, we can understand his relationship with mankind in much the same way as in the above example. As a Father, God created Adam to be his son. He wanted to develop a strong, intimate relationship with Adam. The Father established a covenant with Adam obligating Adam to subdue the earth, increase and multiply, and rule the earth. But Adam did not subdue the earth. Instead, he let it subdue him. In doing so, Adam broke the covenant with his Father and lost the trust of their personal relationship. Although he was still a son, he was now an estranged son, stripped of his previous rights and privileges. God brought the legal sanctions of the covenant against him and made him suffer for his sin. In order to restore the blessings of the covenant, Adam had to regain the rights and privileges of divine sonship; otherwise, the Father would banish him forever.

MORE ON THE FATHER'S COVENANT

Viewing God's relationship with man from the perspective of God as Father helps us understand how the legal dimensions of justification integrate with the personal dimensions. Once we see that the legal dimensions stem from the familial model of God as Father who can take legal action against his sons who break the covenant, we have the proper framework to understand the personal and legal aspects of justification. Viewing God only as a Judge who brings sinners to the bar of justice as in a court of law severely distorts the concept of justification. The separation between the personal and the legal in western society, has caused a strong tendency in Protestant thought to represent justification purely in legal terms which view the individual strictly as a courtroom defendant who is to be acquitted of crimes.

As noted earlier, Scripture does not use courtroom imagery to describe the justification of man before God. This is so because

God is a Father with qualities of justice, not a courtroom judge with fatherly qualities. As 1 Peter 1:17 puts it: "...a *Father* who *judges* each man's work impartially..." One proof of this is that God, in his relationship with the individual, requires personal faith in him. Conversely, a theology based on the courtroom model has no room for faith simply because in any system of law or practice of jurisprudence, the defendant's faith is not a criterion for acquittal or condemnation. If he is guilty he is sentenced, regardless of whether or not he believes in the judge or the judicial system. Or, if one tells a defendant convicted of crimes that another individual has accepted his punishment so as to let the defendant go free, (assuming that the court would allow for such substitution), the defendant's faith, either in the system which provides the substitution or in the individual substituting for him, would not affect the outcome. If the judge allowed another to accept the punishment, then the law would be satisfied and the judge would be forced to release the defendant, whether or not the defendant *believed* in the substitution or wanted to be released. In fact, if the defendant, not believing that the substitute would pay for his crime, insisted on receiving his own sentence, the judge would be forced to call the bailiff to remove him from the courtroom, since the judge could not issue two sentences for the same crime.

As Father, God can love his sons whether they are with him or estranged from him. As Paul says in Romans 5:8, "But God demonstrates his own love for us in this: While we were still sinners, Christ died for us." God does not love us only after we have gone through the bar of justice. As Jesus said of his Father in John 3:16: "For God so loved the world the he gave his only begotten Son, that whosoever believes in him will not perish but have everlasting life." As Father, "God causes his sun to rise on the evil and the good" (Matthew 5:45), and places men in specific times and locations so that they would "seek him and find him, though he is not far from each one of us" (Acts 17:27). Likewise, God tells us to "love our enemies" and "pray for those who persecute you" for the express purpose that "we may be sons of your *Father* in heaven" who shows love to good and bad alike. We are to imitate God's love to such an extent that we "be perfect, therefore, as your heavenly Father is perfect" (Matthew 5:44, 48). But judges cannot show love and forgiveness. They do not love the criminals who appear before them. Only the code of law directs their actions.

We must understand, then, that although faith is not at all involved in the courtroom, it is intimately involved with personal relationships outside of jurisprudence. Within the family, for example, the faithfulness between husband and wife, in the face of temptations to be unfaithful, establishes, strengthens, and solidifies the relationship. Not only their faith in each other, but also their mutual love, sustain them as each looks after the other's needs and desires. They hope in a bright future as their relationship produces offspring and the ultimate blessing of eternal life. Similarly, children are faithful to their parents, obeying the law of respect and honor for the guardians God has placed over them. And friends, too, are also faithful to one another. The whole relationship of friendship is built on trust. Without trust, friendship dies. No "code of law" can make them trust and sacrifice for each other. Rather, in each of these relationships — as spouse, child, or friend — one individual seeks to *please* the other by his faith, hope and love. In essence, our human relationships mirror our relationship to God.

Considering the above principles, we insist that if justification were only a forensic matter, then God could have saved the whole human race by one extrinsic legal action. As God condemned the human race in its solitary representative, Adam, he could easily have saved the whole human race by a solitary legal act. This, however, is not the way the salvation of man occurs. To receive the power of the atonement, man must have faith in God; otherwise, he will remain condemned. This is one of the reasons why the Protestant concept of imputed righteousness is unbiblical. As we have stressed previously, the issue is not a contest between the "alien righteousness of Christ" and the righteousness of man, but how the individual can appropriate and maintain any righteousness, whether of Christ or of himself. As even Protestant sources have stipulated, to receive the benefits of Christ's righteousness, the individual must appropriate and maintain it through faith, and furthermore, through a faith characterized by a firm resolve and outward obedience. The real crux of justification, then, is the individual's *personal response* to his heavenly Father's pleading, not merely an external, legal restitution. As noted above, faith has nothing to do with jurisprudence, since faith denotes the *personal* relationship required between God and his creature that law simply does not provide or have any room to include. Legal adjudication does not depend on whether the defendant believes in the system but only on whether the system has determined him innocent or guilty.

There is another stark contrast between the courtroom model and the familial model. From the courtroom model, Protestants understand justification as a one-time event in which God the Judge sets the accused sinner free. As a result, once the defendant is imputed with another's righteousness, he acquires a kind of "judicial immunity," that is, he will never have to appear in the courtroom again. Thus, belief in the courtroom model inevitably gives rise to the teaching of the individual's "eternal security." As detailed in chapter 5, however, the teaching of eternal security contradicts overwhelming biblical evidence that the individual can fall from his justified state, either by loss of faith or by overt sin, or both. The familial model of justification, on the other hand, readily allows for such a contingency. In the familial model, the son who is no longer faithful and seriously disobeys the father, can be disowned by the family, lose his inheritance, and face the condemnation of the law. The father hands the disowned son over to the legal magistrate and he is punished for his crimes. In effect, the courtroom is reserved until the very end when all personal attempts to bring the son back to the family have failed.

SUMMARY POINTS

1) The Protestant view of forensic imputation uses the model of the courtroom in which God is the Judge convicting the sinner of crimes. As his substitute, Christ takes on the precise guilt and punishment required of the accused, thereby freeing him from condemnation.

2) The Catholic view uses the family model in which God is understood as a Father who either blesses and saves his children or punishes and condemns them. Christ does not take on the precise guilt and punishment required of the individual; rather,

he appeases the Father by his self-sacrifice so that the Father will not bring his judgment upon his disobedient children. The children must, in turn, show faithfulness and love to the Father in order to acquire and maintain his paternal blessing.

3) The familial model includes the possibility that the individual may become disobedient and thus lose his inheritance from the Father, i.e., lose his salvation. On the other hand, a purely forensic model, since the act of adjudication in a court of law is singular and final, has no room within its system to allow for the individual's falling away from his justified state.

4) In the same way, the forensic model has no basis to require *faith* from the individual simply because faith is not a dimension of law. In the courtroom, the individual is not required to believe in the judicial system in order to be acquitted or condemned. The familial model, on the other hand, does require faith; faith and trust are integral parts of familial relationships, and so important that in the familial model it is the loss of these virtues that severs the relationship.

5) Adam was the first adopted son of God. Through his disobedience he became an outcast from the Father's family. God gave him a suspended sentence of death for his insubordination; but in his mercy as a Father still paved a way for Adam to repair his relationship by faith and obedience. Only if Adam failed to become faithful would God finally execute the suspended sentence and finally hand him over to the law for his condemnation.

6) Christ, in being our propitiation, serves to appease the wrath of God against his disobedient sons, and to open the avenue of the Father's gracious mercy upon his children. They must now respond in faith and obedience to their Father in order to attain the inheritance with which he wishes to bless them. If the sons disobey the Father, they are subject to his chastisements and his condemnation.

END NOTES

[1] The Final Judgment will be addressed in Chapter 9.

[2] The Council of Trent described justification in terms of filial restoration and divine sonship. It states: "In these words a description of the justification of the sinner is given as being a translation from that state in which man is born a child of the first Adam to the state of grace and of the "adoption of the sons" of God through the second Adam, Jesus Christ, our Savior" (Session 6, Chapter 4); "...that all men might receive the adoption of sons [Gal. 4:5]" (Session 6, Chapter 2); "...and come to the fellowship of his sons; and are therefore said to be justified gratuitously..." (Session. 6, Chapter 8).

[3] "They [faith, hope, and love] are infused by God into the souls of the faithful to make them capable of acting as his children and of meriting eternal life. They are the pledge of the presence and action of the Holy Spirit in the faculties of the human being" (Catholic Catechism, Section 1813).

[4] See also the Catholic Catechism's remarks on "The Person and Society," Sections 1877-1948.

[5] cf., Genesis 29:14; 37:27; Judges 9:2; 2 Samuel 5:1; 19:12-13; 1 Chronicles 11:1. Even husband and wife share this language; first with Adam and Eve (Gen. 2:23) which then serves as the basis for spouses becoming "one flesh" (Genesis 2:24; Matthew 19:4-6; Ephesians 5:31).

[6] E.g., "In the fifth year of Joram son of Ahab king of Israel, when Jehoshaphat was king of Judah, Jehoram son of Jehoshaphat began his reign as king of Judah" (2 Kings 8:16).

CHAPTER 8

DID GOD CHOOSE ME, OR DID I CHOOSE HIM? (OR DID WE CHOOSE EACH OTHER)?

Any study of justification invariably leads back to the very beginnings of God's program and ultimately back to God himself and how we understand him. Since God is infinite and we are finite, our understanding of God is limited, and to that extent, so is our understanding of salvation. Posing a few simple questions will illustrate the great complexity of the subject we are undertaking. For example, how can God foreknow all events before they occur and still give Adam a free will to obey or disobey in the Garden of Eden? If God knew Adam was going to sin and that people would be sent to hell because of that sin, why did he bother creating the world? Is God himself a determined being or does he also have free will to change a decision he had previously thought otherwise?[1] Whence did evil come? Did God predestine it? We can multiply such questions countless times. Many of them will never be answered until, perhaps, we see God face to face.

Despite these enigmas about God, Scripture does not hesitate to take us back to the very beginning of God's salvation plan. In so many words, it tells us the "thinking process" that went on in God's mind as he planned the creation and the salvation of man. Being infinite in knowledge, certainly God knew that Adam was going to sin before he sinned. It follows that God, if he wanted to save mankind, had to have an eternal plan to deal with that sin. Moreover, God's plan could have no flaws. Everything had to work out in accord with God's calculations and determinations. Nothing could exist outside God's plan and purview. Something that did escape his knowledge and calculations could totally disrupt his and our existence. Hence, it should comfort us that God knows about and controls everything that happens. Although we might not understand how all the pieces fit together, we can rest assured that God has calculated all things out ahead of time.[2]

YOU MEAN WE HAVE TO BELIEVE IN PREDESTINATION!?

The doctrine of predestination is an integral part of the predeterminations and calculations of God. However, because the concept of predestination is intimately dependent on the nature of God in his unfathomable infiniteness, many conflicting ideas of predestination have been proposed by various theologians in Christian history. Suffice it to say, however, that the doctrine of predestination is not a "Calvinistic" idea. The early fathers of the Church taught predestination and incorporated it into the official statements of the Catholic Church early in its history. Prompted by the writings of Augustine in which he had denounced the anti-predestination theology of Pelagius, these Church Councils formulated very strong statements in favor of predestination, which despite challenges to the contrary, continue today as official statements in the Catholic Church.[3] Realizing from the beginning that predestination is an enigmatic subject and that men on both sides of the issue would invariably set forth opposing ideas that could not easily be proved or disproved, the Church, though not explaining all the intricate details concerning the nature of God and predestination, told its people what they *could* say about predestination and what they *could not* say. As we continue in this study, we will discover the "official parameters" which the Church has formulated to help us understand this very important yet puzzling doctrine.

As noted above, Scripture does not hesitate to bring us right to the "thinking process" in the mind of God as he determined the predestination plan. Ephesians 1:4, 5, 11 offer some examples:

> For he chose us in him before the creation of the world to be holy and blameless in his sight. In love he predes-

tined us to be adopted as his sons through Jesus Christ, in accordance with his pleasure and will...In him we were also chosen, having been predestinated according to the plan of him who works out everything in conformity with the purpose of his will.

Paul states clearly in this passage that God has worked out everything ahead of time. God does not guess. Paul specifies that God formulated the predestination plan from his "pleasure and will" showing that God did what pleased himself and what he had determined to do by his own will. Paul also tells us that God has calculated "everything" to be in conformity to his will — nothing escapes his notice or plan. Since God is perfect, we must conclude that everything in and about his creation is the best it could possibly be.

Other Scriptures give the same information. For instance, 1 Peter 1:1-2 states:

To God's elect, strangers in the world, scattered throughout Pontus, Galatia, Cappadocia, Asia, and Bithynia, who have been chosen according to the foreknowledge of God the Father, through the sanctifying work of the Spirit, for obedience to Jesus Christ and sprinkling by his blood.

Here Peter introduces us to the words "elect" and "foreknowledge," both of which become very important in understanding predestination. Scripture often uses the term "foreknowledge" to describe the means by which God provided salvation to man. In Acts 2:22-23, Luke writes, "Jesus of Nazareth was a man accredited by God to you by miracles...This man was handed over to you by God's *set purpose and foreknowledge*; and you with the help of wicked men, put him to death by nailing him to the cross."

Luke 22:22 presents the same conception, that God had predestined the death of Christ: "The Son of Man will go as it has been *decreed*, but woe to that man who betrays him." In this passage, Luke specifies Judas — "that man" — as the main culprit among those whom Peter accuses in Acts 2:23. Here we see that even though God had pre-determined the crucifixion of Christ, nevertheless the man who precipitated that event, namely, Judas Iscariot, was fully culpable for his devilish actions. Acts 4:27-28 presents the same understanding, "...against your holy servant Jesus whom you anointed. They did what your power and will had *decided beforehand* should happen." Is Scripture telling us that God pre-determined the sin of Judas to betray Jesus and yet still holds him guilty and damnable for his action? No, but later in this chapter we will investigate how these seemingly opposing ideas can be reconciled.

Romans 8:28-30 ties predestination to our justification in even more detail:

> And we know that in all things God works for the good of those who love him, who have been called according to his purpose. For those God foreknew he also predestined to be conformed to the likeness of his Son, that he might be the firstborn among many brothers. And those he predestinated, he also called; those he called, he also justified; those he justified, he also glorified.

Here Paul identifies the stages of our Christian life which comprise God's plan of predestination. We can know that everything that happens works out for our good because in God's foreknowledge and predestination he desired that we would become like his Son, both in our present life and in our future life when we are resurrected. It is very clear that those who are justified and glorified were predestined by God. What a comforting doctrine — a doctrine that teaches us not to worry about how everything fits together or whether God has somehow forgotten us in the masses of people on the earth. As Jesus said to the apostles in Matthew 10:30, "And even the very hairs of your head are all numbered."

Continuing in the same context Paul elaborates in detail in Romans 9-11 how God brings his plan of predestination to bear on individual groups and people. For example, in Romans 9:10-13 Paul writes:

> Not only that, but Rebekah's children had one and the same father, our father Isaac. Yet, before the twins were

born or had done anything good or bad — in order that God's purpose in election might stand: not by works but by him who calls — she was told, "The older will serve the younger." Just as it is written: "Jacob I loved, but Esau I hated."

Paul stresses that even before Jacob and Esau had done any good or evil, God chose one over the other. In fact, he chose Jacob over Esau precisely to show that one is not justified by works but because of God's election. God goes so far as to say that he actually "hated" Esau. How can God say such a thing? God reserves such language for the wicked people of the world, as recorded in Psalm 5:5, "The arrogant cannot stand in your presence, you hate all who do wrong,"; Psalm 11:5, "the Lord examines the righteous, but the wicked and those who love violence his soul hates" and Ecclesiasticus 12:6 "For the Most High also hates sinners." Was Esau counted among these whom God hates for their iniquity? Hebrews 12:16-17 leans us in this direction by specifying Esau's wickedness with details that do not appear in the Old Testament:

> See that no one is *sexually immoral* or is *godless* like Esau, who for a single meal sold his inheritance rights as the oldest son. Afterward, as you know, when he wanted to inherit this blessing, he was rejected. He could bring about no change of mind, though he sought the blessing with tears.

Since the context of this passage speaks of those who fall away from the faith, Paul seems to be using Esau as an example of someone who was not ultimately saved. Thus there is evidence to explain the "hate" of God toward Esau as that which ultimately caused his damnation.

Paul realizes that when we first hear these truths of predestination, they immediately raise a question in our minds as to God's fairness. Does God just arbitrarily decide to hate someone, even before they are born, holding them culpable for sin and then damn them to hell? Paul elaborates on this question in Romans 9:14-18:

> What then shall we say? Is God unjust? Not at all! For
> he says to Moses, "I will have mercy on whom I have
> mercy, and I will have compassion on whom I have com-
> passion." It does not, therefore, depend on man's desire
> or effort, but on God's mercy. For the Scripture says to
> Pharaoh: "I raised you up for this very purpose, that I
> might display my power in you and that my name might
> be proclaimed in all the earth." Therefore God has mercy
> on whom he wants to have mercy, and he hardens whom
> he wants to harden.

At forst sight, it appears as if Paul is not giving us a very good
answer. In fact, the quote from Moses concerning God having
mercy on whom he chooses seems to reinforce the accusation of
unfairness. Similarly, the reference to raising up Pharaoh merely
to display God's power seems to make God into a tyrant who uses
men as play toys. (We will see later, however, that this is not the
case at all. There is a good and sufficient reason why God does
what he does).

Paul continues his role as the hypothetical objector in the next
series of verses (Romans 9:19-21). Here he introduces the example
of the potter and his clay:

> One of you will say to me: "Then why does God still
> blame us? For who resists his will?" But who are you,
> O man, to talk back to God? "Shall what is formed say
> to him who formed it, 'Why did you make me like this?'
> Does not the potter have the right to make out of the
> same lump of clay some pottery for noble purposes and
> some for common use?[4]

Now the question of blame or culpability comes to the fore. In
other words, the objector might accept the fact that God does as he
wishes but if that is the case, why does God, who seems to be
controlling me, blame me for the way I am? Having already answered the issue in the previous verses, Paul now says that we no
longer have the right to bring up the subject, let alone require a
more definitive answer from God.

Perhaps purposely, Paul continues the same line of argumentation in the next verses (Romans 9:22-24):

> What if God, choosing to show his wrath and make his power known, bore with great patience the objects of his wrath — prepared for destruction? What if he did this to make the riches of his glories known to the objects of his mercy, whom he prepared in advance for glory — even us whom he also called, not only from the Jews but also from the Gentiles?

Here Paul speaks of those "prepared for destruction," which strongly suggests that God had preordained these people for destruction.[5] We also notice a shift in those to whom he applies this dynamic of God's dealings with men. In verses 10-11 he applied God's election to individuals, e.g., Jacob as opposed to Esau. In verses 24-26 he is applying predestination to groups, e.g., Gentiles as opposed to Jews. Hence we cannot dilute God's plan of predestination by claiming that he only predestines particular ethnic groups or communities, and not individuals within those groups. No, God's predestination is all pervasive; encompassing both the community and the individual. Whether it is communal or individual, however, we still do not know the criterion God uses, in his own mind, for choosing one over the other. Later we will see how Scripture explains this haunting question. For now, we will develop and illuminate the other side of this issue — the free will of man.[6]

BUT DO I HAVE A FREE WILL?

Theologians and philosophers have given various descriptions to the term "free will." Basically, it refers to the capability and freedom of man to choose, from among two or more alternatives, his future course of action. Free will, in order to be free, necessitates the absence of force and coercion. Although the individual may be inclined to one degree or another to make a certain choice, the basic requirement of free will is that man is not programmed to make a choice nor does an entity with greater power force a choice upon him. If one does not define free will in this or a similar way, then there is no use in speaking about a "free will" since in that case it would not be free.[7]

Scripture, complementing its teaching on predestination, also teaches that man's will is presently free to accept or reject God. The first test of man's free will occurred in the Garden of Eden when Adam and Eve were tempted by Satan. God had told Adam and Eve that they could eat of any tree of the Garden except the tree of the knowledge of good and evil. God warned Adam that in the day he ate of the tree, he would die. Adam was a man unencumbered by the effects of sin and physical deterioration that have plagued man ever since. Nevertheless, being a mere man and created out of nothing, Adam still needed God's power for his existence and for his capabilities. In light of this, God did not leave Adam on his own to confront the Devil. He gave him sufficient grace so that he would be able to resist the temptations to sin.[8] In time, Adam confronted the Devil through his wife Eve. Eve had been enticed to think that God was holding something back from the new human couple, that he was not the best caretaker of his own creation, and in essence, was deceiving Adam and Eve. Once she ate of the fruit, Eve told Adam of her decision and convinced him to eat so that he, too, could "be like God." At this point, Adam should have told Eve that she had sinned against God and to ask for His forgiveness. Since Eve was not the head of the human race, the world could still be saved from the curse of sin and death if Adam had obeyed God. When confronted with Eve's decision to eat the fruit, Adam was faced with a cataclysmic decision. He could either bring Eve to God for retribution or he could partake with her in the sin. As we know all too well, Adam chose the latter course. He did so by his own free will. God did not coerce him in any manner. God simply gave Adam a test of faithfulness and he failed. If he had obeyed, the test would have been over and God would have allowed Adam to live on the earth and produce his children in anticipation of a final consummation in which man would be divinized for eternity. Shunning God's grace and his offer of being made like God, Adam sought to become like God on his own terms.

Throughout the course of human history, man has been confronted with situations similar to that of Adam where he must make a choice to serve himself and his own interests or to serve God and His interests. The story of Cain and Abel is the next incident involving man's free will. Cain and Abel had both offered sacrifices to God. According to Hebrews 11:4, Abel's was pleasing to God because of his faithfulness. Cain's was not for the opposite reason. Enraged with jealousy, Cain murdered his brother Abel. Because of the inheritance of original sin from his father Adam, the proclivity to sin was great. Man would be influenced by the working of concupiscence in his body and would find it easier to disobey God and follow in his own way. Yet in keeping with his promise to help man by the power of his grace — a grace that could legitimately be given due to the predestined and anticipated atonement of Christ — man had sufficient power from God to refrain from sin. Abel had apparently succeeded in this endeavor. He used the grace that God had given him and thus was made "pleasing" to God by his faith and works. Cain shunned this grace and decided to take matters into his own hands — to alleviate the problem, so he thought, more quickly and efficiently than reliance on God's grace would afford.

Since Cain and Abel, all the men of the earth have been in similar situations. Under the curse of sin and death, they find themselves with a desire to sin yet a desire that God commands them to overcome (Romans 7:7-25). Scripture does not even remotely question man's ability and responsibility to avoid sin by the power of his own decision. As the Lord told Israel in Zechariah 1:3: "This is what the Lord almighty says: 'Return to me,' declares the Lord Almighty, 'and I will return to you,' says the Lord Almighty." Similarly, in Acts 17:26-27, Paul speaks to all those who came after the sin of Adam:

> From one man he made every nation of men, that they should inhabit the whole earth and he determined the times set for them and the exact places where they should live. God did this so that men would seek him and perhaps reach out for him and find him, though he is not far from each one of us.

Here we have the first indication of an intimate relationship between God's predeterminations and man's free will to choose for God. On the one hand, God "determines" the times and places men inhabit. On the other hand, God does this precisely so that men will have ample opportunity to seek for him. Does God offer himself for men to seek him but not really mean it? To answer "yes" to such a question would be an affront and contradiction to the integrity and character of God. God does not lie or give us the pretense of truth. If he states that he provides man with the environment specifically so that man can choose for him, then we can be assured that God truly desires man to be saved and has given him the ability to respond to the times and places in which God has put him. In short, we must assign as much force to these kinds of Scripture verses as we have done with the verses which speak of predestination.

One of the more important passages showing an intimate relationship between election and free will is 2 Peter 1:9-11. Peter writes:

> But if anyone does not have them, he is nearsighted and blind, and has forgotten that he has been cleansed from his past sins. Therefore, my brothers, be all the more eager to make your calling and election sure. For if you do these things, you will never fall, and you will receive a rich welcome into the eternal kingdom of our Lord and Savior Jesus Christ.

Here Peter says that one can make his calling and election secure by continuing in the virtues he has practiced in the past. The verse assumes that a person has a free will to continue or not continue practicing these virtues. Apparently, there were some who had stopped practicing these virtues. Peter points out that such people are blind and have forgotten their prior cleansing from sin. He spends the next chapter detailing those who have fallen away (2 Peter 2:1-22). This means that at one time their sins were forgiven but they have now decided to enter a sinful life again. What is most intriguing, however, is Peter's decision to bring in the dimension of "calling and election," for we would normally think that such terms are reserved for discussions concerning God's secret plans made before the world was created (Ephesians 1:4-5). Peter could just as easily have warned the wayward Christians that if they continue in sin they will fall away, without adding in the elements of "calling and election." By deliberately adding "calling and election" into the picture, Peter is showing us that man's free will decisions are directly related to God's predestination program. The manner in which they are related, we will investigate momentarily.

Further congruence between God's plan of predestination and the free will of man is evident in Acts 13:46-48. Luke writes:

> Then Paul and Barnabas answered them boldly: "We had to speak the word of God to you first. Since you reject it and do not consider yourselves worthy of eternal life, we now turn to the Gentiles...When the Gentiles heard this, they were glad and honored the word of the Lord; and all who were appointed for eternal life believed.

On the one hand, the Jews to whom Paul and Barnabas spoke had both "rejected" the word and "considered themselves unworthy of eternal life." This speaks plainly of their free will to reject God. On the other hand, the Gentiles believed because they were "appointed to eternal life."

The same relationship between the plan of God and the free will of man is evident in John 1:12-13. John writes, "Yet to all who received him, to those who believed in his name, he gave the right to become the children of God — children born not of natural descent, nor of human decision or a husband's will, but born of God." As used in the original Greek, both "received" and "believed" denote one who is acting on his own volition to accept God. Yet John is also indicating that those who do receive and believe in his name do so because they are born from God's spiritual power, not by man's earthly means.

John's gospel states again the relationship between God's predestination and man's free will as Jesus confronts the Jews. In John 6:39-40 Jesus says:

> And this is the will of him who sent me, that I shall lose none of all that he has given me, but raise them up at the

last day. For my Father's will is that everyone who looks to the Son and believes in him shall have eternal life, and I will raise him up at the last day.

Here John reiterates the same theme noted in Romans 8:28-30. God has calculated his whole plan with such care that he knows the very number of those whom he will give to Jesus to be saved. In John 17:12 Jesus adds, "While I was with them, I protected them and kept them safe by that name you gave me. None has been lost except the one doomed to destruction so that Scripture would be fulfilled." Here Jesus tells us that Judas's betrayal and perdition were foreknown by God and recorded in Scripture. This does not mean, however, that Judas or anyone else who does not come to God did not have a free will to choose for God or that God did not give them the power to respond positively to God. As Jesus says, it is the Father's will that all who believe [choose to believe] will be raised on the last day.

Jesus reiterates these themes in John 6:37,44-45:

All that the Father gives to me will come to me, and whoever comes to me I will never drive away...No one can come to me unless the Father who sent me draws him, and I will raise him up at the last day. It is written in the Prophets: 'They will all be taught by God.' Everyone who listens to the Father and learns from him comes to me.

Again, Jesus states clearly that it is the Father who initiates the salvation process. The Father must draw to Jesus those whom he desires to save. At the same time, however, Jesus specifies that each person has the choice to "listen" to the "teaching of God." When they "listen" and "learn" they will come to Jesus. Yet Jesus is clear in John 5:40 that it is man who decides not to come to God: "These are Scriptures that testify about me, yet *you refuse to come to me* to have life."

Paul teaches the same two dimensions of salvation. On the one hand, Paul's strong predestinarian teaching is very clear in Romans 8:28-30 and Romans 9-11. On the other hand, right in the same context, Paul continually urges people to choose for God. For example, in Romans 10:9-13 he says:

That if you confess with your mouth, "Jesus is Lord," and believe in your heart that God raised him from the dead, you will be saved. For it is with your heart that you believe and are justified, and it is with your mouth that you confess and are saved. As the Scripture says, "Anyone who trusts in him will never be put to shame." For there is no difference between Jew and Gentile — the same Lord is Lord of all and richly blesses all who call on him, for "Everyone who calls on the name of the Lord will be saved."

Here is very clear language that puts the responsibility on the individual to believe in his heart and articulate his conviction in order to be saved. If one is going to respect the face value language of this passage, one can only conclude that the reason a person would not be not saved is precisely because *he* did not choose to call on the name of the Lord.

In the above passage, Paul is using both the communal and individual aspects of God's call to the individual as we have seen earlier with his discussion of predestination in Romans 9:10-29. The call of salvation is for groups, both Jew and Gentile, yet God finally directs the call to each individual within that group. Paul indicates this in Romans 10:9-13 by his use of the singular "you confess" and "everyone who calls."

Later in the same context, Paul gives us at least some answer as to why some people whom God draws do not respond. After explaining in Romans 9:30-10:3 and again in 10:16-21 that though the gospel came to Israel, yet they had rejected it, Paul adds that God is directly involved in the rejection. Recording a conversation that the prophet Elijah had with God, Paul writes in Romans 11:3-8:

"Lord, they have killed your prophets and torn down your altars; I am the only one left, and they are trying to kill me"? And what was God's answer to him? "I have reserved for myself seven thousand who have not bowed the knee to Baal." So too, at the present time there is a remnant chosen by grace. And if by grace, then it is no longer by works, if it were, grace would no longer be grace. What then? What Israel sought so earnestly it did not obtain, but the elect did. The others were hardened, as it is written: 'God gave them a spirit of stupor, eyes so that they could not see and ears so that they could not hear, to this very day.'

This is quite a passage. Now we can see why Paul had to raise the objections against God's determinative will in Romans 9:14-24 and then answer those queries before he came to Romans 11:3-8 by telling us "not to talk back to God." Here we find that the unbelief of the Jews is actually included within God's plan of pre-destination. God is the one who "gave them a spirit of stupor" so they could not believe. Moreover, he elected only a mere seven thousand people out of a nation of millions of people.[9] What kind of God are we dealing with here? The "hardening" of the Jews is the same hardening to which Paul in Romans 9:16-21 attributes Pharaoh's decision not to let Israel leave Egypt. This also explains why Jesus must stress several times to the Jews in John 6 that in order for them to be saved God must "draw" them (John 6:44). In their hearts the Jews are hardened, not believing what Jesus has said about himself and God, and Jesus concludes that they do not believe because the Father has not drawn them but actually blinded them. This look behind the scenes is further detailed in Matthew 13:13-17, indicating that Jesus spoke to the people in parables in order to hide the truth from them:

This is why I speak to them in parables: "Though see-ing, they do not see; though hearing, they do not hear or understand. In them is fulfilled the prophecy of Isaiah: "'You will be ever hearing but never understanding...For this people's heart has become calloused; they hardly hear with their ears, and they have closed their eyes. Otherwise, they might see with their eyes, hear with their ears, understand with their hearts and turn, and I would heal them.

This passage displays the same dynamic we have seen in the other passages. On the one hand, we see that God is not neutral when it concerns belief in Him. If the individual does not accept God from the knowledge and grace that God has given him, God may blind him to the truth so that he cannot understand it.[10] On the other hand, this desperate situation is induced by the individual's free choice, a choice to turn from God which has made his own heart calloused.

Paul alludes to the same dynamic relationship between God and man in discussing God's dealing with Pharaoh in Romans 9:16-18, when he speaks of the hardening of Pharaoh's heart. The account in Exodus 9:34-10:1 reads:

> When Pharaoh saw that the rain and hail and thunder had stopped, he sinned again: *He and his officials hardened their hearts.* So Pharaoh's heart was hard and he would not let the Israelites go, just as the Lord had said through Moses. Then the Lord said to Moses, "Go to Pharaoh, for *I have hardened his heart and the hearts of his officials* so that I may perform these miraculous signs of mine among them...

Again, we are somewhat stunned at the "behind the scenes" information revealed to us. The passage clearly states that Pharaoh and his officials "sinned again" by "hardening their hearts." Apparently, they chose of their own free will to harden their hearts. Yet in the same breath we learn that God specifically tells Moses that HE was the one who did the hardening. What is going on here? Is God making Pharaoh sin? Misguided, some would like to conclude such a thing. But we should not understand Paul's statement in Romans 9:18-20 ("...he hardens whom he wants to harden...Shall what is formed say to him who formed it, 'Why did you make me like this?'") as referring to an arbitrary imposition of God's will on men irrespective of their free will, but precisely an imposition that takes into account or is the result of their free decisions. In this way, one cannot complain to God (i.e., "Then why does God still blame us? For who resists his will?") because as men make decisions, God makes decisions, for he is not neutral with respect to the free acts of men. Scripture makes it clear that God does not make, coerce, or program man to sin. Man sins of his own free will. In James 1:12-15 the apostle writes:

> When tempted, no one should say, "God is tempting me." For God cannot be tempted by evil, nor does he tempt anyone; but each one is tempted when, by his own evil desire, he is dragged away and enticed. Then, after desire has conceived, it gives birth to sin; and sin, when it is full-grown, gives birth to death.

James tells us that when one sins it is because of "his own evil desire." He contemplates his sin for a period of time and then suddenly sin is born. James assures us that God does not have any role in this process because "God cannot be tempted by evil;" that is, since it is evil to tempt someone to sin, God, being all good, cannot be tempted to tempt anyone to sin. Although God has a role in the hardening or spiritual plight of the individual after he sins, God has no role in the individual's sinful thoughts or actual sin. But how does man's free will to sin balance with God's foreknowledge and predestination? Are we not still a product of God's predetermined plan and therefore can we still not plead that we only do what we were made to do? We will attempt to answer that question momentarily. First, we need to see other aspects of God's nature and program.

Sometimes the teaching of free will is implicit in Scripture. For example, in Matthew 11:21-24 Jesus states:

> Woe to you, Korazin! Woe to you, Bethsaida! If the miracles that were performed in you had been performed in Tyre and Sidon, they would have repented long ago in sackcloth and ashes. But I tell you, it will be more bearable for Tyre and Sidon on the day of judgment than for you. And you, Capernaum, will you be lifted up to the skies? No, you will go down to the depths. If the miracles that were performed in you had been performed in Sodom, it would have remained to this day. But I tell

you that it will be more bearable for Sodom on the day of judgment than for you.

Here Jesus teaches a profound truth. Korazin, Bethsaida, and Capernaum were Jewish cities which had witnessed many of Jesus's miracles, yet they remained hardened in their unbelief. One of the purposes of the miracles was to convince the people of Jesus's divinity. Using this premise, Jesus puts forth an alternate scenario for the Gentile cities of Tyre, Sidon, and Sodom other than the destruction they experienced for their unrepentant sin. Jesus asserts that if the same miracles had been done in those cities as was done in the Jewish cities, they would have repented of their sin.[11] This is quite a remarkable statement, since we are very aware of the utter debauchery that was present in the city of Sodom (cf., Genesis 18-20). Since their destruction is a past event, sealed, as it were, in time and space, it should strike us as either odd or illogical that Jesus would make such a bold declaration to the opposite extreme concerning their possible repentance. In respect of Jesus' divinity and integrity, it is unlikely that he is using this possible scenario as a mere hyperbolic teaching tool without any reality to the Sodomite's possible repentance upon seeing the miracles. Moreover, if the Sodomites were "predestined" to reprobation without consideration of their free will, this would contradict the reliance on their free will that Jesus is using to indict the Jews of his day. If we give full force to Jesus's assertion that the Sodomites would have repented, we see again the dynamic relationship Scripture creates between what God has determined and what man has freely chosen.

Another example of the dynamic relationship between God's foreknowledge of all events and man's free will is an incident in David's life recorded in 1 Samuel 23. In this story, Saul, David's father-in-law, is seeking to kill David. In order to thwart Saul's plans, David inquires of God through the traditional ephod of the priest. Verses 10-13 record the event:

David said, 'O Lord, God of Israel, your servant has heard definitely that Saul plans to come to Keilah and destroy the town on account of me. Will the citizens of

Keilah surrender me to him? Will Saul come down, as your servant has heard? O Lord, god of Israel, tell your servant.' And the Lord said, 'He will.' Again David asked, 'Will the citizens of Keilah surrender me and my men to Saul?' And the Lord said, 'They will.' So David and his men, about six hundred in number, left Keilah and kept moving from place to place. When Saul was told that David had escaped Keilah, he did not go there.

Here we see that God gives David information about a potential event, but an event that did not occur because David decided, of his own free will, not to have the event occur. If David had stayed in Keilah, surely God's prediction that Saul would come there to kill David would have come true. Moreover, we must understand that the information God gives to David is more than a prediction. In God's mind, Saul's going to Keilah is a real event that God foresees as occurring. God is not guessing. This shows us that in God's knowledge of the future, it includes all possible events that could occur — events whose fulfillment depends on man's free will decision between two courses of action. Since God knows the potential events in David's life, it is no stretch of the imagination to realize that he knows the potential events in the lives of each and every person that ever existed or will exist, as well as the actual decisions each person will make. In knowing man's free will decisions, God makes his plans accordingly. Yes, he surely is an awesome God.

Finally, one of Scripture's most beautiful passages detailing man's free will, as well as God's insistence that he does not lead men to sin, is found in Ecclesiasticus 15:11-20:

Do not say, 'It was the Lord's doing that I fell away'; for he does not do what he hates. Do not say, 'It was he who led me astray'; for he has no need of the sinful. The Lord hates all abominations; such things are not loved by those who fear him. It was he who created mankind in the beginning, and he left them in the power of their own free choice. If you choose, you can keep the commandments, and to act faithfully is a matter of your own choice. He has placed before you fire and water; stretch out your hand for whichever you choose. Before each person are life and death, and whichever one chooses will be given. For great is the wisdom of the Lord; he is mighty in power and sees everything; his eyes are on those who fear him and he knows every human action. He has not commanded anyone to be wicked, and he has not given anyone permission to sin.

DOES GOD DESIRE ALL MEN TO BE SAVED?

As Scripture is clear about God's plan of predestination and his blinding of people who turn away from him, Scripture is also clear about God's desire to see all men saved. He has no desire to see man, any man, remain in eternal condemnation for their sins. He gives them every opportunity to repent and even blesses them while he waits for them. Ezekiel said as much long ago in Ezekiel 18:21-23,32:

> But if a wicked man turns away from all the sins he has committed and keeps all my decrees and does what is just and right, he will surely live; he will not die. None of the offenses he has committed will be remembered against him. Because of the righteous things he has done he will live. Do I take any pleasure in the death of the wicked? declares the Lord. Rather, am I not pleased when they turn from their ways and live?...For I take no pleasure in the death of anyone, declares the Sovereign Lord. Repent and live!

Speaking for himself, God lets us know quite clearly that he is waiting for man to use his free will and repent of his sins. If he does so, then God in turn will allow him to live. Moreover, in anticipating objections that God enjoys casting judgment upon sinners, God solemnly declares that no such disposition is to be found in him. If we do not repent and live, God takes no pleasure in our death.

Jesus echoed this same sentiment in Matthew 23:37-38 as he contemplated the Jews of Jerusalem:

> O Jerusalem, Jerusalem, you who kill the prophets and stone those sent to you, how often I have longed to gather your children together, as a hen gathers her chicks under her wings, but you were not willing. Look, your house is left to you desolate.

Jesus is certainly not playacting here. He really means it when he says that God sent them prophets in hopes that they would repent of their sins, just as Ezekiel had stated in the previous passage. Jesus also means it when he says that he "longed to gather" them but that "they were not willing." It wasn't because God predestined them to refuse. They refused Jesus of their own free will. They rejected his call and the prompting of God's grace.[12]

Paul expresses the same teaching about God's desire in 1 Timothy 2:1,4:

> I urge, then, first of all, that requests, prayers, intercession and thanksgiving be made for *everyone*...This is good, and pleases God our Savior, who wants *all men* to be saved and to come to a knowledge of the truth. For there is one God and one mediator between God and man, the man Christ Jesus, who gave himself as a ransom for *all men*...

This is exactly what we would expect of a kind, benevolent God — one who shows no respect of persons but desires all men to come to salvation. We see Paul's universal perspective of God's desire for the salvation of all men first by his urging that "prayers" and "intercessions" be made on behalf of "*everyone*," because such prayers are "pleasing" to God who uses the prayers of the faithful to provide salvation for "*all men*." Paul reinforces the inclusion of *everyone* in God's desire to save as he concludes that Christ was given "as a ransom for *all men*," not just a certain few. This echoes the teaching in 1 John 2:2 which states, "He is the atoning sacrifice for our sins, and not only for ours but also for the sins of the *whole world*."

Peter indicates God's sincere desire to save all men in 2 Peter 3:8-9:

But do not forget this one thing, dear friends: With the Lord a day is like a thousand years, and a thousand years are like a day. The Lord is not slow in keeping his promise, as some understand slowness. He is patient with you, not wanting anyone to perish, but everyone to come to repentance.

This passage is in the context of the end of the world. Scoffers, on hearing the prediction that the world will end, ridicule the truth that God is coming back because the world has gone on for thousands of years without so much as a hint of his return. It is typical of man to turn God's care and concern for the world into an indictment against God — that he doesn't really care about man but has left him on his own. However, it is precisely because God loves mankind that he delays his return, allowing them as much opportunity as possible to examine their ways and turn back to God. Peter, as Paul did, emphasizes the *individual* in this call to repentance with words such as "you," "anyone," and "everyone." As Jesus said in John 3:16, "For God so loved the world that *whoever* believes in him shall not perish but have eternal life." This promise applies to every human being, past, present, and future.[13]

WHY DOES GOD CHOOSE SOME AND NOT OTHERS?

Throughout this book we have carefully put together the pieces of the puzzle of God's great plan of salvation. Among other things, we have discovered that one of the primary pieces which helps us understand how salvation is carried out is the very nature of God himself. Simply put, in order to know how to be saved we need to know the God behind the salvation. On the one hand, we have seen that God is transcendent, honorable and holy. There is an infinite distance between his character and ours. As Isaiah 55:8-9 states concerning the human condition, God's ways are as far above ours as the stars are above the earth. Because of this, Christ had to pay a supreme sacrifice in order for God to open the doors of salvation for mankind. But we have also seen that God is our Father, not a force in outer space, not an ogre who seeks to hurt people, but a loving Father who wants all his lost children to be made right. God's love is real love. It is not an abstract concept or a mechanical calculation. By the same token, God's anger is real anger. God really gets angry when men sin and he either punishes or destroys them. These passionate qualities are all part of God's personal nature, or for lack of a better term, his personality. God's personality is not imaginary or metaphorical. It is very real and he deals with people according to the personal dimensions of his divine character. Because we are made in God's image, we can have a glimpse of God's personality by knowing and observing ourselves, except that God's personality is perfect, without sin, and perfectly suited to his divinity.[14]

In possessing personality, God is affected by the response of his creatures. Accordingly, God will give or withhold his blessing depending on how his creature has pleased or displeased him. A dramatic example of this dynamic quality is noted in God's dealing with Moses and Israel in Exodus 32-33. In Exodus 32, the Israelites have just come out of Egypt and are traveling through the desert. While Moses is on the mountain obtaining the Ten Commandments, the Jews sin grievously by making and worshiping a golden calf. God becomes so angry that he wants to destroy them all. But Moses pleads with God, reasoning that the Egyptians will mock the God of Israel for destroying his people so quickly. He also reminds God that he had made a promise to Abraham for the Israelites to inherit the land of Canaan. Because of Moses's plea, God changes his mind and does not destroy Israel (Exodus 32:14). What is so special about Moses that he could plead with God and actually persuade him to change his mind?

The answer to this question comes in the next chapter, Exodus 33. Still very angry over the sin of the Israelites, God tells Moses that he won't go with the people on the way to Canaan because if he did go he "might destroy them on the way" (33:3-5). Although God desires to keep his distance from the people, he treats Moses very differently. Exodus 33:11 says, "The Lord would speak to Moses face to face, as a man speaks to his friend." Here we see a description of a very intimate relationship between God and Moses. Colloquially speaking, we could say that God liked Moses very much, and of course, loved him as well. Moses was a humble man, the

most humble man on the earth at that time (Numbers 12:3). He had
a very similar character to that of Abraham, his ancestor, who was
humble, feared God, and was also called God's "friend." (James 2:23).
But in being a friend, Moses, for the second time, respectfully challenges God to reconsider his refusal to follow the people through
the desert (Exodus 33:12-17). Once again, God accepts Moses's plea
and determines that he will go with the people. The most important
part of this exchange, however, is the reason God gives to Moses for
changing his mind. In verses 17-19, the conversation is recorded:

> And the Lord said to Moses, 'I will do the very thing
> you have asked, because I am pleased with you and I
> know you by name.' Then Moses said, 'Now show me
> you glory.' And the Lord said, 'I will cause all my good-
> ness to pass in front of you, and I will proclaim my name,
> the Lord, in your presence. I will have mercy on whom
> I will have mercy, and I will have compassion on whom
> I will have compassion.'

Notice several things here. First, God says he will respond to
Moses's request because he is *pleased with Moses*, and second,
because he *knows Moses by name*. God decides his course of action based on the intimate relationship he has with Moses. It is
obvious that God takes extreme delight in righteous people who
seek him and honor him. God reacts this way because he is a personal being, a being who is moved by the humble disposition and
positive response of his creatures. In being so moved, God also
agrees to show his glory to Moses, something very few men have
seen. Moreover, just as God knew Moses by name, God says that
he will "proclaim" his name, "The Lord," to Moses. In Hebrew
culture, this 'name exchange' is a sign of the deep personal relationship between God and Moses. God is putting his relationship
with Moses on the highest order possible.

What is even more important, especially for our present discussion concerning God's reasons for election, is the choice of
language God uses in favoring Moses. In verse 19, he tells Moses
that he "will have mercy on whom he will have mercy and compassion on whom he will have compassion." These words are not

just filler for the story. They stem from the personality of God, a God who has divine emotions of mercy and compassion for those that please him.

Even more intriguing, is that the apostle Paul quotes this section of Exodus 33:19 when he is addressing the rationale for why God elects one person over the other. Paul writes in Romans 9:14,18:

> What then shall we say? Is God unjust? Not at all! For he says to Moses, 'I will have mercy on whom I have mercy, and I will have compassion on whom I have compassion.' ...Therefore God has mercy on whom he wants to have mercy, and he hardens whom he wants to harden.

If we read Paul's words without the benefit of the exchange between God and Moses in Exodus 33 we might be tempted to conclude that God is some kind of despot, arbitrarily handing out mercy and hardness without taking into account the disposition of his creatures. But since these sayings are a direct quote from God's encounter with Moses, we must use the information in that text to help understand what Paul means. Exodus 33 certainly does not portray God as a despot who, out of a capricious whim, decides to grant mercy to one or hardness to another. No, God is very careful to whom he gives his mercy and whom he hardens. According to Exodus 33:17-19, God shows mercy because Moses pleased God and God new him by name.

Of course, on the other side of this issue are those who do not receive God's mercy and compassion. In this case, Paul refers to Pharaoh in Romans 9:17 who was raised up not for himself but merely to show God's power. God hardened Pharaoh's heart so that Pharaoh would not release the Israelites from Egypt. This led to the ten devastating plagues God cast on the Egyptians. We saw earlier, however, that God did not arbitrarily harden Pharaoh's heart. In Exodus 9:34, the text records that Pharaoh and his officials hardened their own heart, God did not coerce them. God hardens Pharaoh's heart only after Pharaoh hardened his own heart (10:1). Pharaoh acts and God reacts. If not, then surely God could come under suspicion of being a tyrant. No, God hardens because he sees men refuse his wishes, and then he punishes them by reinforcing and continuing their hardness. He then proclaims his power for all the world to hear so that they will humble themselves before him.

Thus, God's decisions are sovereign but they are not arbitrary. As Ephesians 1:4-5 says that, "In love he predestined us...in accordance with his pleasure and will," God's "pleasure and will" are a product of his personal nature and they are not manifested without taking into account the actions and responses of his creatures. Arbitrarily choosing to save or to damn would give God no pleasure. What pleases God is the joy he experiences in rewarding those who diligently seek after him. As we saw with Moses, God is "pleased" when he sees his creatures respond to his grace and humble themselves before him. God is so pleased with them that he will consider their every desire.

WHAT ABOUT JACOB AND ESAU?

If what we have stated above is true, then how do we explain Paul's teaching about Jacob and Esau in Romans 9:10-13? Paul emphasizes that even before the twins were born or had done anything good or bad, God told Rebecca that Esau (the elder son) would serve Jacob (the younger son). Quoting from Malachi 1:2-3, Paul also says that God loved Jacob and hated Esau. God is not placating our human sensibilities when he declares his love and hate. No, God really loves Jacob, better than Jacob loves himself. Although Jacob sinned from time to time, he was devoted to God just like his father Isaac and his grandfather Abraham. God was pleased with that devotion. Conversely, Esau was, and continued to be, a godless and sexually immoral person who never submitted himself to the God of his forefathers (Hebrews 12:16-17).[15]

Why, then, does Paul make a point to say that God chose Jacob over Esau even before they were born or had done anything good or bad? The first answer lies in what Paul is trying to accomplish in his teaching to the Jews. As we learned in chapter 1, the Jews had a distorted concept of the law. They did not really love God for who he was, rather, they only wanted him for what they could get out of him. They based their religion on doing work, devoid of a personal relationship with God based on grace and faith. They lived by a "written code" and expected God to pay them a "wage," the same as an employee demands from his employer. As Paul says later in Romans 9:32, "...they pursued it not by faith but as if it were by works..." In much of their history, the Jews demanded God's blessings and they complained bitterly when they did not receive his goods immediately (Exodus 16-17). They thought that God owed them something for just being alive. This kind of response is precisely what God hates most — those who puff themselves up and pretend they are more noble than God. In his usual ingenious way, Paul focuses on God's pre-choosing of Jacob over Esau because, having not yet been born, Jacob and Esau could never have put God 'under contract' to pay them a wage for their works. Jacob and Esau's pre-born state, then, serves as an overstatement of Paul's case so that he can make the deepest impression on the Jews of their wretched state.

This is not to say that any of the elect, including Jacob, have earned their place. God owes nothing to Jacob and he does not base his election on Jacob's merits. If he chooses anyone, it is out of his grace, but a grace, as we saw with Moses, that is in conjunction with humble faith and obedience to God's desires. Thus Paul can rightly conclude in Romans 9:16 that "It does not, therefore, depend on man's desire or effort, but on God's mercy." What Paul means is man can never thrust his self-righteous efforts in God's face and expect a legal payment, as if God were merely an employer. It is only by the mercy of God, stemming from his own personal nature, that anyone receives salvation. God alone will determine whether a man deserves his mercy, but God's mercy is neither arbitrary nor without thought of the disposition of the person to whom he gives it. No, God is completely just and he gives his mercy to those he judges best to receive it, without violating their freedom.

Second, God can choose Jacob over Esau even before they are born because, as the Catholic Catechism says, "To God, all moments of time are present in their immediacy. When therefore he establishes his eternal plan of 'predestination,' he includes in it each person's free response to his grace" (Section 600).[16] God foreknew that Esau, out of his own free will, would choose to remain in godlessness. We know God is basing his decision on his foreknowledge of the future, since in Genesis 25:22-23 God foretells the future to Rebecca. God reveals to her that two nations will be produced from her womb and that the older (Esau) will serve the younger (Jacob). Since God knows these future events, surely he knows all the events in Esau's life, including Esau's free will decision to reject God's graces and become a godless person (Hebrews 12:16-17). Moreover, not only is Esau godless, but he produces a whole nation (Edom) that is godless. This is noted in the remaining context of Paul's quote from Malachi 1, which in verse 4 says:

> Edom may say, 'Though we have been crushed, we will rebuild the ruins.' But this is what the Lord Almighty says: 'They will build, but I will demolish. They will be called the Wicked Land, a people always under the wrath of the Lord.

Hence, we see that God's "hate" and wrath on Esau extends to his future descendants who also despised God and became a wicked nation. In turn, we must acknowledge that God foreknows all the decisions and events of all individuals and all nations of the world, and predestines his plans accordingly.

PREDESTINED TO HOLINESS

One final facet we should know about the relationship between predestination and free will is that, curiously, the Scriptural passages on predestination are not specific to heaven. Heaven certainly is the end result of predestination, but the New Testament writers have something far more profound in mind. For example, in Romans 8:29 Paul says "those whom God foreknew he also predestined to be conformed to the likeness of his Son..." Here we see that the primary function of predestination is to conform us to Christ's image. Similarly, in Ephesians 1:4-5 Paul says, "For he chose us in him before the creation of the world to be holy and blameless in his sight...to be adopted as his sons..." Again, the primary emphasis is on becoming "holy and blameless" not on a guaranteed entrance into heaven. Additional verses confirm this intention. 2 Timothy 1:9-10 says, "God, who has saved us and called us to a holy life ... this grace was given us in Christ Jesus before the beginning of time..." 1 Peter 1:2 says, "who have been chosen according to the foreknowledge of God ... for obedience to Jesus Christ." 1 Thessalonians 1:4,6 says, "...he has chosen you ... you became imitators of us and of the Lord; in spite of severe suffering..."

Why do the New Testament writers describe predestination in terms of becoming holy rather than as a guaranteed entrance into heaven? As we have seen throughout this study, the answer lies in the relationship between God's predestination and man's free response. More specifically, God has laid out a "predestined" path in order for man to enter the kingdom of heaven and there is no other way God will allow us to enter. That predestined path includes: suffering (Romans 8:18-28; Acts 14:22); maintaining faith in spite of not being able to see God or when life appears too hard (Romans 4:18-25; Hebrews 11:1-40; 1 Peter 1:6-9); obedience in spite of sin and concupiscence (Romans 7:7- 25; 8:1-17); perseverance in spite of harsh treatment and ridicule (James 5:1-12; 1 Peter 3:8-4:19); submission to authority (Romans 13:1-8; 1 Peter 2:13-25); loving your enemies and praying for those who persecute you (Matthew 5:43-48; 1 John 3:11-4:21); repenting of sin (Acts 2:38-41); giving riches to the poor (Matthew 19:16-26); self-denial and shunning the world (1 John 2:15-17); receiving the sacraments and attending church (Hebrews 10:19-25); and any other thing related to the spiritual life. All these conform us to the image of Christ, and thus Romans 8:29 is fulfilled.

Even Jesus took part in God's predestination. Lets look at Romans 8:29 again. Paul says, "those God foreknew he also predestined ... that he [Christ] might be the firstborn among many brothers." This shows us that Jesus was the first person who participated in and accomplished the predestination plan of God. God chose Christ to follow the predestined path "before the creation of the world but was revealed in these last times for your sake" (1 Peter 1:20). Christ's life on earth showed that he performed each of the items listed above: suffering, faith, obedience, perseverance, submission, love, etc. Christ's acceptance of God's predestined plan reached its climax in the Garden of Gethsemane as Jesus asked the Father if there was another way *another path* he could follow other than the cup of suffering and death he was ordained to undergo. No answer came, except the entrance of his betrayer (Matthew 26:36-45). As Paul says in Hebrews 5:4-9:

No one takes this honor upon himself; he must be called
by God... During the days of Jesus' life on earth, he
offered up prayers and petitions with loud cries and tears
to the one who could save him from death, and he was
heard because of his reverent submission. Although he
was a son, he learned obedience from what he suffered
and, once made perfect, he became the source of eternal salvation for all who obey him...

In all this we learn that Jesus was the prime object of God's
election and the first to complete the predestined path to heaven.
As Paul says in Colossians 1:15-16, "...the firstborn over all creation ... all things were created by him and for him." Our goal is to
follow the same predestined path and be "conformed to his likeness." In following the predestined path, we will be glorified with
Christ in heaven, for "those he called, he also justified; those he
justified, he also glorified" (Romans 8:30). The glorification is the
end product of our free response in conjunction with God's election, as Paul says in 2 Timothy 2:10-12:

Therefore I endure everything for the sake of the elect,
that they too may obtain the salvation that is in Christ
Jesus, with eternal glory... If we died with him, we will
also live with him; if we endure, we will also reign with
him. If he disown him, he will disown us...

In God's plan of predestination, he is seeking those who will
accept the predestined path of submission and holiness in order to
enter the kingdom of heaven. In his foreknowledge, God knows
who will accept and who will not accept his course to heaven. Thus,
as the Catechism says, "When therefore he establishes his eternal
plan of 'predestination,' he includes in it each person's free response
to his grace." God will predestine those who from their "free response" accept God's preordained path to heaven. Those who do
not accept are destined to damnation (1 Peter 2:8; Romans 9:22).

This principle of predestination also applies to the angels. God
knew which angels would accept his path and which would not.
The angels were given a choice to serve God and to minister to
man. Not willing to submit to God's design, in their pride, Satan

and his angels decided that it would be better to commiserate in hell than to assist God and man. God foreknew their choice and made all his plans accordingly. However, God also knew which angels would accept the role of service. Scripture calls them "the elect angels" (1 Timothy 5:21).

Once in heaven, we will be completely "conformed to the likeness of Christ." We will fully "participate in the divine nature" and God's plan of predestination will reach its fruition (2 Peter 1:4). The goal of predestination is to rid the universe of every evil once and for all, thus we will live eternally in the likeness of God himself.

In the end, we bow our heads and exclaim with Paul:

> Oh, the depth of the riches of the wisdom and knowledge of God! How unsearchable his judgments and his paths beyond tracing out! Who has known the mind of the Lord? Or who has been his counselor? Who has ever given to God, that God should repay him? For from him and through him and to him are all things. To him be the glory forever! Amen (Romans 11:33-36).

SUMMARY POINTS

1) The doctrine of Predestination is an integral part of Catholic theology and was taught in the beginning of the Church's history and to the present day.

2) All events, without exception, are included in God's foreknowledge. God makes plans and decrees based on his foreknowledge.

3) God predestines the salvation of the elect and the punishment of the wicked.[19]

4) Although God predestines, this is in conjunction with man's free will to accept or reject God.

5) God does not cause, coerce or predestine men to sin. However, God's plan of predestination includes the foreknowledge that men will sin of their own volition.

6) God gives each man the power to accept or reject God and desires that all men, without exception, become saved. If they are damned, it is their own fault.

7) God chooses whom he will save and whom he will damn based on his sovereign will, but the decision is not arbitrary.

8) In the New Testament, predestination is specific to being "conformed to the likeness of Christ," which, in conjunction with our free response to God's grace, will reach its fruition in heaven.

END NOTES

[1] One of the more remarkable Scriptural passages in this regard is Genesis 6:6, "The Lord was sorry that he had made man on the earth, and his heart was filled with pain." Here we see regret in God. In addition, the Hebrew uses the hitpa'el verb form which denotes intense pain.

[2] Catholic Catechism: "The witness of Scripture is unanimous that the solicitude of divine providence is concrete and immediate; God cares for all, from the least things to the great events of the world and its history. The sacred books powerfully affirm God's absolute sovereignty over the course of events" (Section 303). "From the beginning to the end of time he can see everything...For the Most High knows all that may be known; he sees from of old the things that are to come...No thought escapes him, and nothing is hidden from him...We could say more but could never say enough; let the final word be: He is the all" (Ecclesiasticus 39:20; 42:18-20; 43:27).

[3] Although the Catholic catechism (1994) does not have any index references to the topics of predestination or election, the doctrine nevertheless permeates the catechism's teaching, many times very explicitly (Sections 600, 602, 769, 969, 1037, 1045, 1308).

[4] "Some he blessed and exalted, and some he made holy and brought near to himself; but some he cursed and brought low, and turned them out of their place. Like clay in the hand of the potter, to be molded as he pleases, so all are in the hand of their Maker, to be given whatever he decides" (Ecclesiasticus 33:12-14).

5 See also 1 Peter 2:8 — "they stumble because they disobey the message — which is also what they were destined for."

6 Other passages that explicitly or implicitly teach predestination are Matthew 25:34; John 6:65; 10:28; 15:16; 17:12; 18:9; 1 Corinthians 2:7; Galatians 1:4; 1 Thess. 1:4; 2 Thess 2:13-14; 2 Timothy 1:9-10.

7 "To be human, 'man's response to God by faith must be free, and...therefore nobody is to be forced to embrace the faith against his will. The act of faith is of its very nature a free act.' 'God calls men to serve him in spirit and in truth. Consequently they are bound to him in conscience, but not coerced...' Indeed, Christ invited people to faith and conversion, but never coerced them. 'For he bore witness to the truth but refused to use force to impose it on those who spoke against it" (Catholic Catechism, Section 160; see also Sections 1730-1742).

8 The Council of Trent stated: "...although free will was not extinguished in them, however weakened and debased in its powers..." (Session 6, Chapter 1); "If anyone shall say that man's free will moved and aroused by God does not cooperate by assenting to God who rouses and calls, whereby it disposes and prepares itself to obtain the grace of justification, and that it cannot dissent, if it wishes, but that like something inanimate it does nothing at all and is merely in a passive state; let him be anathema" (Session 6, Canon 4); "If anyone shall say that after the sin of Adam man's free will was lost or destroyed, or that it is a thing in name only, indeed a title without a reality, a fiction, moreover, brought into the Church by Satan; let him be anathema" (Canon 5)

9 According to Numbers 1-2; Ecclesiasticus 46:8, over 600,000 Israelite men left Egypt during the exodus. Assigning one wife and one child to each, this would bring the total to 1.8 million people. The exodus took place in the 15th century BC. Elijah is a prophet in the 9th century BC. We can estimate that the population of Israel during these six centuries grew to several million. A conservative estimate of 5 million would then make the 7,000 who did not bow to Baal, a mere 14% of the total population.

10 Other passages which indicate similar blinding are: Isaiah 6:9-10; 44:18; Jeremiah 6:21; Matthew 11:25; John 12:40; Romans

1:28; 11:8; 2 Thess. 2:11. Other passages show God controlling or influencing the thoughts of men, e.g., Lev. 26:36; Deut. 28:28, 65-67; 1 Sam. 16:14; 26:12; Prov. 21:1; Job 12:24; Is. 29:10, 14; Ezk. 7:26; 14:9; Zech. 12:4.

[11] This is similar to the account in Luke 4:24-30 in which Jesus reminds the Jews that the miracle worker, Elijah, was not sent to any of the widows of Israel but was sent to the Gentile woman of Zarephath in Sidon, and that his successor, Elisha, was not sent to cure any of the lepers in Israel but was sent to the Gentile, Naaman from Syria.

[12] The early Fathers taught that God gives sufficient grace to everyone for faith and salvation: Clement, *Letter to the Corinthians*; Arnobius, *Against the Pagans*; Chrysostom, *On John*; Ambrose, *On Psalms*; Augustine, *Psalms*; *Genesis Defended*; *Nature and Grace*; *Corrections*; *Predestination of the Saints*; Prosper of Aquitane, *The Call of All Nations*.

[13] Council of Trent, Session 6, Canon 17: "If anyone shall say that the grace of justification is attained by those only who are predestined unto life, but that all others who are called, are called indeed, but do not receive grace, as if they are by divine power predestined to evil: let him be anathema."

[14] cf., Deut. 5:9-10; Psalm 103:13; Hosea 11:4.

[15] James 4:6; 2 Timothy 3:8; Acts 13:46-48; Matthew 13:11-15.

[16] Augustine says: "How could you have consented when you did not exist? But He who made you without your consent does not justify you without your consent. He made you without your knowledge, but He does not justify you without your willing it" (Jurgens, vol. 3, no. 1515).

[17] See also Colossians 3:12; Titus 1:1-3.

[18] See also Isaiah 42:1; 43:10; Acts 2:23; 4:28; Luke 9:35; 22:22; 1 Peter 2:4-6; Revelation 13:8.

[19] Council of Valence, 855 AD, Canon 3.

HOW CAN i GET TO HEAVEN

CHAPTER 9

CAN I KNOW FOR SURE IF I'M GOING TO HEAVEN?

THE FINAL JUDGMENT

*S*ince justification is a process that begins when God infuses his Spirit into the individual, continuing as the individual co-operates with that same Spirit to increase in grace, so must justification come to an end as the individual finally attains his heavenly inheritance. As the name implies, *final justification* is the time when God makes his ultimate evaluation of the individual's life. If one has been a faithful son, he will indeed be completely justified and receive the inheritance. If he has been unfaithful and finds himself without the grace that was infused into him at his initial justification, he will be eternally condemned. In regard to condemnation, the picture of God as "Judge" is especially prominent in contexts of Christians on the verge of sin. This appears often in the epistle of James. James 4:11-12 states: "Brothers, do not slander one another...There is only one Lawgiver and Judge, the one who is able to save and destroy. But you — who are you to judge your neighbor?" Again, in James 5:9: "You too, be patient and stand firm, because the Lord's coming is near. Don't grumble against each other, brothers, or you will be judged. The Judge is standing at the door." These passages remind us of Jesus' admonition in John 10:28: "Do not be afraid of those who kill the body but cannot kill the soul. Rather, be afraid of the One who can destroy both soul and body in hell." Peter also tells us about the judgments of the Father: "Since you call on a Father who judges

279

each man's work impartially, live your lives as strangers here in reverent fear" (1 Peter 1:17).

These passages remove all doubt that while God is a kind Father to his Christian sons, he can turn into a wrathful Father and Judge very quickly when serious sin is present. Other passages such as Acts 10:42 ("he is the one that God appointed as judge of the living and the dead") or Hebrews 12:23 ("you have come to God the judge of all men") show us that God is King over all creation and holds men accountable for his righteous laws. For those who have not received the grace of God, or who have rejected that grace after once having it, God will be the ultimate Judge — "a consuming fire," as Paul says, who will eternally destroy his enemies and all those who have been unfaithful. There is no worse punishment than to be banished by one's Father for eternity. For those who have remained in the state of grace, however, God will continue forever to be their kind heavenly Father.

Indeed, the New Testament's description of God's judgment upon the wicked and unfaithful is awesome and frightening, yet for the faithful, unspeakably comforting. In 2 Thessalonians 1:5-10 Paul writes:

All this is evidence that God's judgement is right, and as a result you will be counted worthy of the kingdom of God, for which you are suffering. God is just: He will pay back trouble to those who trouble you and give relief to you who are troubled, and to us as well. This will happen when the Lord Jesus is revealed from heaven in blazing fire with his powerful angels. He will punish those who do not know God and do not obey the gospel of our Lord Jesus. They will be punished with everlasting destruction and shut out from the presence of the Lord and from the majesty of his power on the day he comes to be glorified in his holy people and to be marveled at among all those who have believed. This includes you, because you believe our testimony to you.

Revelation 20:11-15 records another ominous scene:

> Then I saw a great white throne and him who was seated
> on it. Earth and sky fled from his presence, and there
> was no place for them. And I saw the dead, great and
> small, standing before the throne, and books were
> opened. Another book was opened, which is the book
> of life. The dead were judged according to what they
> had done as recorded in the books. The sea gave up the
> dead that were in it, and death and Hades gave up the
> dead that were in them, and each person was judged
> according to what he had done. Then death and Hades
> were thrown into the lake of fire. The lake of fire is the
> second death. If anyone's name was not found written
> in the book of life, he was thrown into the lake of fire.

In this passage, the apostle John refers twice to being "judged according to what they had done," the first time indicating that the deeds of each person were written in "the books." Here the plural "books" is used to indicate the massive volumes, as it were, which are needed to record all the deeds of each person, thus leaving the reader with the impression that nothing escapes the scrutiny of God. Every thought, word and deed has been documented. This closely resembles the prophecy Jesus gave in Matthew 12:36-37, "But I tell you that men will have to give an account on the day of judgment for *every careless word* they have spoken. For by your words you will be justified and by your words you will be condemned." As Ecclesiasticus 28:1 states, "...for he keeps a strict account of their sins."

Most importantly, the above passage speaks of the "day of judgment." Whether this is the general judgment when all souls will stand before God, or the particular judgment when individuals will stand for judgment at death, is not specified.[1] Nevertheless, it is specified that the *justification* takes place at the final judgment of that individual.

In regard to the final justification about which Jesus speaks in Matthew 12:37, such an end-time judgment that alone determines whether the individual is ultimately justified forces the Protestant concept of the one-time imputed act of justification into an acute contradiction. Protestant theology understands justification, once applied, as a past event never to be repeated. In Matthew 12:37, however, Jesus is using *justification* as continuing far beyond the initial stage of becoming a Christian, making it last, in fact, until the end of the person's life, at which time it will determined whether that person will be justified or not. Hence, justification cannot be a one-time event never to be repeated again, but must be understood as a continual process with its final outcome reserved for judgment day. The above passage also makes it clear that the criterion for the final justification is the individual's *works*.

Paul used a similar context to explain the final justification in Romans 2:5-8,13:

> But because of your stubbornness and your unrepentant heart, you are storing up wrath against yourself for the day of God's wrath, when his righteous judgment will be revealed. *God will give to each person according to what he has done.* To those who by persistence in doing good seek glory, honor and immortality, he will give eternal life. But for those who are self-seeking and who reject the truth and follow evil, there will be wrath and anger...For it is not the hearers of the law who *are just* with God, but the *doers of the law will be justified.*

Here Paul connects God's positive evaluation of an individual's good deeds with the fact that they are presently "just," adding that they will also be "justified" in the future. Although a present justification is implicit in the phrase "will be justified," it cannot be confined only to the present given the unmistakable reference to the future judgment in the context of Romans 2:5-13. Paul couples the justification with "the day of God's wrath," which can only refer to the final judgment. Hence we see again that Scripture uses the term justification as a past, present and future event. This agrees with what we have learned in Chapter 4 that justification is a process with a beginning, middle, and end.

In previous chapters we have already cited many New Testament judgment passages. Some we will mention again, others we will look at in more detail to gain a more precise picture of the future judgment.

Jesus' teaching contains several references to judgment based on works as determining one's eternal destiny. John 5:28-29 states: "Do not be amazed at this, for a time is coming when all who are in their graves will hear his voice and come out — *those who have done good* will rise to live, and *those who have done evil* will rise to be condemned." In John 6:40 Jesus adds faith to works: "For my Father's will is that everyone who looks to the Son and believe in him shall have eternal life, and I will raise him up at the last day." Similarly, in John 12:48 Jesus states: "There is a judge for the one who rejects me and does not accept my words; that very word which I spoke will condemn him at the last day." Jesus says in Matthew 16:27: "For the Son of Man is going to come in his Father's glory with his angels, and then he will reward each person *according to what he had done.*"

In Matthew 25:41-46, Jesus vividly describes the final judgment:

> Then he will say to those on his left, 'Depart from me, you who are cursed into the eternal fire prepared for the devil and his angels. For I was hungry and you gave me nothing to eat, I was thirsty and you gave me nothing to drink'...They also will answer, 'Lord, when did we see you hungry or thirsty'...He will reply, 'I tell you the truth, *whatever you did not do for one of the least of these*, you did not do for me.' Then they will go away to eternal punishment, but the righteous to eternal life.

We have also noted that Paul clearly teaches a judgment based on works that determines one's eternal destiny. First, in Romans 2:6-8:

> *God will give to each person according to what he has done.* To those who by persistence in doing good seek glory, honor, and immortality, he will give eternal life. But for those who are self-seeking and who reject the truth and follow evil, there will be wrath and anger.[2]

Though Romans 2 is more a general description of judgment, Paul in Romans 14 orients the same message specifically to his Christian audience. In Romans 14:10-12 he states:

> You, then, why do you judge your brother? Or why do you look down on your brother? For we will all stand before God's judgment seat. It is written, "'As surely as I live,' says the Lord, 'every knee will bow before me; every tongue will confess to God.'" So then, *each of us will give an account of himself to God.*

Similarly in 2 Corinthians 5:10: "For we must all appear before the judgment seat of Christ, that each one may receive what is due him for the *things done while in the body, whether good or bad.*" 1 Corinthians 3:12-15 also uses similar language:

> If any man builds on this foundation using gold, silver, costly stones, wood hay or straw, his work will be shown for what it is, because the Day will bring it to light. It will be revealed with fire, and the *fire will test the quality of each man's work.* If what he has built survives, he will receive his reward. If it is burned up, he will suffer loss; he himself will be saved, but only as one escaping through the flames.

In interpreting these passages, many Protestants have attempted to confine them to a judgment solely for the determination of personal rewards in heaven. The better the Christian's works, the better his reward. Consequently, any judgment for sin, or anything concerning eternal punishment, is conveniently eliminated from the passage. Since the Christian has already been justified and forgiven of sin by *faith alone* in Christ, he cannot be judged for sin any longer. If this were not the case, it would create a severe contradiction in *faith alone* theology. In order to arrive at this interpretation, these commentators must assume certain premises. First and foremost, they must hold that the passages which speak of judging an individual's bad works are not referring to sin. If sin is not in view, there can be no threat of eternal punishment but only a withholding of personal rewards. In this way, faith alone theology is salvaged.[3]

There is a fatal flaw in this theory: Scripture *never* makes a distinction between bad works and sins. Each time bad works are mentioned they are in the context of sin. In light of this, it is no coincidence that proponents of the distinction between sins and bad works do not offer any definition of what constitutes a "bad work" in contradistinction to what constitutes "sin," nor do they offer any Scriptural evidence for the distinction. They deliberately leave the categories of distinction ambiguous, because, as becomes apparent, they are making the distinction on purely arbitrary grounds. Since Protestant theology demands that a Christian not be judged for his sins, the only possible means to avoid the eventuality of his judgment for sin is to categorize his bad deeds as something other than sin. Such analysis forces the reader to come away with a distinction that sounds theologically plausible, yet the authors offer not the slightest lexical or biblical analysis to prove their point.

Some try to support a distinction between sins and bad works by saying that the latter are characterized chiefly by bad motives.[4] The intent here is to minimize the impropriety by confining the bad work to a mere mental process. But this attempt is futile. Scripture never classifies "motives" as sinless occurrences. In fact, motives are potentially some of the worst kinds of sins. Scripture condemns anyone who does a "good deed" in front of others while harboring bad intentions or motives, and treats it as one of the highest forms of hypocrisy. Scripture admonishes us that motives and intentions must be as pure as the act itself. We must not be menpleasers but God-pleasers. We must not show outward pleasantries and yet secretly despise the person for whom it is done or hope that by such external performance others we will recognize us as holy. In fact, the entire Sermon on the Mount deals with the very issue of personal motives, showing that sin resides deep within the intentions of the heart, whether or not they reach fruition. For example, Jesus says it is not good enough to refrain from physical adultery, rather, one must also refrain from lust in the heart (Matthew 5:27-28). Both are sins. When we give alms, the motivation can never be to gain the accolades of men; rather, we are to give in secret for our heavenly Father who sees in secret (Matthew 6:2-4). In short, whether an action is sinful or not depends on the individual's motivation in doing that action.[5] Moreover, in defining sin, Scripture provides very wide parameters. On the one hand, Paul states in Romans 14:23 that "everything that does not come from faith is sin." Again, we see that unless the proper mental attitude is present, the action performed is sinful. On the other hand, James expands the boundaries of sin even further when he says in James 4:17, "Anyone, then, who knows the good he ought to do and doesn't do it, sins." Here again, the attitude of the individual is at the forefront. He "knows" what is good and what he ought to do but refuses to put his thoughts into action. Thereby he sins in his own thoughts — without ever lifting a figure to harm someone.[6] Hence, Scripture certainly does not give any room for a distinction between "bad deeds" and sins, or between "bad motivations" and sins. Such distinctions arise purely because a *faith alone* theology demands them.

1 CORINTHIANS 1-4
BE CAREFUL HOW YOU BUILD GOD'S TEMPLE

Not only does the general information in Scripture fail to support a distinction between "bad deeds" and sins, neither do the contexts of the verses in question. Paul introduces his teaching on the judgment of works in 1 Corinthians 3:12-17, and begins the chapter in 1 Corinthians 3:3 by pointing out the sins of "jealousy and quarreling" among the Corinthians: "You are still worldly. For since there is *jealousy and quarreling* among you, are you not worldly? Are you not acting like mere men? For when one says, 'I follow Paul,' and another, 'I follow Apollos,' are you not mere men?" Such is the context that begins his pericope concerning building on the foundation with gold, silver and costly stones or wood, hay and straw in 3:12 and leads into his description of the passing of that work through the fire in 3:13-15. Clearly the "fire tested works" are directly related to their "jealousy and quarreling" over Paul and Apollos, since Paul continues with the same theme of quarreling with one another over certain men in the church immediately following the passing through fire in 3:21-22: "So then, no more boasting about men! All things are yours, whether Paul or Apollos or Cephas or the world..."

In fact, the first four chapters of 1 Corinthians deal specifically with the sinful factions occurring in the Corinthian church. Already in 1:11-12, Paul mentions the "quarrels" created over the allegiances they are giving to certain men: "My brothers, some from Chloe's household have informed me that there are *quarrels* among you. What I mean is this: One of you says, 'I follow Paul,' another, 'I follow Apollos,' another, 'I follow Cephas,' another, 'I follow Christ.'" Three chapters later, Paul concludes on the same theme in 1 Corinthians 4:6: "Now, brothers, I have applied these things to myself and Apollos for your benefit so that...you will not take pride in one man over against another." All in all, the first four chapters of the epistle contain four interspersed references to these false allegiances. In the midst of these is Paul's specific warning that their works will be tested by fire. It is apparent, then, that his warning of a judgment for works has something to do with the divisive disturbances going on in the church. In any case, he understands *jealousy* and *quarreling* as sins, as Scripture plainly teaches. In fact, Paul mentions the same sins of jealousy and quarreling in 2 Corinthians 12:20 in addition to other sins in the Corinthian church that greatly concerned him: "I fear that there may be *quarreling, jealousy*, outbursts of anger, factions, slander, gossip, arrogance, and disorder." To these Paul adds in verse 21 the sins of a sexual nature that were prevalent in the church: "I am afraid that when I come again my God will humble me before you, and I will be grieved over many who have sinned earlier and have not repented of the impurity, sexual sin, and debauchery in which they have indulged."

It is also obvious that Paul was competing against ideas and teachings of worldly philosophy and wisdom. He notes this in a momentary discussion in 1 Corinthians 1:18-2:16. Here Paul emphasizes the apparent "foolishness of the cross of Christ" over against the wisdom of the world or the quests of miracle seekers (1:18-24). Paul says that God chose the things that appear weak, (e.g., the cross and the gospel), to frustrate the wise of the world. Such apparent "weakness" is the Lord's strength and wisdom. Paul's conclusion: rather than boast in men as they were so prone to do (1

Cor. 3:21), he exhorts them: "Therefore, as it is written: 'Let him who boasts boast in the Lord'" (1 Cor. 2:31). Paul continues to reiterate the same theme in 1 Cor. 2:1-16, making a sharp contrast between how the world thinks and how God thinks. The world simply does not understand God's ways.

Since Paul's digression to the discussion of worldly wisdom appears in the context of his warnings against the in-house quarreling of the Corinthians regarding their human allegiances, we can safely assume that some of these prominent and eloquent teachers in Corinth were either mixing the gospel of Christ with the philosophies and wisdom of the world, or, emasculating the gospel altogether. Since the gospel seemed weak and unattractive to the sensibilities of the cosmopolitan city of Corinth — a center of various Greek and Roman mythologies and cults — the Corinthian teachers may well have been tempted to placate their larger audience by integrating ideas from these false religions into Christianity. Different views of the Christian gospel led to different messages. Combined with the divisive personalities of the various teachers, the potential for factions and quarreling within the church was very great. It is no wonder, then, that Paul warns them, using himself as an example, that a teacher must only do God's bidding. They can't make the church grow by artificial means because only "God gives the increase" (1 Cor. 3:6-8). Not only is it futile to preach any other gospel than the one that God gives, God also exacts a stiff penalty for those who pervert the gospel. After warning them to build on the foundation of Christ alone, he charges them to examine their own work of building the temple of God. In so many words, 1 Corinthians 3:12 asks: Have they been building with gold, silver and costly stones, or have they been building with wood, hay, and straw? Paul implies that the jealousy and quarreling that resulted in the esteeming of men and the creation of factions and division, and the incorporation of worldly wisdom into the gospel of Christ crucified, are building the temple with wood, hay, and straw. Paul warns the Corinthians that they will be judged for such false building. On the one hand, he says that some will be judged and yet still be saved (1 Cor. 3:15). On the other hand, he warns that some will receive God's ultimate punishment of destruction. In 1 Cor. 3:17 he writes, "If anyone destroys God's temple, *God will destroy him*; for God's temple is sacred; and you are that temple."[7]

In the next verses (1 Corinthians 3:18-21), Paul reiterates that both the worldly wisdom that has crept into the gospel and the factions created by esteeming men, are the two main reasons for God's destructive wrath. He writes: "Do not deceive yourselves. If any one of you thinks he is wise by the standards of this age, he should become a fool that he may be wise. For the wisdom of this world is foolishness in God's sight...So then, no more boasting about men."

To return to our main point, the context of 1 Corinthians 1-4 makes it abundantly clear that Paul considers the Corinthian's behavior as anything but non-sinful. It is precisely because of the Corinthian's sins that God could ultimately "destroy" them for destroying his church.

DOES MY SALVATION REALLY DEPEND ON MY WORKS?

Romans 14 conveys the same message regarding sin in the midst of the church. This passage is significant since, as noted previously, verses 10-12 describe the final judgment of both those in the church and those in the world. As they do with 1 Corinthians 3:12-17, many Protestants view the *judgment seat of God* as a judgment set aside exclusively for Christians in which a personal reward is allocated to each deserving recipient. Again, they accomplish this by claiming that God is not including the Christian's sins in the judgment, only his "good and bad deeds." As in 1 Corinthians 3 just analyzed, however, the context of Romans 14 does not support a distinction between sins and bad deeds which this view requires.

First, in the context of Romans 13:13-15:4, Paul takes great pains to list his grievances against the Romans, much having to do with the despising and mistreatment of the weaker brother. Paul begins in 13:13-14 by referring directly to their potential of sin:

> Let us behave decently, as in the daytime, not in orgies
> and drunkenness, not in sexual immorality and debauch-
> ery, not in *dissension and jealousy*. Rather, clothe your-

selves with the Lord Jesus Christ, and do not think about how to gratify the desires of the *sinful nature.*

Here we see the same sins that Paul mentioned in the Corinthian church, "dissension and jealousy." Paul calls these the "desires of the sinful nature." He then leads into his discussion of the weaker brother in Romans 14:1: "Accept him whose faith is weak, without passing judgment on disputable matters...The man who eats everything must not look down on him who does not, and the man who does not eat everything must not condemn the man who does." Apparently, the one who did not have a strict diet was "looking down on him" who did, and those with strict religious diets were "condemning" those who did not refrain from certain foods. This seriously divided the church, with each side hurling epithets at the other. Paul reiterates this in Romans 14:13 telling them to "stop passing judgment on one another" or "not to put a stumbling block or obstacle in your brother's way." In 14:15 he tells those who persist in this behavior that they are "no longer acting in love" and are "destroy[ing] your brother for whom Christ died." In 14:20 he warns them, "Do not destroy the work of God for the sake of food" and "it is wrong for a man to eat anything that causes someone else to stumble."

With all these descriptions of sinful activity, especially under the heading of "dissension and jealousy" which are termed "sinful desires," we can only conclude that what is being evaluated at the judgment seat of Christ in Romans 14:10-12 is sin, and serious sin at that. Judging, destroying, not acting in love, putting stumbling blocks in the way, and condemning are all sinful attitudes and actions that will receive harsh judgment from God. The Roman Christians have exhibited just as much potential of "destroying the temple of God" as the Corinthians, and they too will "be destroyed" if they persist in such activity.

We must also point out that in Romans 14:10-12 Paul has in view a judgment not merely for Christians but for the whole world. The context of Romans 14 refers mainly to Christians only because that is Paul's major concern — keeping Christians faithful to their commitments so that they don't fall away. He has, however, a global concern which he notes in Romans 14:11 by quoting Isaiah

45:23: "It is written: As surely as I live, says the Lord, every knee will bow before me; every tongue will confess to God." Paul's emphasis on "every knee" and "every tongue" carries an ominous tone for it implies that whether willingly or unwillingly, sinful or not sinful, everyone will appear in this judgment to be evaluated and to confess to God. Just prior to this warning in Isaiah 45:23, Isaiah warns Israel to turn from her idols and speaks of God as the Savior for them and the whole world, pleading with all men to turn to him and be saved:

> I am the Lord and there is no other. I have not spoken in secret, from somewhere in a land of darkness; I have not said to Jacob's descendants, 'Seek me in vain.'...a righteous God and a Savior; there is none but me. Turn to me and be saved, all you ends of the earth...by myself I have sworn, my mouth has uttered in all integrity, a word that will not be revoked; Before me every knee will bow; by me every tongue will swear. (Isaiah 45:18-23).

Isaiah 45:24 describes two outcomes to God's judgment in Isaiah 45:23: First: "They will say of me, 'In the Lord alone are righteousness and strength...in the Lord all the descendants of Israel will be found righteous and will exult." Second, "All who have raged against him will come to him and be put to shame." The context makes clear that those who will be "put to shame" are the Egyptians, Cushites and Sabeans of verse 45:14 and who will be "put to shame and disgraced" in verse 45:16. Conversely, the hand of Cyrus in 45:1, a type of Christ, saves those in Israel.

We see from the universal context in Isaiah 45, which describes the two opposing outcomes of the judgment of God, i.e., salvation and damnation, that the context of the judgment seat of God in Romans 14:10-12 is more than one in which God merely issues rewards for good Christians. Rather it is a judgment in which God determines who is saved and who is not. If there are rewards to be given for the saved God will determine at that time, but inescapable is the fact that one must first pass the judgment of salvation before God gives him any further rewards.

2 CORINTHIANS 5:10
GOD WILL JUDGE OUR GOOD
AND BAD WORKS

Paul writes: "For we must all appear before the judgment seat of Christ that each one may receive what is due him for the things done while in the body, whether good or bad."[8] This is the second time Paul refers to the "judgment seat of Christ." It is sometimes referred to as the *beema seat* since it comes from the same Greek word.[9] Unlike Romans 14:10, 2 Corinthians 5:10 specifies the "good or bad things done in the body." Thus, there is a definite polarity in the judgment. Paul assumes that some people will have good deeds and others bad, or that each person will have a mixture of good and bad deeds. Since, as noted in the study of 1 Corinthians 3:12-17, there is no distinction between "bad deeds" and sin, Paul's reference to "things done in the body" that are "bad" must refer to sin.

Paul introduces the concept of judgment in 2 Corinthians 5:9 when he says: "So we make it our goal to please him, whether we are at home in the body or away from it." As we have learned previously in this study, the New Testament strongly emphasizes "pleasing" the Lord. Paul uses the same word in Romans 14:18 ("because anyone who serves Christ in this way is pleasing to God and approved by men"), referring to the "judgment seat of God" in Romans 14:10. Those who did not mistreat their brother did not anticipate being condemned at the judgment seat of God, and thus God considered them "pleasing." This shows us that "pleasing God" is more than just making God feel good; it entails our committed obedience to him, which, in turn, means that disobedience carries the ominous potential of condemnation. As Paul stated, "without faith it is impossible to *please* God." Faith is the beginning of our quest to please God. After faith we continue to obey him even as Paul says of Abraham, "by faith he obeyed." The same is true in 2 Corinthians 5:9-10. Paul says we must "please" God (by faith and obedience) while in the body because someday we must all stand before his judgment seat. If we are not pleasing to him, then we will be like the Israelites Paul mentions in 1 Corinthians 10:5: "God *was not pleased* with most of them; their bodies were scattered over the desert."

Since "pleasing" God implies we can also "displease" him, Paul continues in 2 Corinthians 5:11 with, "Since, then, we know what it is to fear the Lord, we try to persuade men." Although there may be some question whether Paul, as suggested by verses 12-13, is trying to persuade the members of the Corinthian church of his apostolic commission or perform his evangelical duty to warn the ungodly of God's future judgment, the latter seems the more likely since Paul uses the general reference "we persuade men" as opposed to the more specific "we persuade you."[10] Reinforcing this evangelical perspective, other New Testament references to judging good and bad deeds include *all* men.[11] The "fear" that is instilled in Paul because of this judgment is what motivates him to complete his task as an apostle. Similarly, he writes of himself in 1 Corinthians 4:4-5:

> My conscience is clear, but that does not make me innocent. It is the Lord who judges me. Therefore judge nothing before the appointed time; wait till the Lord comes. He will bring to light what is hidden in darkness and will expose the motives of men's hearts. At that time each will receive his praise from God.

Here Paul states that "the Lord...judges me" but he further stipulates that judgment is at "the appointed time...when the Lord comes." In other words, this future judgment takes place at the same time as the "judgment seat of Christ" in 2 Corinthians 5:10 which Paul says he "fears." The "bringing to light what is hidden in darkness" in 1 Corinthians 4:4 is the same as the judgment of the "bad deeds done in the body" in 2 Corinthians 5:10. Similarly, the "receiving his praise from God" is the same as being rewarded for "good deeds done in the body."

That Paul is concerned not only about fulfilling his evangelical duty to the world of men but also about keeping the Corinthians on the straight and narrow road to Christ is evident in how he speaks to the Corinthians in the remaining context. First, in 2 Corinthians 5:15, he suggests that there are some who have come to "live" in Christ but who must learn not to "live for themselves but for him who died for them..." He follows this in 5:20 with the plea, "We implore you on Christ's behalf: Be reconciled to God." One does not say this to a group of Christians unless he is worried about their spiritual disposition. In the next verses, 2 Corinthians 6:1-2, confirm this concern; Paul does nothing short of warning them to be saved: "...we urge you not to receive God's grace in vain...I tell you, now is the time of God's favor, now is the day of salvation."

This is not the first time Paul issued such an ultimatum to the Corinthians. In 1 Corinthians 15:2 he writes: "By this gospel you are saved, if you hold firmly to the word I preached to you. Otherwise, you have believed in vain." In 2 Corinthians 13:2,5 his warning is even more direct:

> On my return I will not spare those who sinned earlier or any of the others...Examine yourselves to see whether you are in the faith; test yourselves. Do you not realize that Christ Jesus is in you — unless, of course, you fail the test.[12]

One of the more important questions arising from the above passage, as regards the present discussion, is what sins Paul has in view. Elsewhere, in 2 Corinthians 12:20, Paul lists the sins:

> I fear that there may be *quarreling, jealousy*, outbursts of anger, factions, slander, gossip, arrogance and disorder. I am afraid that when I come again my God will humble me before you, and I will be grieved over many who have sinned earlier and have not repented of the impurity, sexual sin and debauchery in which they have indulged.

This admonition has two significant dimensions. First, Paul specifies that "many" in the Corinthian congregation have sinned in these ways. Second, the admonition comes at the end of Paul's second letter, indicating that after a year's passage of time the Corinthians have not heeded the warnings of Paul from his first letter.

We see, then, that (1) the context of 2 Corinthians 5-6, (2) the general warnings in the Corinthian epistles; and (3) the reference to the *beema seat* the New Testament uses exclusively to determine the guilt or innocence of the party in question rather than to issue rewards, that none of these references treat the judgment seat of Christ as a time or place in which God ignores the sins of Christians in favor of giving rewards for their good works. God will certainly reward good works, with the inheritance of heaven, with the beatific vision, and with the personal honor God will bestow individually on his faithful. However, there is no escaping the fact that God judges bad works as sins. If the sins are serious enough, the Scriptures stipulating a judgment for bad works specify that eternal damnation awaits him. In order to enter heaven, the Christian must show that he, in the state of grace, has "pleased" his Father by his faith and obedience. If he has not, he will be condemned with the wicked.

BUT CAN I HAVE ANY ASSURANCE THAT I WILL GET TO HEAVEN?

Although Paul makes it clear from 2 Corinthians 5:9-11 and other passages that we must both *please* God and *fear* his judgment at the same time, nevertheless the faithful and obedient Christian need not stand in abject terror of the future judgment. As we have learned throughout this study, God is a loving Father who does not evaluate us by the strict and uncompromising standards of law. Under his grace, God tolerates many of our sins and faults just as a father would do for his children. As we saw in Hebrews 12, God disciplines his sons. Though we fear his discipline, we also treasure it for it shows our Father's cares for us, otherwise, we would be like illegitimate orphans.

Scripture instructs us to be both confident and cautious as we anticipate the final judgment. In 1 John 4:16-17 the apostle writes:

> And so we know and rely on the love God has for us. God is love. Whoever lives in love lives in God, and God in him. In this way, love is made complete among us so that we will have confidence on the day of judgment, because in this world we are like him.

Here John establishes the same truth found in Hebrews 12. God loves us dearly. In fact, he *is* Love. As his children, we strive to imitate his love. As we show more and more love to God and our neighbor we are perfecting our love. The more we love the more we become like God. We have already noted that God shows his love for all mankind in both giving his Son for a redeemer and by causing his sun to shine on the good and bad alike. So too, we reflect the Son in our lives both by expressing our faith to others and by helping them in their needs. We must do this to friend and foe alike. The more we perfect this love, John says, the more we can then have "confidence in the day of judgment." The people in Corinth who had committed sins of jealousy and quarreling were not loving each other. Similarly, the people in Rome who were looking down upon and condemning their brothers for the kind of food they ate were not loving each other. It was precisely because of those unloving actions that Paul warned them about the judgment seat of Christ and how the fire will test their works. Simply put, "those who do not love will not see the kingdom of God."[13] John says we can have "confidence" in judgment only if we see ourselves imitating our heavenly Father's love.

John speaks of the same confidence in 1 John 2:28: "And now dear children, continue in him so that when he appears we may be *confident* and unashamed before him at his coming," and in 1 John 3:21: "Dear friends, if our hearts do not condemn us, we have *confidence* before God." Most such passages focus on the *feeling* a Christian can have toward his salvation and relationship with God. The opposite, according to 1 John 2:28, is feeling "ashamed" — a feeling our first parents had when they sinned against God (Gen. 3:8-10). John also speaks of "knowing" our salvation. In 1 John 5:13 he says, "I write these things to you who believe in the name of the Son of God; so that you may *know* that you will have eternal life, and that you may believe on the name of the Son of God."[14]

Paul, speaking of one of his friends who showed great love to him, hopes this friend, too, can be confident on the day of judgment. In 2 Timothy 1:16-18 Paul writes:

> May the Lord show mercy to the household of Onesiphorus, because he often refreshed me and was not ashamed of my chains. On the contrary, when he

was in Rome, he searched hard for me until he found me. *May the Lord grant that he will find mercy from the Lord on that day!* You know very well in how many ways he helped me in Ephesus.

Apparently, Onesiphorus was a man of great love. In two cities, Rome and Ephesus, he was right by Paul's side. It is Paul's desire that Onesiphorus find mercy from the Lord on "that day," i.e., judgment day. Even then, notice the reserve that Paul uses in his statement, "*May* the Lord grant..." He is not stating absolutely that Onesiphorus will find mercy. Mercy entails pardon of sin and overlooking of faults. Only the Lord who sees into every dark corner of our lives can judge whether we deserve his mercy. In all probability Onesiphorus did find mercy from the Lord and entered the kingdom. But our point in fact is that he had to wait till that final day for the complete mercy of God to be applied to him.

As we have noted 1 Corinthians 4:4-5, Paul also spoke in a guarded manner about himself. He reflected on the fact that while his own conscience was clear, God was the final judge of whether he was faithful to his ministry, because it is God alone who "exposes the motives of men's hearts." In 1 Corinthians 9:27, Paul admonishes himself to "beat his body and make it his slave" so that he does not become a "reprobate."[15] This passage is especially significant because the following context in 1 Corinthians 10:1-13 deals entirely with those Israelites who did fall away from their faith. Paul, who does not want to be like one of them, "beats his body" into submission so that it won't sin. He wants the wayward Corinthians to do the same.

Yet, despite this caution, Paul later shows a robust confidence about his life and what he expects God to do for him. In 2 Timothy 4:8 he writes:

I have fought the good fight, I have finished the race, I have kept the faith. Now there is in store for me the crown of righteousness, which the Lord, the righteous Judge, will award to me on that day — and not only to me, but to all who have loved for his appearing.

Here Paul uses the same imagery of the boxer and runner in a race that he used in 1 Corinthians 9:27. There is a definite air of confidence here. Paul, as he writes the pastoral epistle of Timothy from prison in Rome, has come to the end of his life. He says as much in 2 Timothy 4:6: "...the time has come for my departure." Apparently, Paul knew of his impending martyrdom at the hands of the Roman officials. He could look back on his life now and know with confidence that he had been faithful and obedient to the Lord. Though God was his final judge, Paul's conscience was clear and his expectations were high. As far as he knew, he had not sinned grievously against the Lord. He knew that he loved the Lord with every fiber of his being and he knew that God loved him even more. With that confidence he was ready to meet his maker. Paul wants each of us to have the same confidence. However, we must note that it is not by faith *alone* that Paul has this confidence. Although Paul refers to "keeping the faith," this is accompanied by "fighting the good fight" and "loving his appearing." His confidence is based on the fulfillment of his work and on his continual love, not on faith alone.

BUT WHAT ABOUT PURGATORY? DOES THE BIBLE TEACH IT?

While the apostle John speaks of "confidence in the day of judgment," he says this in an epistle that consistently emphasizes understanding, avoidance and confession of sin.[16] No matter how high our confidence, no matter how high our aspirations, sin is constantly with us in this life. Although we fight mightily against it, what happens when sin enters our life? How does it affect our relationship with God and what are its consequences? We have already answered these questions to a large degree in the preceding chapters. We have discovered that for those who make shipwreck of their faith or sin grievously against God, God will judge them with eternal condemnation. God will no longer be a loving Father, but a wrathful Father who finally and completely disinherits his wayward children.

God also deals with the sins of his sons on earth by disciplining them, as Hebrews 12 teaches. The father's discipline of his children has a twofold purpose. On the one hand, discipline shows the child what he has done wrong and sets him on the path of obedience. It strengthens and purifies him. It makes him ready for the next event in life. On the other hand, discipline also punishes the child for his disobedience. While fathers are kind and merciful, they are also just. Their sense of justice demands that the child undergo a certain degree of payment for his infraction, however minor the infraction may have been. The father may spank the child, confine him to his room, take away his allowance, etc. Whatever the choice of punishment, it is for the good both of the child and the family. In order to make a proper entrance into the society and be a fine upstanding citizen, the child must be self-disciplined. It is the parent's job, by instilling this self-discipline, to prepare the child for the future.

God works the same way with his Christian children, except that he needs to prepare them for citizenship in the kingdom of heaven. Everything that God does prior to heaven he does to prepare us for heaven. Through the infusion of the grace of his Spirit at baptism, God renovates the inner essence of his children, extending it throughout their whole lives in preparation for the kingdom. For many, physical suffering plays a great part in that preparation. It refines the soul. For others, the everyday trials of life play a greater part in their preparation. Whatever the mode, God uses each event of life to mold us to be conformed to the image of his Son in preparation for his kingdom. Wisdom 12:2 states, "Therefore you correct little by little those who trespass, and you remind and warn them of the things through which they sin..." God cannot allow anyone into heaven who is not prepared for it. As the apostle John said in Revelation 21:27, "Nothing impure will ever enter it..."

In order to be an upstanding citizen in the kingdom of heaven, the child of God must be disciplined, with punishment, for his infractions against the rules of the Father's house. This is for his own good and the good of all the people with whom he will interact for eternity. Part of this discipline is accomplished on earth. Frequently, the Scripture speaks of this discipline and punishment as purging fire. In 1 Peter 1:7 the apostle writes:

> ...until the coming of the salvation that is ready to be revealed in the last time. In this you greatly rejoice, though now for a little while you may have had to suffer grief in

all kinds of trials. These have come so that your faith — of greater worth than gold, which perishes even though *refined by fire* — may be proved genuine and may result in praise, glory and honor when Jesus Christ is revealed.

Peter uses the same imagery in 1 Peter 4:12: "Dear friends, do not be surprised at the *fiery* trial you are suffering, as though something strange were happening to you."

God's fire can be used in two ways: for purification or for destruction. Scripture often refers to the latter as the "unquenchable fire" of eternal destruction.[17] The former is used by Peter in both of the above passages as he describes the trials, and thus the discipline, from the Lord as equivalent to being passed through fire like gold. Just as one removes impurities of gold by passing it through fire so that the dross will melt away, so God passes us through fire to dissipate our sinful impurities.[18] This fire is "quenchable" because when the impurities are dissipated the fire is removed.

Scripture also speaks of a purging fire after death. It is a fire similar to the purging fires we sustain on earth, for this fire also prepares us to take our place in the heavenly kingdom.[19] Paul alludes to these postmortem fires in 1 Corinthians 3:13, 15:

> The work of each person will become manifest, for the Day will declare it because it will be revealed by fire and the fire will test each person's work of what sort it is. If anyone's work remains which he built on, he will receive a reward. If anyone's work is consumed, he will suffer a penalty,[20] but he will be saved in the same way as through fire.[21]

Various modern translators, not understanding the intent of 1 Corinthians 3:15 and trying to fit it into a *faith alone* theology, have had much difficulty in giving an accurate picture of what Paul is saying. The major difficulty these translators face is the explicit reference to a judgment of the individual's works. As noted earlier in this chapter, many resolve this anomaly by relegating the judgment of works to the arena of personal rewards for Christians, claiming that the bad works implied in the passage do not refer to sin. In dealing with these difficulties, some translators have attempted to picture the fire of 1 Corinthians 3:15 as one which singes the coattails, as it were, of one escaping from a burning building. This is evident in the New International Version's rendering, "he himself shall be saved, but only as one escaping through the flames"; the New English Bible's "and yet he will escape with his life, as one might from a fire" and the Today's English Version's "as if he had escaped through the fire."[22] The impression is that the individual was saved, but just barely. The flames, though perhaps singeing him, did not harm or change him in any way. The major problem with this conception, especially with the connotation that the salvation was "just barely attained," is that it contradicts the major dictum of *faith alone* theology, i.e., that works do not serve as a criterion for one's salvation. There is no room in *faith alone* theology for salvation to come by degrees.

Relating, to the general context, the connection between 1 Cor. 3:15 and 1 Cor. 3:17 which speak of testing and destruction by fire, we see that 1 Corinthians 1-4 emphasizes the false allegiances, the jealousy and quarreling, and the dabbling in worldly wisdom. Instead of working together, the Corinthians were competing against one another, vying for leadership in the church at the expense and subjugation of their brothers. Using planting-and-watering imagery, Paul explains that there should be no such competition; rather, each should realize that it is God's field and God's building and only he can make things grow. In verses 5-9 Paul writes:

> What, after all, is Apollos? And what is Paul? Only servants through whom you came to believe — as the Lord has assigned to each his task. I planted the seed, Apollos watered it, but God made it grow. So neither he who plants nor he who waters is anything, but only God, who makes things grow. The man who plants and the man who waters have one purpose, and each will be rewarded according to his own labor. For we are God's fellow workers; you are God's field, God's building.

Clearly Paul's concern is people. He calls them "God's building" in 3:9, reinforces it in 3:16 by the question, "Don't you know that *you yourselves are God's temple...*" and reiterates it again in 3:17 in the phrase, "and *you are that temple*." Since the temple is God's, they must be extremely careful how they help construct that building. In 1 Corinthians 3:10-11, Paul warns each one to "be careful how he builds" on the "foundation of Jesus Christ." If they perpetuate a gospel of quarreling rather than love, a gospel of division rather than unity, or a gospel of worldly wisdom rather than the message of Christ crucified, then either they have "laid another foundation" or they have begun to build on the present foundation with wood, hay, and straw instead of gold, silver, and costly stones. Ezekiel had used similar imagery in his address to Israel. In Ezekiel 13:10-16 the prophet writes:

> ...and one builds a boundary wall, and they plaster it with untempered mortar — say to those who plaster it with untempered mortar, that it will fall...Surely, when the wall has fallen, will it not be said of you, 'Where is the mortar with which you plastered it...So I will break down the wall you have plastered with untempered mortar and bring it to the ground, so that its foundation will be uncovered; it will fall, and you shall be consumed in the midst of it. Then you shall know that I am the Lord. (NKJV.)

Ezekiel 28:28-30 uses similar language:

> Her prophets plastered them with untempered mortar, seeing false visions and divining lies for them, saying, 'Thus says the Lord God,' when the Lord had not spoken...Therefore I have poured out My indignation on them; I have consumed them with the fire of My wrath; and I have recompensed their deeds on their own heads, says the Lord. (NKJV.)

Here we see an uncanny resemblance to the language of Paul in 1 Corinthians 3:10-17. Building with "untempered mortar" is the same as building the temple of God with "wood, hay and straw." The "false visions" and the pseudo-prophets who say, 'Thus saith the Lord' in Ezekiel's time resemble those in Corinth who come with a gospel of worldly wisdom instead of "Christ crucified." The "uncovering of the foundation" is similar to Paul telling the Corinthians to be certain they are building on the "foundation of Jesus Christ." The "fire of his wrath that will consume them" resembles the warning of Paul in 1 Cor. 3:17 that God will "destroy those who destroy his temple." The same problems and the same warnings exist — just at different times. Hence, it comes as no surprise that Paul takes great pains to compare the plight of Israel to that of the Corinthians in 1 Corinthians 10:1-13, and in particular in verses 5-6,11:

> Nevertheless, God was not pleased with *most* of them; their bodies were scattered over the desert...We should not commit *sexual immorality*, as some of them did — and in one day twenty-three thousand of them died...Now these things occurred as examples to keep us from setting our hearts on evil things as they did...These things happened to them as examples and were written down as warnings for us, on whom the fulfillment of the ages has come.

We have already noted that these were not just idle warnings from Paul. The Corinthians were already engaging in sexual immorality, as 2 Corinthians 12:21 makes clear: "I am afraid when I come again...I will be grieved over *many* who have sinned earlier and have not repented of the impurity, *sexual sin,* and debauchery in which they have indulged." Obviously, the Corinthians had already fallen into the same sexual sins as Israel. A remarkable feature in this comparison is Paul's statement in 1 Corinthians 10:5 that God was not pleased with "most" of the Israelites, and then his reference in 2 Corinthians 12:21 to "many" in the Corinthian church who have likewise sinned. Further, those in Corinth were refusing to repent of their sin, just as the people in Israel who were eventually destroyed.

In all these warnings Paul is trying to show the Corinthians that they cannot just "play church." To be a custodian of the gospel is serious business. The eternal destiny of every individual who comes in contact with the gospel hangs in the balance. That being the case, the custodian must be absolutely faithful in the propagation of that gospel as God gave it, as well as obedient to it himself. If not, then he will face destruction by God for destroying the temple, as 1 Corinthians 3:17 makes clear.

God, as a merciful Father who looks at his children through the eyes of grace, does not penalize every single infraction with eternal damnation. Such punishment is reserved for continual or very serious offenses against his temple. For offenses within the category of eternal damnation, however, it is just a matter of measuring the extent of the damage done and meting out its appropriate punishment. The more one destroys God's temple, the harsher will be his eternal punishment. In 1 Corinthians 3:13-15, however, the person has sinned and produced some bad works that are burned in the fire, yet his improprieties are not so great as to incur the "destruction" in 1 Corinthians 3:17. Naturally the question arises: if a man suffers penalty for his bad works, will God still allow him to be saved? The answer is "yes," but it is a *qualified* yes. He can only be saved by going through the same fire that burned away his bad works. The bad works were his, not another's and thus the responsibility is his. He is the source of the works; therefore the source must also be purified of evil. Hence, he, as well as his works, must pass through the fire. If all he is is evil, then the fire will consume him in eternal destruction. If his constitution is only partly evil, then the fire will purge him of any remaining evil in order to prepare him to be a member and builder of God's eternal temple — a man of pure gold, silver, and costly stones who produces the same.

This understanding of the context also shows why the notion conveyed by the translation "suffer loss" in 1 Corinthians 3:15 is somewhat inadequate. One could suffer loss of work without the question being raised whether he would still be saved. When penalty is introduced into the picture, however, one would then have to know the degree of penalty to be suffered, which, according to the context of the passage, depends on the degree of the offense. We must know whether the individual will be given a temporary sentence and eventually set free or sentenced to eternal imprisonment. If the focus of the passage were only on whether the individual will receive a personal reward, then the matter of salvation in 3:15 would not be an issue, and certainly the eternal destruction of 3:17 would

be a totally foreign element in the discussion. However, it is precisely the reference to the gain or loss of salvation (i.e., "he will still
be *saved*") that puts this passage into a totally different dimension
than one merely concerning the degree of personal reward. Moreover, because 3:17 requires a severe penalty for sin, then it is only
logical that 3:15 would also require a penalty, albeit, less severe.
Although reward is certainly a facet of the passage, it is only sec-
ondary. The main question is whether the individual being judged
will, in the end, be at the place where rewards will finally be issued.
If he is "destroyed" as verse 3:17 stipulates, he certainly will not be
there. As the false prophets in Ezekiel's time were destroyed by God
for building with defective material, Paul tells the Corinthians in 1
Corinthians 10:6,11 that such incidents were written down precisely
to warn those in the new age that they, too, will be destroyed if they
build with defective material and thereby destroy God's temple.

In conclusion, we see that 1 Corinthians 3:10-17 specifies the
three destinations which will be the ultimate outcomes of judgment day. Those in 3:14 whose work survives the fire receive their
reward immediately. Although part of the reward may be the eternal companionship of the very people that we persuaded to seek
the kingdom of God,[23] the ultimate reward is the kingdom of God
itself. Second, those in 3:15 who see some of their works burned
and yet have not committed capital sins against God, must first
pass through the purging fires both as a penalty for their sins and as
a preparation for the eternal kingdom, for, as the apostle John said,
"nothing impure will enter." In fact, the degree of purgation on
earth to which we do not submit or from which we do not learn,
will be the same discipline and purification we will be required to
experience in Purgatory. Finally, those in 3:17 who, without repentance, have deliberately and maliciously destroyed the temple of
God, will themselves be destroyed in the eternal and unquenchable
fire of God, never to escape.

SUMMARY POINTS

1) Justification is a process with beginning, middle, and end. The
end of justification takes place at the final judgment. It is here
that the entire life of the individual is judged by God. The Scrip-

ture often speaks of God judging our works at the end time judgment to determine our eternal destiny. If the individual is in serious, unrepentant sin when he meets the judgment he will be eternally condemned. If the individual has "pleased" God by his faith and works, he will receive the eternal inheritance.

2) Attempts to confine the end-time judgment of the individual's works to the receiving of personal rewards are thoroughly unbiblical. Often such attempts are made by positing a distinction between sin and bad works in an effort to dismiss sins from being judged at the final judgment. Scripture, however, does not support a distinction between sin and bad works. The evaluation of bad works is for the primary purpose of determining the eternal destiny of the individual, and secondarily to determine his personal reward.

3) If he is living a good Christian life, loving God, and his neighbor as he should, the Christian can have confidence that God will completely justify him. He cannot, however, have absolute assurance that he will be saved precisely because he may fall into sin, depart from the faith, and remain unrepentant until death.

4) God is a merciful Father who desires to prepare his sons and daughters for citizenship in the kingdom of heaven. In order to prepare us, God sends us firey trials and sufferings in this life so that we may grow in his grace. God will also purge any remaining corruption from us in post-mortem purgatorial fires.

END NOTES

[1] The judgment in which all men must take part is called the general judgment (cf., John 5:28-29; 6:40, 44; 12:48; Acts 24:15; Romans 14:10-12; 1 Cor. 3:13-17; 2 Cor. 5:10; 2 Tim. 4:8; Rev. 20:11-15, Eccles. 16:12-14, 2 Macc. 7:14; et al). Catholic theology also teaches a "particular" judgment which determines the destiny of each man upon his death (Hebrews 9:27; Luke 16:22; 23:43; 2 Cor. 5:8; Council of Trent, Ch. 7; Catholic Catechism, Sections 1021-1022). The judgment for sin at the particular judgment is analogous to the temporary detaining of a criminal in jail

without bail prior to his formal trial date and conviction. He is put in temporary detention since the evidence against him is very great.

2   This passage may be taken from Psalm 62:12, "...Surely you will reward each person to what he has done" (cf., Job 34:11, Jeremiah 17:10, Daniel 12:1-2; Ecclesiasticus 35:24).

3   James R. White, *The Fatal Flaw* (Southbridge, MA: Crowne Publications, 1990) pp. 179-180. Norman Geisler and Ralph MacKenzie, *Romans Catholics and Evangelicals: Agreements and Differences* (Grand Rapids, MI: Baker Book House, 1995) p. 237.

4   James R. White, *The Fatal Flaw*, pp. 179-180.

5   See Catholic Catechism, Sections 1752-1753.

6   "But all mortal sins, even those of thought, make men children of wrath and enemies of God..." (Council of Trent, DS 1680).

7   "...and in another those who at one time freed from the servitude of sin and the devil, and on receiving the gift of the Holy Spirit, did not fear to 'violate the temple of God knowingly' (Council of Trent, DS, 1690).

8   "...the souls of those who depart in actual mortal sin immediately after their death descend to hell where they are tortured by infernal punishments, and that nevertheless on the day of judgment all men with their bodies will make themselves ready to render an account of their own deeds before the tribunal of Christ, 'so that everyone may receive the proper things of the body according as he has done whether it be good or evil' [II Cor. 5:10]" (*Benedictus Deus*, Benedict XII, DS 1002).

9   The word "beema" is used 12 times in the New Testament, referring twice to Jesus standing before Pilate (Mt. 27:19; John 19:13); the throne of Herod (Acts 12:21); the court of Gallio where Paul was taken (Acts 18:12,16,17); the court of Festus where Paul was taken (Acts 25:6,10,17).

10   The word "persuade" is used frequently in situations of witnessing to the ungodly, e.g., Acts 17:4; 18:4; 19:26; 26:28; 28:23.

11   Romans 2:5-13; Matthew 16:27; John 5:28-29; Revelation 22:11-12.

12   The phrase, "fail the test" is from the Greek "adokimos" which is used 8 times in the New Testament in reference to extreme

evil or apostasy (Rom. 1:28; 2 Tim. 3:8; Tit. 1:16; Heb. 6:8, 1 Cor. 9:27; 2 Cor. 13:5-7).

13 Or, as St John of the Cross said, "At the evening of life, we shall be judged on our love" (*Dichos* 64). Catholic Catechism, Section 678: "Our attitude about our neighbor will disclose acceptance or refusal of grace and divine love. On the last day Jesus will say: 'Truly I say to you, as you did it to one of the least of these my brethren, you did it to me.'"

14 This kind of "knowing" is not absolute. It is conditioned by the entity doing the knowing and the thing known. John frequently speaks of factual knowledge about the Christian faith that can be known absolutely (e.g., 1 John 3:15 — "we know that no murderer has eternal life"; 1 John 5:20 — "we know also that the Son of God has come"), yet knowledge that is also conditioned on how God wishes to reveal it to us (e.g., 1 John 5:15 — "And if we know that he hears us, whatever we ask, we know we have what we have asked of him."). In any case, except for one instance, John invariably uses "know" in the plural verb form, denoting that it is the *community of believers* who possess the factual knowledge of the aspects of the Christian faith, not the individual possessing factual certainty of his own salvation without contingencies (cf., 1 John 2:20, 21, 29; 3:2, 5, 14, 15; 5:13, 15, 16, 18, 19, 20; 3 John 12, 14). John's use of "know" in the singular appears only in 1 John 2:11. Here, however, he is speaking of an individual in sin who does not know where he is going.

15 As noted previously, the word translated by the NIV as "disqualified for the prize" is the Greek "adokimos" which is used preponderantly in the New Testament in reference to evil, apostasy and falling away from the faith.

16 1 John 1:7-10; 2:1-2; 3:4-9; 4:10; 5:16-18.

17 cf., Ezekiel 22:17-22; Mark 9:43-49; Luke 3:17; Matt. 18:8-9; 25:41.

18 The Old Testament also uses the same imagery of "purging fire," e.g., Zechariah 13:9; Malachi 3:2; Daniel 12:10; Isaiah 48:10; Wisdom 3:5-9.

19 "...but after death they undergo purification, so as to achieve the holiness necessary to enter the joy of heaven" (Catholic Catechism, Section 1030). "The Church gives the name *Purgatory*

to this final purification of the elect, which is entirely different from the punishment of the damned" (CC, Section 1031).

[20] Greek: *zemioo*. Although "suffering loss" or "damage" for the laborer could certainly be in view in 1 Cor. 3:15 due to the fact that the work is destroyed by fire, penalty for the laborer can also be in view due to the meaning of *zemioo* in reference to punishment. The Septuagint frequently uses this meaning of *zemioo* (e.g., Exodus 21:22 — "the offender must be fined"; Deut. 22:19 — "they shall fine him"; Prov. 17:26 — "to punish" (coupled with "flogging officers"); Prov. 19:19 — "a hot tempered man must pay the penalty"; Prov. 21:11 — "when a mocker is punished"; Prov. 22:3 — "the simple keep going and suffer for it" could mean either that stupidity has natural consequences or that one will eventually face civil punishment for his folly. Various translations render *zemioo* in Prov. 22:3 as "punishment" (eg., KJV, NASB, NEB), or as "suffer" (e.g., ASV, RSV, NIV, Douay-Rheims)). In any case, the variances in these translations show the semantic range of the word *zemioo*. Either *zemioo* can refer to suffering loss or punishment, or to suffering as a form of punishment. The LXX uses the noun cognate *zemia* three times: once in 2 Kings 23:33 in reference to the imposition of tribute money; another in Prov. 22:3 in reference to the suffering of the simple minded; the last in Ezra 7:26, in a more revealing translation of *zemia* as "confiscation of property" or "fining of property." More significant is the context of *punishment* within which *zemia* is contained. The entire verse reads, "And whosoever shall not do the law of God, and the law of the king readily, judgment shall be taken upon him, whether for death or for chastisement, or for a fine of his property, or casting into prison." Here we see clearly that *zemia* can mean corporal punishment for sins against God and crimes against the society. Greek lexicons also recognize this distinction, defining *zemioo* as "punishment." Significantly, Bauer references 1 Cor. 3:15 as the New Testament support for this alternate meaning. (Bauer, p. 338).

[21] The translation "in the same way" is used in place of the traditional "yet so" in order to bring out the grammatical force of the Greek adverb. It can be translated as "even so" (Matt. 24:33; Luke 21:31); "in the same way" (Matt. 17:12; Luke 15:7,10;

17:10; Rom. 6:11; 1 Cor. 2:11), or simply "so" (John 3:16). It is pointing out in what manner the person is saved, e.g., "he is saved thusly." The complete connection between the subordinate phrase ("as through fire") and its preceding verb ("shall be saved") is understood by the utilization of "fire" in the previous verse, 1 Cor. 3:13. The fire tests or refines the *work* of the individual. The fire of 3:15 is also proving or refining, but with its object of purification or consumption in the individual himself. Hence, the thrust of the passage can be stated thus: as the *work* of the individual is brought through the fire to be tested, "in the same way," the *individual* is brought through the fire in order to be saved. The time reference for bringing the individual through the fire is limited to "the day" (in this case, the particular judgment) and prior to his entrance into heaven.

22 Other translations have not taken such liberties: KJV: "yet so as by fire"; RSV: "but only as through fire"; NASB: "yet so as through fire"; Douay-Rheims: "yet so as by fire."

23 In certain passages, e.g., 1 Corinthians 9:18-23; Philippians 4:1, Paul speaks of the people who were converted and remained faithful as his "reward."

Scriptural index

Old Testament

Genesis

2:23	244
2:24	244
3:8-10	296
3:15	8, 235
3:22-24	7
4:4-5	46
4:26	32, 160
5:24	44
6:3	47
6:6	65, 275
6:8-9	47
6:9	47, 200
7:1	47
10	160
12	32, 33, 34, 35, 96, 98, 103, 110, 151, 152, 165, 219
12-22	220
12:1	32
12:1-3	86, 114
12:1-8	151
12:3	36
12:4	86
12:5	32
12:6	33

12:7	114
12-17	94
12-21	86
12-22	94
13	87, 88, 92, 109
13:14-17	114
14	88
15	32, 33, 34, 35, 85, 86, 89, 98, 99, 109, 114, 151, 152, 165, 219
15:1-6	151
15:2	90
15:4	90
15:6	36, 43, 85, 89, 89, 90, 92, 94, 96, 96, 98, 99, 100, 105, 110, 152, 157, 166
15:7	89
15:15	237
15:16	43
15:16-21	114
15-17	33
16	90, 92, 109
16:1f	92
16:12	91
17	90, 99, 114

24:5	120
24:9	120
26:36	277

Numbers

1-2	276
5:7	126
6:25	226
11:1	66
11:10	66
12:3	267
13:31	87
14:4	87
15:25-28	67
15:27-36	114
22:22	66
25	157
25:3-4	66
25:11	10
32:10	66
32:13	66
32:14	66

Deuteronomy

2:20	87
2:26-36	33
5:9-10	277
6:15	66
6:25	48, 49
7:4	66
9:5f	105
9:13-29	91
13:17	66
21:18-21	238
22:19	309

22:22	114
24:13	48, 49
28:28	277
28:65-67	277
29:19-21	114
29:20-28	66
31:17	66
32:21	65
32:22	66

Joshua

1-2	104
2:9-11	106
2:10-11	106
7:1	66
7:16-18	237
7:26	66

Judges

2:14	66
2:20	66
9:22	244

1 Samuel

1	165
13:14	104, 154
15:22	118
16:7-13	104
16:14	277
17	154
21:6	120
23	261
23:10-13	261
26:12	277

2 Samuel	
2	165
5:1	244
6:7	66
11:27	45
11-12	152
12:6	126
12:11-12	155
12:13	227
12:15-23	155
19:12-13	244
24:1	66
1 Kings	
14:13	167
2 Kings	
6:16	244
13:3	66
20:1-6	167
23:33	309
24:20	66
1 Chronicles	
1-10	237
11:1	244
21:8	227
29:17	65
2 Chronicles	
12:12	167
19:3	167

20:7	103, 104
24:16	167
30:18-20	167
Ezra	
7:26	309
Job	
1:1	200
1:5	60
2:9	79
2:10	79
12:24	277
34:11	307
Psalms	
2:4	65
5:5	65, 249
6:1	66
11:5	65, 249
14	159
14:5	159
14:4-6	159
18	155
18:20-24	48
25:7	155
32	153, 154, 155, 165, 211
32:1	152, 211
32:2	227
37:4-9	167
51	152, 211
51:2	211, 227
51:5	155
51:6	211

Malachi

1:2-3	269
1:4	271
3:2	308

Wisdom

1:24	174
3:5-9	308
11:23	167
12:2	299

Ecclesiasticus (Sirach)

2:10-14	66
2:26	45
12:6	249
15:11-20	262
16:7-8	33
16:12-14	306
25:10-11	93
28:1	281
28:12-18	113

33:12-14	275
35:20	45
35:24	307
39:20	275
39:28	66
42:18-20	275
43:27	275
44:16	44
44:17	47
44:19-21	66
45:19	45, 66
46:8	276
49:14	44

Susanna

1:3	200

2 Maccabees

5:17	67
6:14	43
7:14	306
7:33	67

NEW TESTAMENT

Matthew

1:19	199
3:17	57
5	201
5:3-12	128
5:18	129
5:18-19	129
5:20	128, 129, 200, 201
5:21	201

5:21-48	128
5:27-28	285
5:28	201
5:32	201
5:34	201
5:39	201
5:43-48	272
5:44	201, 240
5:45	200, 201, 240
5:48	119, 240

6:1-18	129	18:21-35	129
6:2-4	286	18:34-35	129
6:3	226	19:4-6	244
6:12	129	19:16-26	xii, 19, 144, 272
6:14-15	129	19:21	119
7:21-23	176	19:28	216
7:22-23	170	21:31	105
8:11-12	175	22:37-40	49
9:2-8	147	23	128
9:21	135	23:14	118
9:22	147	23:14-15	113
10:22	140, 176	23:29	200
10:27	140	23:35	200
10:28	176	23:37-38	263
10:30	248	24:12-13	176
10:32	121	24:13	140, 146
10:33	176	24:29-31	140
11:19	102, 103, 109	24:33	309
11:20	147	24:36	140
11:21-24	260	24:44	140
11:25	276	24:45-51	140
12:1-12	120	24:50	140
12:7	118	25	141, 143
12:36-37	123, 131, 144, 281	25:1-13	141
12:36-39	147	25:13	140
12:37	102, 227, 282	25:14-30	141
12:39	113	25:31-46	83, 142
13:11	175	25:34	276
13:11-15	277	25:34-36	142
13:11-17	175	25:37-38	142
13:13-17	258	25:40	142
13:17	200	25:41	308
15:32	65	25:41-45	142, 283
16:19	113	25:46	147
16:27	142, 147, 283, 307	26:36-45	272
17:12	309	26:38	65
18:8-9	308	26:30	65
18:18	113	27:19	307

2:29	125, 127	4:4	6, 8, 10, 20, 22, 24, 95, 210
3	22, 159		
3-4	126	4:5	154, 155, 218
3-6	22	4:5-6	153
3-6:23	22	4:5-8	126, 166, 212
3:2	226	4:6	156
3:3	204	4:7	67
3:4	102	4:9-11	16
3:5	204, 226	4:10-16	99
3:6	23	4:11	95
3:7	204	4:12	38, 64, 96, 127, 222
3:9	53	4:13-15	65
3:9-11	8	4:15	53
3:9-20	65	4:16	37, 64
3:10	159, 199	4:16f	66, 219
3:11	159	4:17	37, 38
3:13-17	147	4:17-21	38, 220
3:19	9	4:18	220, 222
3:19-20	207	4:18-21	31, 95
3:20	16, 17, 25, 65	4:18-25	272
3:21	226	4:19-20	42, 222
3:21-22	62, 207	4:20-21	222
3:22	226	4:21	42, 95
3:22-24	12	4:22	220, 224
3:23	9	4:23	64
3:23-25	126	4:23-24	38
3:24	207	4:24	221
3:25	40, 62, 66, 156, 222	4:25	39, 55
3:26	53	5:1	217, 227
3:27	11, 66	5:1-5	217
3:28	3, 5, 13, 65, 226	5:5	217
3:29	64	5:8	240
4	35, 85, 89, 95, 96, 152, 153, 165, 210	5:12	8, 54
		5:18-19	54
4:1-8	65	6	22, 217
4:2	11, 66	6:1-4	65, 217
4:3	85, 109, 223	6:1-6	219
4:3-4	162, 207	6:5	219

5:3	19
5:3-4	65
5:6	4, 26, 79, 84, 132
5:13	26, 64
5:14	26, 49, 80
5:15-26	80
5:16	80
5:16-17	50
5:18	51
5:19-21	50, 114, 180
5:21	26, 50, 80, 81, 155, 173
5:25	37
6:7-9	180
6:8	50
6:16	37, 215

Ephesians

1:4	246
1:4-5	254, 269, 271
1:5	230, 246
1:11	246
2:1-3	54
2:7	66
2:8	14
2:8-9	12, 66
2:15	18, 55
4:7	195
4:30	65
5:2	56, 58, 66
5:5	114, 173
5:5-6	180
5:10	45
5:31	244
6:8	147

Philippians

2:12-13	194
2:12	225
2:13	225
3:5-6	28
3:6	163
3:9	28, 65, 226
3:10	214, 219
3:10-12	214
3:10-16	180
3:13	195, 226
4:1	310
4:8	226
4:18	45

Colossians

1:4-5	112
1:10	45
1:15-16	273
1:21-23	181
2:5	112
2:11-12	65
2:14	18, 25, 55
2:16-17	15
3:10	214
3:12	277
3:20	45

1 Thessalonians

1:4	276
1:4-6	272
2:4	45
2:16	43, 114
4:1-8	181
4:3	227

HOW CAN I GET TO HEAVEN

HOW CAN I GET TO HEAVEN